Praise, Praise, Praise for Joyce Lain Kennedy's For Dummies® Books

"Take it from an insurance guy: *Resumes For Dummies* Is the job insurance of the new millennium."

— Al Ferrari, St. Louis, Mo.

"I never thought writing resumes could be fun and easy! *Resumes For Dummies* shows many magic formulas to create unbeatable resumes that get interviews! Highly recommended by the Professional Association of Resume writers, it is a must reference for all pro writers."

— Paul Chin, Papua, New Guinea

"I first would like to say that you are awesome. After buying my *Resumes For Dummies* book, I realized my interviewing skills are really poor. I just had to buy your *Job Interviews For Dummies* book. I am reading it like a novel now. You rock!!"

— G. B., San Francisco, Calif.

"*Resumes For Dummies* is an all-purpose, content-filled resume book that has enough humor to focus your interest on what is a very serious matter: You as a marketable product. One chapter (Chapter 3) stood out for me. It clarifies the use of hooks — when to use an objective and when to use a skills summary, citing advantages and disadvantages of each. I also liked the detailed chart on updating your resume for scanning technology and for sending it online. A very timely read!"

— Patricia S. Pigg, Florissant, Mo.

"A book I like is *Resumes for Dummies.* Joyce keeps very current on all things career-related and this book reflects that kind of professionalism."

— D.S., Milwaukee, Wisc.

"Dear Joyce: I just finished your book *Cover Letters For Dummies.* It was terrific. I laughed and I cried when I saw some of my writing habits as the things not to do."

— Gretchen Nordby, Leesburg, Va.

"Joyce's book *Job Interviews For Dummies* is out and I think it's terrific! Joyce's job-interview directions should get you on an employer's Top Choice list every time."

— Jack Chapman, Wilmette, Ill.

"I love *Resumes For Dummies*! It's my job search bible."

— Bonnie J. Mclurg, Mayfield, Ohio

"My sister Peggy recommended I read *Job Interviews For Dummies.* The night before my interview, I reread several chapters and also took it with me in the car and refreshed myself before the interview. The interview went great. One of the things that Ms. Kennedy mentions in her book that attracted my attention was "You have the determination, the willingness to work hard, and the quick-learning skills to make up for any lack of experience." I walked into that interview with my head held high — and got the job. I believe in Joyce Lain Kennedy's wisdom."

— Julie Beecroft, Portland, Ore.

"I'm writing to show my appreciation to your book Job Interviews For Dummies. I had been working for a company for 5 years and being retrenched due to the bad economy condition in Asia countries.

Being through several job interviews but in vain, I was totally depressed and eager to know what was the problem. After finished reading your book, I realized that I had made several mistakes during job interviews. I decided to follow your guidance for my last job interview. And what happened, I got the job offer and the pay was (equivalent to) my last drawn salary."

Thank you for your book for giving me confidence and guidance."

— Lim Lie Ching, Singapore

"Wow! *Resumes For Dummies* is a great resource. Since it has been 15 years since I wrote my last resume, I was at a definite loss as to where to begin — this book was the perfect resource for creating my resume. I really like the Web-oriented resume information. Now I need to get *Cover Letters For Dummies* and *Job Interviews For Dummies*."

— Tracy Pipkin, Houston, Tex.

"I have read *Resumes For Dummies* with joy, laughter, and a deep sense of gratitude. What a godsend you are to those of us who are resuming a career. Thanks for you gifted advice."

— Carol Treadwell, San Diego, Calif.

BESTSELLING BOOK SERIES

Resumes For Dummies,®
4th Edition

Cheat Sheet

Ten Reasons to Get Your Resume Ready to Lead Your Charge

Of the 56 percent of people in the U.S. workforce open to changing jobs, 12 percent are actively looking or planning to leave, while 44 percent aren't on the market but would consider a better offer. If you're in that 56 percent, get your StandOut resume up and running if any of the following are true about you:

✔ You feel antsy to move on to a better job.

✔ You see job-loss writing on the wall.

✔ You were passed over, blocked, and are dying on the vine.

✔ You discover your boss is a dinosaur brain or was indicted.

✔ You notice less-talented people earning more than you.

✔ You are a techie and stuck with aging technology.

✔ You feel betrayed by job and training misrepresentation.

✔ You suspect your coworkers are from another planet.

✔ You get calls from headhunters.

✔ You know that successful people always keep resumes updated.

If you want to change your job, start by learning how to create a StandOut resume. That's what all parts of this book are about.

Ten Ways to Give Resume Deadweight the Heave-Ho

Make sure your resume packs a wallop by trashing excess baggage. Fill the precious space you save with information that sells you. Here's what to snip, snip, snip.

✔ **Salary needs and history:** Employers push 24/7 to make you reveal your pay requirements and history before the interview. Your interests are better served by resisting until the interview. But new online screening software often makes you talk money upfront or it will ignore your resume. Otherwise, don't include salary figures on your resume. Period. Never!

✔ **Reasons for leaving other jobs:** Goodbye explanations could raise negative questions. Today's exception: You've had a slew of job layoffs that aren't your fault. Rather than look like a job hopper, consider putting brief reasons — (Business closed) (Business left town) (Company downsized) — after each former job.

✔ **Avoidable negative information:** From a firing to a recovery from a breakdown, avoiding a problem in your history takes less space on your resume than trying to explain it.

✔ **References:** Write them in a separate document and release only when requested to avoid wearing out your allies. Don't add "References available upon request." That's a given.

✔ **Unnecessary headings:** Skip extraneous labels such as "Resume." You know. They know. We all know.

✔ **Unexplained time gaps:** These black holes of uncertainty give rise to wild suspicions of exorcisms, time served for Money Train robberies and illness so severe it will break the employer's bank of already unaffordable health insurance. See Part II.

✔ **Genealogical information:** Don't include marital status, age, parents' occupations, children's names and ages, ethnicity or national origin. None of that stuff is job related.

✔ **Photograph or physical description:** Concerned about charges of discrimination, smart companies don't want to see what you look like unless you're a model or actor.

✔ **Health:** The Americans with Disabilities Act directs employers to avoid health questions per se. Overseas, mention your excellent health status; in the U.S., say nothing (no one ever writes "sickly health").

✔ **Leisure activities:** Don't waste your valuable space on hobbies that are not job related. If you can't figure out a cross-connection, neither will an employer.

Part II tells you what to put in your resume as well as elaborates on what to leave out.

65014
Ken

For Dummies: Bestselling Book Series for Beginners

Resumes For Dummies, 4th Edition

Cheat Sheet

Three Incredibly Useful Technology Tips

Old days, old ways are fading. New technology is changing the face of finding work in ways sometimes helpful for job seekers, sometimes not so helpful. See Part I.

✔ **New Technology Tip #1:** Find out what type of system will receive your resume. Call a company and ask "Can I submit my resume to your company electronically?" If yes, then ask "Can I send my resume as an attachment?" If so, send it fully formatted as an attachment (MS Word or WordPerfect) to your e-mail. Get more details in Parts I and IV.

✔ **New Technology Tip #2:** By using smart job-agent features offered by most job sites, instead of looking for a better job, you encourage a better job to look for you. See Part IV.

✔ **New Technology Tip #3:** Mastering new online screening techniques is often necessary before employers and job sites will pay attention to your resume. Learn more about the "e-gatekeeper" language of competencies and other critical e-resume facts in Parts I, III, and IV.

Four Suggestions to Enhance Your Resume

✔ Research, research, research to know the skills, education, and experience you need for the job you want.

✔ Include a Job Objective or Asset Statement (Skills Summary) targeted to the job you want.

✔ Include the correct name, title, and address of your resume recipient.

✔ Proofread your resume as well as relying on your computer spell-checker.

Your Brisk Resume Review

Find the full, industrial-strength Resume Checklist in Part VI. As a quick review, ask yourself these questions:

✔ Have I selected the best format for my background and goals?

✔ Does my resume illustrate to an employer the benefits of interviewing me — how I can handle the job, have positive work attitudes, get along well with others?

✔ Does my resume stress my accomplishments and skills?

✔ Does my resume contain negative information?

✔ Are all my claims believable, backed up by measurable results and true examples?

✔ Does my resume have adequate keywords to retrieve my resume and bring me to a searcher's attention?

✔ Is my resume inviting to read with good, clean layout and adequate white space?

Tell the truth. After a fair evaluation, do you have a StandOut resume? Or must you call in the smoke-jumpers and paramedics to save a sorry piece of pap? If the latter, gentle reader, you need this book!

For Dummies: Bestselling Book Series for Beginners

"I'm an engineering/computer science college senior and have had several internships in college. For my last interview I prepared by reading Joyce's *Job Interviews For Dummies*. It is spectacular! I thought I knew how to interview but now I know how much I didn't know — from making a "commercial" about myself, gathering information on companies, telling about my strong points, and negotiating my salary. Thank you, thank you. This book is THE interviewing book!"

> — Carole Beaudoin, Tottenham, Ontario

"Joyce Lain Kennedy: I love your books. Because I used a cover letter that you suggested, I got my job. You mean a lot to my career."

> — Pilar Mendiola Fernandez, Washington, D.C.

"I borrowed a copy of *Job Interviews For Dummies* from the public library. After reading the book, I am now willing to invest in a personal copy for myself. It is an excellent book and I think you did such a fabulous job with presentations that now I actually look forward to job interviews."

> — Sherry Akbar, Brampton, Ontario

"I have just finished reading *Resumes For Dummies*. I found it very informative and I plan to start an online resume business based mostly on the information you provided."

> — J.A.B., Chicago, Ill.

"I really did love *Job Interviews For Dummies*. It was the first book that actually taught me how to answer specific questions. It was VERY valuable in my job search process. I have a lot of experience, but was always lacking in interview skills. (I would get really nervous before and during the interview, and would bomb it because of this.) I can see why this book won the year's best career book award."

> — Susan Postma, Burnaby, British Columbia

"After a disappointing job search I picked up Job Interviews For Dummies. In two days I read the first eight chapters, went to the interview and my answers flowed very smoothly — I showed confidence when meeting with three key people individually for three hours. The next day I had an offer for the pay I wanted plus stock options. I am overjoyed — your book was a tremendous help. Thanks for writing the book the way you did."

> — Ali Khan, Fairfax, Va.

"I wish to thank Joyce Lain Kennedy for writing the books *Job Interviews For Dummies* and *Cover Letters For Dummies*. I relied solely on the two books in my attempt at a career move.

I have been driving a truck for eight years and just recently finished night school with a Magna Cum Laude BS degree in accounting. Every job interview and cover letter were tailored by Joyce.

I'm now a portfolio accountant with an investments company in Andover, Mass. I have begun my dream career thanks to you and your effective material.

[second letter]

Joyce's book saved me again. I had been interviewing for the past couple of months to take my career to the next level. After an interview that went awry, I dug out *Job Interviews For Dummies* and crammed all the pertinent chapters the night before the next big interview for a job I really wanted. The interview the next day with the director of human resources went PERFECTLY. For each forthcoming interview, I read this book again the night before interviews with the supervisor, manager and director of the department. I began working at my present great job a month ago, thanks to Joyce and her book.

I was so excited about the results that I let two co-workers at my previous employer borrow it before their interviews. They both received offers after those interviews. I'm touting the praises of Joyce's book all over Boston and it's having a great effect."

— Mark W. Emmith, Newburyport, Mass.

Resumes

FOR

DUMMIES®

4TH EDITION

Resumes
FOR
DUMMIES®
4TH EDITION

by Joyce Lain Kennedy

Wiley Publishing, Inc.

Resumes For Dummies, 4th Edition

Published by
Wiley Publishing, Inc.
909 Third Avenue
New York, NY 10022
www.wiley.com

Copyright © 2003 by Joyce Lain Kennedy

Published by Wiley Publishing, Inc., Indianapolis, Indiana

Published simultaneously in Canada

For general information on our other products and services or to obtain technical support, please contact our Customer Care Department within the U.S. at 800-762-2974, outside the U.S. at 317-572-3993, or fax 317-572-4002.

Wiley also publishes its books in a variety of electronic formats. Some content that appears in print may not be available in electronic books.

Library of Congress Control Number: 2002110290

ISBN: 0-7645-5471-9

Manufactured in the United States of America

10 9 8 7 6 5 4 3 2

About the Author

Joyce Lain Kennedy is the author of the Tribune Media Service's twice-weekly column CAREERS NOW, in its 35th year and appearing in more than 100 newspapers and Web sites.

As America's original careers columnist, Joyce has received more than three million reader letters. In her column, she has answered in excess of 4,800 queries from readers.

She is the author or senior author of seven career books, including *Joyce Lain Kennedy's Career Book* (McGraw-Hill), and *Electronic Job Search Revolution*, *Electronic Resume Revolution*, and *Hook Up, Get Hired! The Internet Job Search Revolution* (the last three published by John Wiley & Sons). *Resumes For Dummies* is one of a trio of job market books published under Wiley's wildly popular *For Dummies* imprint. The others are *Cover Letters For Dummies* and *Job Interviews For Dummies*.

Writing from Carlsbad, California, a San Diego suburb, the dean of careers columnists is a graduate of Washington University in St. Louis. Contact Joyce at jlk@sunfeatures.com.

About the Technical Reviewer

James M. Lemke is internationally known as a leader in directing staffing strategies and staffing process reengineering. A human resources adviser to major organizations, examples of his clients are Northrop Grumman, Southwest Airlines, the White House, New York State, Resumix (Yahoo.com), Peoplesoft, and Recruitsoft. Jim formerly was an executive with TRW, UCLA, Disney Imagineering, and Raytheon. He resides with his wife Viki, a recruiting professional, in Lake Arrowhead, California. Contact Jim at jmlemke@aol.com.

Author's Acknowledgments

This is one of those books where everyone is better than anyone. I toss enormous bouquets of appreciation to the following people:

James M. Lemke, the awesome technical reviewer, who for the fifth book has kept my pages turning with hot marketplace news.

Walter Tamulis, my technically savvy editorial associate without whom I could not have made death-defying leaps across tall cyberbuildings and who is quickly finding his editorial legs.

Kathleen Dobie, this edition's gifted and unflappable project editor, who knows a thing or two about book organization, and her enthusiastic outrider whose inquiring mind sharpened my work, copy editor **Chrissy Guthrie.**

Kathy Cox, the acquisitions editor for this edition, whose valued and expert help far exceeded her job description.

Gail Ross, literary agent supreme and my representative.

My special thanks to the following aces for a wide range of editorial contributions:

Adrian Barbour	**Paul Hawkinson**
Richard Beatty	**Ron Krannich, PhD**
Jack Chapman	**Mark Mehler**
Gerry Crispin	**Ed Struzik**
Michael R. Forrest	**Kathryn Troutman**
Bill Gaul	**Wendell Williams, PhD**

Publisher's Acknowledgments

We're proud of this book; please send us your comments through our Dummies online registration form located at www.dummies.com/register/.

Some of the people who helped bring this book to market include the following:

Acquisitions, Editorial, and Media Development

Project Editor: Kathleen A. Dobie

(Previous Edition: Linda M. Brandon)

Acquisitions Editor: Kathy Cox

Copy Editor: Chrissy Guthrie

Technical Editor: James M. Lemke

Editorial Manager: Christine Meloy Beck

Editorial Assistant: Melissa Bennett

Cartoons: Rich Tennant, www.the5thwave.com

Project Coordinator: Maridee Ennis

Layout and Graphics: Joyce Haughey, Barry Offringa, Heather Pope, Jacque Schneider

Proofreaders: Laura Albert, David Faust, Andy Hollandbeck, Carl Pierce, TECHBOOKS Production Services

Indexer: TECHBOOKS Production Services

Special Help Chad Sievers

Publishing and Editorial for Consumer Dummies

    Diane Graves Steele, Vice President and Publisher, Consumer Dummies

    Joyce Pepple, Acquisitions Director, Consumer Dummies

    Kristin A. Cocks, Product Development Director, Consumer Dummies

    Michael Spring, Vice President and Publisher, Travel

    Brice Gosnell, Publishing Director, Travel

    Suzanne Jannetta, Editorial Director, Travel

Publishing for Technology Dummies

    Andy Cummings, Vice President and Publisher, Dummies Technology/General User

Composition Services

    Gerry Fahey, Vice President of Production Services

    Debbie Stailey, Director of Composition Services

Contents at a Glance

Table of Contents

Part III: The Making of a StandOut Resume 115

Chapter 8: Market Yourself with a StandOut Resume 117

Chapter 9: Format Means So Much: Choose Wisely 125

Introduction

Shades of déjà vu. While preparing this new edition I often felt like a time traveler pulled back to the first half of the last decade trying to explain to a reading audience what an electronic resume is when they'd never heard of *keywords* or *scannable resumes* or *optical character recognition software*.

At other times, I relived the writing struggles of the second half of the last decade when scannable self-marketing documents found less favor and resumes began their frenzied dart across the Internet, where, to assure safe arrival, they came dressed in the pedestrian garb of *plain text* (ASCII) embodied within e-mail. Coming up with attractive sample plain text resumes that didn't look like a telephone book without boldface type was a challenge neither I nor anyone else mastered.

But now, change is upon us once again in this fourth edition. Big, spectacular change. Since the last edition of this book, which was written in late 1999 and published in 2000, I found that the software designers in the recruitment industry have been working overtime — like 24/7. (Hey, software wizards, cool it! How about taking a long nap while the rest of us catch up with you?)

This edition reports on the third big dramatic technological wave in the recruiting industry:

- **First wave:** Scannable resumes.
- **Second wave:** Internet plain text resumes.
- **Third wave:** The return of the handsome resume made portable, and the emergence of online screening quizzes that determine whether your resume is accepted by recruiters and employers or buried at the bottom of the pile.

Chapter 1 has the intriguing details.

And for good measure, this edition still tells you how to deal with first- and second-wave technologies.

About This Book

Odds are that you are holding this book because you feel a need to discover what works and what doesn't work in representing yourself with a resume. This need is true whether you are:

- ✔ A new graduate starting out, a person in the big arch of main working years, or a seasoned ace

- ✔ A downsized job searcher, an individual writing a resume to support a career change, a transitioning military member, or a displaced information technology professional

- ✔ A novice resume writer or a well-experienced professional resume writer

No matter your experience, set of circumstances, or familiarity with resume writing, you've hit the mother lode with *Resumes For Dummies,* 4th Edition.

In these pages, the updated technical information — gathered from a wide variety of recruiting professionals — paired with classic strategies and smooth moves I've learned in three decades of career reporting, show you how to develop and distribute a state-of-the-art resume that says you're too superior to ignore.

It's a different job market out there: This book is the resume-writing tool that you need to stand out.

Technology Transition and Your Resume

Our world is bigger and more diverse than when the employment marketplace began to move from print to electronics about 20 years ago. People have more specific needs and opportunities — and deeper pitfalls to avoid.

Take just one aspect of the recruitment practice as an example: resume processing and applicant management. That activity is becoming ever more structured. Unless you are an A-list candidate — one employers fall all over themselves to hire — you may be better advised to avoid the rigid e-structures entirely or to use online resources in limited, specific ways described throughout this book.

My mission here is to help you master change in your written word, whether you're an A-list candidate or not. The tool you'll use is a StandOut resume.

What Is a StandOut Resume?

A StandOut resume is

- ✔ Carefully constructed to compete, compel, and capture attention

- ✔ Too skills-rich to overlook

- ✔ Targeted to the job, showing that you can and will do the work

- ✔ As good looking online as it is on paper

How This Book Is Organized

This book is divided into six distinct parts, and each part is divided into chapters. Here's the drill on what each part covers.

Part 1: Resumes in the Changing Job Search Environment

This part discusses the big-picture trends and developments, and what you should do to get your resume in the right hands to be hired.

Part II: StandOut Resumes for Affinity Groups

In this part, special attention is paid to recognizable groups of people who have been laid off, are feeling the bias against aging baby boomers, are information technology professionals who are not being hired, are leaving the military and reinventing themselves in the civilian job world, and are newly graduated and jobless.

Part III: The Making of a StandOut Resume

The elements of presenting yourself as a StandOut candidate appear in this part. It explains which format to choose, offers worksheets to help you organize your information, suggests essential content material to include (and omit), describes the most powerful words to use, and explains how to think your way through deadly resume dilemmas.

Part IV: StandOut Resumes Online

Three chapters in this part take you into the dimension of e-resumes, give you a script to use to determine which technology your target employer is using, point out how atypical e-resumes can work, and review the rules for scannable and plain text resumes for use in older systems.

Part V: Samples of StandOut Resumes

This part presents examples of annotated StandOut resumes, arranged by career fields. Special needs resumes are included.

Part VI: The Part of Tens

For Dummies readers know that The Part of Tens is a collection of single-subject chapters that cut to the chase in a ten-point format.

In these lists of ten, I offer ways to back up your resume claims, identify actions that drive recruiters to mayhem, suggest simple adjustments to quickly improve your resume, give tips on choosing a professional resume writer, and give you a resume checklist to rate your work.

Icons Used in This Book

For Dummies signature icons are those little round pictures you see in the margins of the book. I use them to rivet your attention on key bits of information. Here's a list of the icons you find in this book and what they mean.

This icon directs your undivided attention to resume techniques that make you stand out from the crowd.

Differences of opinion are found throughout recruitment and resume writing. Nothing works 100 percent of the time for everyone in every walk of life. This icon reminds you to try to make the best choice for your situation.

Some of the points in this book are so basic or important that you'll want to commit them to memory. This icon alerts you to those points.

This icon flags information that can make a difference in the outcome of your job search.

The dinosaur icon chomps away at job-killing goofs. Ignore these warnings, and you may be eaten alive.

Where to Go from Here

If you're writing your first resume, the chapters in Part III offer worksheets, words, and formats to help you get it right the first time. These chapters are also a good place to get reacquainted with the world of resumes if you've been out of the job market or are unexpectedly job hunting after a layoff.

To be in tune with current standards and practices, you must check out Chapters 1 and 2, then go to Part IV for the latest on e-resumes.

Otherwise, jump in where the topic and samples look inviting and applicable — I've done my best to make it all outstanding.

Part I

Resumes in the Changing Job Search Environment

The 5th Wave   By Rich Tennant

"It's a pretty good resume, but I would have liked to see more bells and whistles."

In this part . . .

You find trends and developments impacting your resume that you absolutely, positively must know about to remain competitive in the whirling landscape that is recruitment today. Starting with the return of the handsome resume and the growing adoption of online screening, this part presents easy understanding of the best resume moves in an era of technology transition.

Chapter 1

New Realities: Ten Big Changes in the World of Resumes

In This Chapter

▶ A welcome back for good-looking resumes

▶ Online screening as a danger to your resume

▶ The growth industry of background checks

▶ The rise of specialty sites and company portals

▶ Regimentation in the Information Age

▶ A place for human interaction and paper resumes

*H*eads up! Here comes the initial splash of the third big technological wave revolutionizing the employment landscape. Advance warning: Your stake in the new way of doing things is more critical than you may imagine.

Historically speaking, we raced through the first two waves in record time. In the single decade of the 1990s job seekers learned to write (1) scannable resumes and (2) ASCII plain text resumes. Now — with front-line news reported by the book's technical reviewer Jim Lemke — this book is the first to describe still newer technology that's the basis for rethinking how you prepare your resume and collateral materials — and how you market them for maximum effect.

Formatted e-resumes and *online screening* are the two most dramatic developments turning up in large- and medium-sized companies in developed nations across the globe. I tell you about these two big changes in some detail and how they impact your resume. Then, in the remainder of this chapter, I overview other big changes coming your way.

But first, please read about the current state of the recruiting industry, so you can better understand what's happening now and what will happen next to your resume as it makes its way in the workplace chase.

Unintended Consequences from a Resume Revolution

In our networked employment world of online resumes, e-mail, and applicant management systems, some of the vaunted technologies of the 1990s that were created to save recruiters' time and effort have measured up. But other technologies have produced unintended consequences brought about by staggering numbers of online resumes. The glut of resumes overloads recruiters, who are struggling to separate qualified from unqualified applicants for the jobs they're trying to fill.

From where are all these resumes coming? The resumes are plucked from cyberspace by many elements of online recruiting that include: search engines, Web-savvy recruiters, job sites, corporate Web sites with career portals, resume distribution services, and newsgroups.

As one recruiter complained to colleagues in a recent online discussion:

> *Most job searchers no longer read job descriptions. Job ads have become a lot like horoscopes: Every applicant thinks a job description describes him or her perfectly. Or if there isn't a fit at all, many job seekers reason that if they're not right for this position, maybe there's something else within the company that they're good for. Armed with an Internet connection, a list of job boards, and a resume, a job searcher can crank out about 100 applications in less than four hours.*

Job searchers aren't solely responsible for the high resume volume in cyberspace. Corporate human resources (HR) departments contribute to the nearly unmanageable workload when they fail to develop clear job requirements or use puzzling company jargon. These deficiencies force job searchers to work blindfolded, attempting to decipher inadequate postings of who or what a company is seeking.

Sometimes, the company is vague or purposely paints a rosier cast on a job than reality supports. A number of my newspaper column readers have written to me complaining that the positions they accepted are very different from their job descriptions; a single example is an unrevealed requirement to travel frequently and wear a beeper 24 hours a day.

Meet the recruiting tribe

The term *recruiter* in this book is used to indicate any professional who plays a role in bringing candidates to a hiring manager's attention. The recruiter *screens* candidates, and the hiring manager *selects* candidates. The presumption is that candidates brought to a hiring manager have been checked out and possess the qualifications to do the job being filled. All recruiters read resumes.

✔ **Internal recruiters** employed by a company are also called *in-house recruiters, corporate recruiters, or talent managers.* They are salaried and eligible for bonuses based on production.

✔ **External recruiters,** commonly called *headhunters* or *executive search consultants,* may also be called *third-party recruiters,* (recruiting) *agency recruiters,* or *independent recruiters.* They recruit for a variety of

companies and are further divided by the way they are paid for their services.

✔ **Retained recruiters** are paid fees whether or not a search produces the candidate hired for the job. Retained recruiters may work on yearly retainer contracts and, like outside lawyers, are called upon when their help is needed.

✔ **Contingency recruiters** are paid on the transactional model — they get their money only when they deliver a candidate who is hired by their client.

Contingency recruiters vastly outnumber retained recruiters. Until the mid-management level, contingency recruiters may produce better results for your career advancement, but retained recruiters may offer the best opportunities at upper-management levels.

The end result is that because of job seekers who apply for virtually every published job they come across — regardless of qualifications — and employers who write fuzzy job descriptions, the recruiting system is awash in resumes. Recruiters say most of them are unusable.

Many called, few chosen

A West Coast recruiter working a career fair complains that of 8,000 resumes left at his company's booth, about 60 made the cut back to the company's HR office. The others failed to meet the requirements of the open positions.

A Midwest recruiter reports a recent experience in which his agency posted a position for a project manager on major job boards and other free job-related sites. Some 654 applicants responded, of which 6 percent met 80 percent or more of the job's requirements and 11 percent met 51–79 percent of the job's requirements. But 82 percent failed to meet 50 percent of the job's requirements, and it took the recruiter two days to review the resumes to determine whether they were useful.

From the recruiter's viewpoint, taking the time to filter out about eight of ten applicants who weren't at all qualified for the job means that much less time could be spent doing in-depth assessments and negotiating and closing offers to the right candidates.

Plain text is hard on the eyes

The vast number of e-resumes "on ice" in resume databases are spun in plain text. Reading through 50 or 60 ASCII resumes is a task that can cause your chin to sag and your eyes to glaze over. "At the end of some days, I feel like I'm circling the drain," moans a bleary-eyed recruiter. Fortunately, help is here through better technology.

Hooray! The Return of the Handsome Resume

Do you remember — or perhaps you're too young to remember — those handsome resumes with the compelling embellishments: attractive formatting, appealing typefaces and fonts, boldfaced headings, italics, bullets, and underlining? Embellishments that were refreshing to read until technology all but killed them off a decade ago in favor of the electronically-correct but truly-blah online ASCII plain text resume? (See Chapter 15.)

The handsome resume was wonderful and is sorely missed by resume readers who grow bleary-eyed looking at pure text the livelong day.

Well, saints preserve us! Smart technology is bringing back those good-looking specimens we grudgingly gave up in the 1990s to make sure our resumes arrived intact over the Internet.

The new technology gang

The thrust for updated technology permitting handsome resumes to flourish comes from vendors selling technology known as *applicant tracking systems* (ATS) and *applicant management systems* (AMS). An ATS is any system, whether in software form or paper, that manages both a company's job posting and its data collection (of resumes and applications) to efficiently match prospective candidates to appropriate job openings. An AMS includes features of ATSs plus other functions, such as automated online screening.

Goodbye plain text, farewell scanning

As resume management technology evolves at breakneck speed, the end approaches not only for ASCII plain text resumes but also for scanning resumes into a system. The new paradigm allows you to attach your fully formatted, word-processed, handsome resume directly into the applicant system from a Web portal. (A portal is an entryway. A Web portal for resume submission is either a company Web site's career portal; a job site, such as HotJobs or Monster; or another Web site, such as one operated by a college career center or professional society.)

Submitting your resume through a Web portal eliminates the labor-intensive, error-plagued scanning process and allows line (department) managers who make hiring decisions to view an aesthetically pleasing formatted resume in its full glory with boldings, underlinings, and pleasing fonts.

How the systems work

In older applicant tracking systems, resumes are routed to managers by e-mail. If the resume is scanned and converted to a text file, the result is an eyesore, full of errors introduced through the scanning process (optical character recognition software makes mistakes).

Many reviewing managers see an error-studded resume and either assume that the applicant is not a detail-oriented person or that HR did a slovenly job in screening. Another feature of older systems is managerial overload. A manager could easily receive more than 20 e-mailed resumes daily in addition to all his or her other e-mail.

The new systems send the manager only one e-mail: "Check your manager's portal. You have resumes to review." When the manager opens the portal, all the resumes are listed with a hot link to either the MS Word document, or an HTML (*Hypertext Markup Language;* see Chapter 16 for more info on HTML resumes) version of the Word document. If the system includes an online screening component, the manager may choose not to look at all the resumes, but reduce their number by looking for certain specific requirements.

When the manager finishes reviewing the resumes, the appropriate recruiter in HR is automatically advised of the manager's interview choices. This streamlined process improves the staffing workflow and shortens the time it takes to bring a new employee onboard.

The rush to get onboard

New software releases by the major vendors of applicant management systems allow you to take advantage of the handsome resume option. Smaller vendors are expected to follow suit quickly or be placed at a competitive disadvantage. All major software programs accommodate these functions:

- ✔ **Take in fully formatted, word-processed (MS Word, WordPerfect, for instance) resumes as an attachment**

- ✔ **Inventory the resumes in the original format (most often MS Word)**

- ✔ **Send resumes downstream to hiring managers in their original formats**

The fact remains that plenty of older systems that cannot handle the formatted handsome resume are still in use. These older systems continue to put new resumes into plain text database storage.

If your resume is already in a database at a company that has recently upgraded its applicant management system technology, your resume will remain in plain text. If you hope to work for a particular employer that already has your plain text resume in its database, should you bother to send in a handsome resume? I would.

See Chapter 14 for suggestions on how to find out if a prospective employer is using technology that will accommodate handsome resumes, and, if not, what to do about it.

Online Screening Comes of Age

Traditionally, employers checked out candidates' qualifications for a position during or after a job interview. Today's emerging technology moves big chunks of the checking-out process upfront and automates it.

The online screening technology is a direct response to the congested resume marketplace. Online screening has an enormous effect on your resume's acceptance and, if you flunk online screening, the technology can banish your resume to the database basement.

Online screening is known by various terms — *prescreening* and *pre-employment screening,* to mention two. By any name, the purpose of online screening is to verify that you are, in fact, a good fit for the position and that you haven't lied about your background. Employers use online screening tools (tests, assessment instruments, questionnaires, and so forth) to reduce and sort applicants against criteria and competencies that are important to their organizations.

If you apply online through major job sites or many company Web site career portals, you will be asked to respond yes or no to job-related questions, such as:

- ✔ Are you willing to relocate?
- ✔ Do you have two or more years' experience managing a corporate communications department?
- ✔ Is your salary requirement between $55,000–$60,000/year?

Answering "no" to any of these questions disqualifies you for the listed position, an automated decision that helps the recruiters thin the herd of resumes more quickly but that could be a distinct disadvantage to you, the job searcher. (Without human interaction, you may not show enough of the stated qualifications, but you may have compensatory qualifications that a machine won't allow you to communicate.)

On the other hand, professionals in shortage categories will benefit by a quick response, such as nursing. Example: *Are you an RN?* If the answer is "yes," the immediate response, according to a recruiter's joke, is "When can you start?"

Online screening can be described as an automated process of creating a blueprint of known requirements for a given job, then collecting information from each applicant in a standardized manner to see if the applicant matches the blueprint. The outcomes are sent to recruiters and hiring managers.

Sample components of online screening

The following examples of online screening are not exhaustive, but they are illustrations of the most commonly encountered upfront filtering techniques.

- ✔ **Basic evaluation:** The system automatically evaluates the match between a resume's content and a job's requirement and ranks the most qualified resumes at the top.
- ✔ **Skills and knowledge testing:** The system uses tests that require applicants to prove their knowledge and skills in a specific area of expertise. Online skills and knowledge testing is especially prevalent in information technology jobs where dealing with given computer programs is basic to job performance. Like the old-time typing tests in an HR office, there's nothing subjective about this type of quiz: You know the answers, or you don't.
- ✔ **Personality assessment:** The attempt to measure work-related personality traits to predict job success is one of the more controversial types of online testing. Dr. Wendell Williams, a leading testing expert based in the Atlanta area, says that personality tests expressly designed for hiring are

in a totally different league than tests designed to measure things like communication style or personality type: "Job-related personality testing is highly job specific and tends to change with both task and job," he says. "If you are taking a generic personality test, a good rule is to either pick answers that fall in the middle of the scale or ones you think best fit the job description. This is not deception. Employers rarely conduct studies of personality test scores versus job performance and so, it really does not make much difference."

✔ **Behavioral assessment:** The system asks questions aimed at uncovering your past experience applying core competencies the organization requires (such as fostering teamwork, managing change) and position specific competencies (such as persuasion for sales, attention to detail for accountants). Chapter 10 further describes competencies.

✔ **Managerial assessments:** The system presents applicants with typical managerial scenarios and asks them to react. Proponents say that managerial assessments are effective for predicting performance on competencies, such as interpersonal skills, business acumen, and decision making. Dr. Williams identifies the many forms these assessments can take:

- **In-basket exercises** where the applicant is given an in-basket full of problems and told to solve them

- **Analysis case studies** where the applicant is asked to read a problem and recommend a solution

- **Planning case studies** where the applicant is asked to read about a problem and recommend a step-by-step solution

- **Interaction simulations** where the applicant is asked to work out a problem with a skilled role player

- **Presentation exercises** where the applicant is asked to prepare, deliver, and defend a presentation

✔ **Integrity tests:** The system attempts to measure your honesty with a series of questions. You can probably spot the best answers without too much trouble.

Pros and cons

From your viewpoint, here's a snapshot of the advantages and disadvantages of online screening:

✔ **Advantages:** (A) In theory, a perfect online screening is totally job-based and fair to all people with equal skills. Your resume would survive the first cut based only on your ability to do well in the job. (B) You are screened out of consideration for any job you may not be able to do, saving yourself stress and keeping your track record free of false starts. (C) If you're judged a close match, you're halfway through the hiring door.

✔ **Disadvantages:** (A) The creation of an online process is vulnerable to human misjudgment; I'm still looking for an example of the perfect online screening system. (B) You have no chance to "make up" missing competencies or skills. (An analogy: You can read music but you don't know how to play a specific song. You can learn it quickly, but there's no space to write "quick learner.") (C) Tests may lead to test faking — not you, but job searchers who do find ways to cheat put you at a disadvantage. (D) You may be screened out of contention by impersonal software because you aren't Web savvy, but with a little computer coaching, you could do very well in the job.

Level playing field for salaries

When employers demand your salary requirements before they'll schedule an interview, you are at a disadvantage in negotiating strength. But with hundreds of Web sites broadcasting the compensation information supplied by Salary.com (salary.com), the tables are turning.

You can, with a few clicks, get a ballpark estimate of your market worth. For an additional sum, you can get a detailed report on your market value. Now, you become a more informed and more equal partner in the negotiation. If your market rate is $75,000/year and you answer the question earlier in this section, "Is your salary requirement between $55,000 and $60,000 per year?" you can answer "no" and keep looking.

Background checks

Background checks are another component of online screening. They're booming in this era of ongoing security concerns. With your permission, employers can dig deeply into your personal and employment history.

Background verifications are done after a hiring manager narrows the search to a few candidates (the "short" list) and hires Web investigators to check them out on databases of public records. Sometimes the employer owns the software to do in-house background checks.

Verification is highly regulated, but the following question is a wild card: How widespread are databases that bend the rules, such as ones that offer booking and arrest records, which, unlike convictions, are unproven accusations? Privacy experts say "gray market" databases can be found without exhaustive searching.

So that you will be very careful about the accuracy of the information you convey during an online screening, here are sample topics that are available for a price by Web-based investigators:

- **Employment history:** A history of an individual's employment for up to the past 20 years.

- **Education verifications:** A confirmation that an individual did indeed receive the diploma, degree, or other educational credential claimed.

- **Personal profile report:** Records of parties to federal, state, and county actions, including felony, misdemeanor, or civil actions.

- **Booking and arrest records:** Available in some states.

- **Civil lawsuits and divorce records:** Available by county.

- **Medical treatment history:** Medical visits for 10 years, with the name and address of the treating facility and the dates of treatments. The exact purpose of the patient's visit is not provided. Workers' compensation claims are also available.

- **Credit report:** An individual's credit-worthiness, financial stability, spending habits, prior addresses, and more.

- **Driving record:** A driving abstract for an individual; usually three years.

- **Address history by SSN:** Names and addresses for a given social security number as reported to credit bureaus during the past seven years.

- **Bankruptcies, liens, and judgments:** Records of court-ordered financial obligations by state.

- **Military service:** Determines or verifies the branch and dates of U.S. military service.

- **Bank account history:** A log of activity in a given checking or savings account; requires legitimate and documented purpose for access.

When online screening questions ask for your social security number, think before supplying it. You can't be sure who is reading the information. A social security number and a resume are all the data a crook needs to steal your identity. Substitute a series of "9"s in the space where the SSN is a required field. Give your SSN only when you're confident that the data is going to the right place.

Your rights in background checks

Finding derogatory information about you is not necessarily sufficient to officially disqualify you from employment. The EEOC (Equal Employment Opportunity Commission) says the deficiencies must be shown to be job-related.

Background screening must be done by the books, both at the federal and state levels. On the federal level, the main governing legislation is the Fair Credit Reporting Act (FCRA). The bulk of the credit reports are "investigative consumer reports" (such as character, general reputation, personal characteristics, or mode of living), rather than pure credit reports (financial records). Some states also have credit reporting requirements and privacy laws. Your rights include these rules:

- ✔ You must give signed permission for background screening.

- ✔ You must be told if your record is used to deny your application.

- ✔ You can insist that inaccurate information be corrected or deleted and that outdated information be stripped from your record.

Find out more about federal and state laws as they apply to pre-employment background screening. Use Google.com, or another search engine, to search on "Fair Credit Report Act" and by state, such as "California + credit reporting law."

Watch your back in screening rejection

The first thing to do to get your resume on the favored short list of candidates: Be sure that you don't get knocked out by online screening simply because you are unknowledgeable about the topic. Spend enough time cruising job sites and company Web site career portals to get a feel for the kinds of online screening that are apt to come your way. Take a few tests on company career portals where you really don't want to work to gain experience and increase your comfort level.

What about the online free psychology tests that aren't job specific? Don't bother with these baseless pop psychology instruments for this purpose — unless you feel you just need to get some practice interacting with online tests.

As for background checks, what can you do to protect your career against harm? Before you sign releases permitting the screening to take place, make sure your records in credit bureaus are correct. You can order a credit report from one or more of the three national credit bureaus — Equifax, Experian, and TransUnion — to correct errors. You can also order a credit report from each of the three bureaus (they may have differing information about you) from one Web site, 3bureaureport.com, for about $35.

Can your resume be turned away?

What if you get low grades on answering the screening questions — can the employer's system tell you to take your resume and get lost? No, not legally. Adrian Barbour, the Western recruiting manager for a major defense contractor, explains:

> Anyone can leave a resume, but if they do not pass the screening, the resume will be ranked at the bottom of the list in the database. Employers should maintain all resumes for a minimum of two years in case of an EEO (Equal Employment Opportunity) audit, especially firms that receive federal dollars. Some private employers may not accept resumes from applicants who do not meet minimum standards, but they are vulnerable to discrimination lawsuits, especially if minimum requirements are not explicitly detailed in published job descriptions.

The bottom line: If you don't score well in screening questions, your resume will be exiled to an electronic no-hire zone even if it isn't physically turned away.

The future of online screening

If all the online screening technology is beginning to feel like Big Brother, unfortunately, you can do little to avoid it entirely if you submit e-resumes through the portals specified by job ads.

But take heart: The vast majority of employers in the United States do not use the online screening technologies yet. And when, as demographers predict, the job market again becomes employee-driven, the rush to do online screening may slow down.

Employers who haven't adopted online screening say they forego the technology for a number of reasons. The two big ones: a lack of knowledge of online screening and skepticism about the results that its advocates claim.

Jumping through hoops

Job seekers complain that recruiters expect you to do far too much work before giving you an inkling that you're a contender for a position. When you post your resume, you may be instructed to also fill out a lengthy job application, breaking down your resume item by item, and filling out a long skills summary. You may be asked to do all this task online or through autoresponder e-mail.

When these demands are made, turn to your completed worksheets (in Chapter 13) for a quick tool.

More Big Changes on the Workplace Horizon

In addition to the handsome resume and online screening trends, other developments also influence how effectively your resume travels.

Job sites

Surveys report that the big general employment sites (Monster, HotJobs and CareerBuilder) aren't responsible for high numbers of job offers. Newly favored for higher job-offer rates: specialty sites and company Web career portals. (See Chapter 2.)

Company Web career portals

Almost all big corporations now operate company Web sites with career portals. This makes it easy to directly apply to the companies that you'd most like to work for.

Employee referral programs

The practice of employers asking their own workforce, "Do you know anyone who might be good for this job?" has blossomed into widely used formal employee referral programs where sizeable bonuses are paid for each candidate hired. A strongly referred candidate is usually seen as preferable to someone off the street. In tempo with advertising, employee referral programs rise when too few unemployed look for work and slow down when too many unemployed look for work.

Profile-based systems

Profile-based systems are designed to bypass keyword searches entirely by standardizing data fields on which the recruiter can search. (The e-forms described in Chapter 15 are also short forms, but profiles contain far more structured details.)

Basically, you dissect small pieces of your overall self-marketing information into specific data fields (boxes), which are filed in a company or job site database. You may use the site's automated resume-builder, answer lengthy questionnaires, cut-and-paste data from your plain text resume — or, in some systems you may be asked to build a profile of yourself online.

Profiles often require you express your preferences by naming your desired salary range, work location, job function, travel, work schedule, and so forth (a version of online screening).

Some companies, such as Predict Success.com and HR Technologies specialize in helping employers develop online competency questions (see Chapter 10) used to develop the applicant's profile. The profile is measured against a position model to predict whether a person has what it takes to succeed in a position.

Creating a standardized format that compares apples to apples is done for the convenience of recruiters. If you have superb qualifications, profiles can lift you above the competition.

But, because the vast majority of job seekers don't fall in that rarified category, profiling can work against you. In profiling, you are negotiating 100 percent on the employer's terms without the opportunity to express unique skills, an uncommon experience mix, or compensatory characteristics if certain requirements of data fields are missing in your background. The image of robo resume comes to mind when I think of profiles.

XML technology

A decade ago everyone thought that *Hypertext Markup Language* (HTML) resumes would be the next big thing, but the technology never really took off. Most employers tell me that they receive less than 1 percent of their resumes in HTML.

XML *(eXtensible Markup Language)* is the new technology that allows staffing systems and payroll systems to talk to each other. An independent, nonprofit world-wide consortium of companies, HR-XML, is attempting to develop standards for exchanging workforce staffing and management information between HR specialists.

Although XML is thought by some recruiting insiders to be the next big new thing, other observers predict that this technology, too, will be underused just like its predecessor, HTML.

Barbara Ling, a leading authority on e-recruiting, says HTML is about displaying information, while XML is about describing information because you can define your own metatags for your own purposes and share those tags with other users.

Ling says that you can find a good Web site explanation about XML at
www.w3schools.com/xml/xml_whatis.asp.

Volatile job market

Economists say the *human capital marketplace* (latest buzz word for job
market) should expect endless cycles of hiring/layoff at the same company.
This prediction seems reasonable if the past decade is a clue, suggesting you
keep your resume current, register with online job agents, maintain a network of employment contacts, remain visible in professional organizations,
and follow tips for handling temporary jobs on your resume (see Chapters
4 and 12).

Paper resumes

Professionals in the e-recruiting industry have been trying to exterminate
paper resumes for a half-dozen years, proclaiming them all but dead. But
paper resumes are alive and well and will survive for use in local or regional
job markets during the next decade — perhaps even longer. Among reasons
why paper survives:

- **Paper to have and to hold:** Hiring managers, as well as recruiters, may
  like a tangible paper to feel, view, and save.

- **Job fairs:** Using e-resumes at some brick-and-mortar job fairs is possible, but paper resumes are the norm because they're easy to distribute.

- **Advertising mail address:** Job ads that include postal addresses keep
  the paper alternative in place.

- **Employee referral programs:** Companies that haven't converted
  employee referrals to Web processes often retain a form that instructs
  referring workers to clip a paper resume to the form before submitting a
  name to the HR department.

Human networking

If you are a job seeker with doubts about your job qualifications, age, or
employability problems and fear you may run into a brick wall on the Web,
stick with human-based job search. Only half the U.S. population uses the
Internet for any form of job search, and the majority of small businesses
don't use electronic methods. You can find tips on finding employment the
old-fashioned way throughout this book.

Ten Big Changes at a Glance

1. Return of the handsome resume
2. Emergence of online screening
3. Changed job site mix
4. Booming company Web career portals
5. Formalization of employee referral programs
6. Regimentation through e-profiles
7. Development of XML technology
8. Forecasted change in human capital market
9. Still a force: paper resumes
10. The human antidote for e-recruiting rigidity

The key trends and developments addressed in this chapter render other resume books obsolete. Keep these big changes in mind as you dig into the rest of the book.

Chapter 2

Get Your Resume Out There

In This Chapter

▶ Succeeding with a ten-step placement plan

▶ Using personal job agents

▶ Unraveling the real deal about job sites

▶ Safeguarding your privacy and credentials online

▶ Networking inside and outside companies

▶ Following up in professional style

This chapter puts the cart before the horse. The water skier before the boat. The train before the engine.

Suggestions on how to distribute your StandOut resumes before you've written a word come up front in this edition because so much has changed during the past couple of years that knowing how you'll *use* your resume could help you do a better job of *writing* your resume.

Ready? Try on these ideas for size.

Market Your Resume in Ten Steps

Follow these steps to get your resume to the right place.

1. Target your job market.

You may not know precisely what you want, but having one to three choices will shorten your search. Choose an occupation, industry, company size, and locale you think you'd like. For example, you may want a job, using your education in electrical engineering, in a medium-sized company in Chicago or Milwaukee. Or you may want to work in a non-profit organization as an event planner in Washington, D.C. In both cases, you'd want to check out specialty sites for your occupation.

You can be flexible and change directions if opportunity strikes.

2. Make a master list of job leads.

Identify and research potential employers that might be a good fit. Try to uncover the name of the individual at each company who is responsible for hiring people for the position you want. Here are resources for your list:

- **Job sites:** Big super sites like HotJobs, Career Builder, and Monster, and specialty sites that relate to your occupation and job title, industry, and geographic location.

- **Newspapers:** Classified and larger display job ads, plus business page articles.

- **Business directories, trade publications, and other sources of company information:** CorporateInformation (corporate information.com), Hoover's Online (hoovers.com), and PR Newswire (prnewswire.com), are three examples.

- **Networking groups:** Both local and functional; both online and offline.

- **Recruiting firms:** Independent, third-party.

- **Professional organizations:** In your career field.

- **College or university:** Garner alumni names and contact information from your school's alumni directory.

- **People:** Family, friends, neighbors, former co-workers, bankers, social organization members, job club members, former professors.

- **Referrals:** Acquaintances and friends who work at companies you admire, and referrals from people you contact who don't know of a job opening but can give you more names to contact.

3. Take care of housekeeping chores.

Such as:

- **Get a free e-mail address:** You can get a free e-mail address from Hotmail (hotmail.com) or Yahoo!Mail (yahoomail.com). Be sure to check each and every one of your e-mailboxes every day.

  Rent a post office box and install a phone with an answering machine if you intend to add that layer of privacy to your search.

- **College students:** Get another e-mail address. Most college students get a free e-mail address on campus that ends with the extension ".edu" — a dead giveaway for student status. Many employers, who really want from one to three years' experience, won't consider resumes with .edu in the e-mail address. Get another address for job hunting, so that you can at least make the first cut.

- **Consider using split personalities:** Suppose you want to present yourself as a candidate in two occupations or career fields in the same database. You're looking for a job as a convention planner or a market representative. Or as a controller or internal auditor. Most databases are programmed to replace resume number one with resume number two, under the assumption that resume number two is an update.

If you wish to be considered for two types of jobs, consideration may come automatically as a job computer searches the resume database for keywords. But if you want to double up to be sure, use your full name on resume number one. On resume number two, cut back your first and middle names to initials and change telephone numbers and e-mail addresses.

- **Self-send first:** Before sending out your resume, send it to yourself and a friend to compare and correct.

- **Double-check your Web page:** Before making your Web resume address public by putting it on other types of resumes, review your site for links that you may have forgotten you added in a more carefree period. Stories of links to employment-killing naked lady pictures and bawdy jokes continue to circulate. And don't provide links to your school class or professional society; employers may slip out and find better candidates than you. Finally, if confidentiality is important, don't forget to password-protect your Web page. When employers call, give them the password. If you don't know how to password-protect your site, ask your Web site host or Internet service provider for instructions.

- **Practice online testing:** Some employers, weary of having their databases crammed with candidates who don't meet their skill standards, are requiring that jobs seekers take a screening test before their resumes are allowed inside (see Chapter 1).

- **Be mindful of legal issues:** Remember that resume banks must obey civil rights laws: Don't reveal any potentially discriminatory information (age, race, gender, religion, ethnicity) by e-mail to a representative of a resume bank or job site that you would not reveal in a telephone call or during an in-person job interview. Assume the information will be passed on to employers.

- **Use consolidator sites to save time:** Flipdog (`www.flipdog.com`) and Career Builder (`www.careerbuilder.com`) are two free services that pull together job listings from many job sites and put them in one place. Additionally, infoGIST CareerInfoFinder (`infogist.com/careerxroads.htm`) is a fee resource that searches hundreds of job banks, employment sites, and company Web sites for job leads and company research; a trial period is free.

- **Bookmark favorite job sites and search tools:** Bookmark favorite sites and, on a regular basis, make a focused search by job title, industry, or geographic location. You could, for example, ask a site to show a list of all open jobs for emergency medical technicians in Illinois.

4. Draft your resume(s).

Create more than one resume if possible (see Chapter 8). Shape several different resumes: one general version plus several others that address the finer points of functions you want to do — for example, accountant, internal auditor, tax specialist.

Make sure your resume contains the relevant keywords (see Chapter 11) because, in a word-matching keyword search, your resume will be stuck to the bottom of a database if it lacks the required words.

5. Draft back-up self-marketing resume content.

Create mix-and-match text blocks for a fast tune-up of your resumes and cover letters. Write a variety of paragraphs and store them on your computer. Need ideas of what to say in the paragraphs? Read over resumes of others in your field and be inspired. Then, when you must quickly put together a resume targeted to a specific job — and none of your full-blown resume versions are perfect — your inventory of text blocks gives you a running start.

6. Draft your cover letters and cover notes.

Draft several cover letters and the shorter version, cover notes. My book, *Cover Letters For Dummies* (Wiley), offers state-of-the-art tips on writing dynamic statements.

7. Review today's submission technology.

The handsome resume is making a comeback (see Chapter 1). But until the new technology pretty much drives out the old, telephone an employer about any job that's very important to you and inquire about that specific company's technology (see Chapter 14). When in doubt, paste your ASCII text cover letter and resume in the body of the e-mail message and attach a formatted Word or WordPerfect resume. The ASCII resume is backup in case the employer is using an old system and can't or doesn't download your formatted resume.

8. Save your resumes and cover letters in useful formats.

Ready your resume packages for battle by saving them on your hard drive, and a disk if you transmit resumes from more than one location. One version should be in MS Word or WordPerfect and the other in ASCII plain text. See Chapter 14 for specifics.

9. Determine your online resume strategy.

If privacy issues are of concern to you, you may choose any of several strategies:

- **Conservatively confidential:** No online posting of your resume, except as a response to specific job listings, or to a targeted mailing list of potential employers. You take care to protect your identity. You plan to work with one or more recruiters (you understand that third-party recruiters are paid for finding the best candidates and will likely ignore you if you are spread all over the Net and can be hired for free).

- **Moderate exposure:** In addition to the conservative exposure just mentioned, you are highly selective about the resume databases and personal job agents to which you submit your resume. You may or may not cloak your identity. You understand the privacy policy of the job sites you select.

- **Full visibility:** You are unemployed and need a job quickly. You post to every logical job site you can find. You want immediate action and are pulling out all the stops. You have read this chapter and know the pros and cons of such a move.

10. **Keep track of your progress.**

Don't let important aspects of your online activity get away from you. Keep records of where you databanked your resume, which personal job search agents are alerting you to the best job posts, and which source of job listings are proving to hold the most potential for you. Make mid-course corrections when needed.

When should your resume arrive? Mondays are busy days, and Fridays are termination days. Try for arrival on Tuesday, Wednesday, or Thursday.

Send Your Resume the Right Way to the Right Places

Deciding whether to post your resume at a big job site or stick with the traditional paper resume is a decision deserving some thought. I explore the options in the following sections.

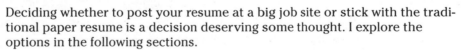

Making sure that the right people get it

If you send your resume to a hiring manager (good idea), send a duplicate to the human resource department. Note this effort in your cover letter to the hiring manager, which means that not only is the human resource professional not treated disrespectfully, but the hiring manager gets to keep your resume as a constant reminder of you instead of having to send it down to HR.

Warning: Watch out for the black hole at major job boards

Recruiter Mary Nurrenbrock doesn't sugarcoat it when describing her view of the practice of responding to jobs advertised on the major job boards:

"When you respond to openings directly through job boards, your resume usually ends up in a black hole, a passive database. If you are responding right from the board, it's going to HR. Bad move. These guys are up to their eyeballs and usually don't even really know what the hiring manager is looking for. That is, if the HR person even sees the resume in the passive database.

"You need to get to the hiring manager, not HR. How? When you visit a job board and see a job that looks like it's a fit (you notice I didn't say that it looks interesting), go to that company's Web site and get a name. Most of the corporate sites have profiles. Get the name of the VP Marketing, CEO, CMO — whomever the open position is likely to report to.

"Figuring out the address isn't hard. Look under the press releases where you'll usually find a company contact e-mail address. Use the same format — john_doe@, john.doe@, jdoe@ — to send your resume. If it bounces back, try a different format. If that doesn't work, try to wrangle the address from the company receptionist. If all else fails, snail mail it.

"What usually happens next is that the hiring manager sends your resume to HR. But we are trying to avoid that, right? No, we are trying to avoid the black hole. Now the HR person is looking at a resume that came to her from an internal source. Big difference!"

Be aware: Big online job sites get small slice of hiring pie

Even Net-savvy job searchers write to my column telling me they're becoming disenchanted with big online job sites.

I've been looking for a job, using big job boards for three months. Offers for interviews: zilch! I need help. What's going on?

I keep sending resumes for jobs to big job boards (generalized super sites), however I never hear anything back from them. As yet, I have never been contacted. I fill out the resume and make it specific to the job advertised. What am I doing wrong?

I have sent out my resume to a number of positions posted on sites like (big job board), and I have noticed that a number of these positions stay posted for weeks on end. What is the average response to jobs posted on the Web? Are people actually hired from these responses?

Back in 1995, a zillion years ago in Internet time, advisers, including myself, urged job seekers to get aboard the Web train or be left behind. The message was received around the world. Nearly a decade later, the online novelty has vanished as millions of job seekers found out how easy it is to pop a resume online and have done so.

As an unintended consequence, the crush of resumes has muted the ability of hiring managers to respond effectively. The online job sites are delivering virtual bodies but not many job offers and acceptances, according to recent studies. *In short, recruiting industry insiders now believe that job boards account for less than 8 percent of hires in the United States.* Depending on which research — none of it is flawless — you read, the stronger online hiring ratios belong to specialty job boards and corporate Web sites.

The giant job boards do offer several advantages when you're floating your resume:

✓ Excellent for entry-level jobs with big corporations like Microsoft and Procter & Gamble.

✓ Excellent for job searchers with broadly applicable skills, such as sales and marketing.

✓ Excellent for a number of fancy tools, such as job title converters that help job seekers figure out what their job title would be in other companies or career fields.

✓ More focused sections or channels (like healthcare and legal jobs) are being added to emulate the appeal of the niche job sites.

You shouldn't decide that, because of the low rate of hires, you're never going to speak to the Web again and that's that. As unsatisfying as the Web is for the actual hook-up of people and jobs at the moment, the clock won't be turned back. Consider online searching as merely one more option in your tool kit.

My recommendation: Use one or two major job boards, and otherwise, devote your online time to the specialty sites and the corporate sites.

Post on specialty Web sites: Why smaller may be better for your resume

The super-generalized job sites — Career Builder, Monster, HotJobs, and the government-sponsored America's Job Bank are good examples — have been compared to a broadcast model similar to the TV networks, appealing to a very wide, diverse audience.

Specialty sites, by contrast, operate a narrowcast model similar to the cable networks where channels like Comedy Central, Animal Planet, and MTV are targeted to very specific groups of viewers.

The future of online job searching: Specialty and specificity

Generic broad-based Web recruiting is giving way to narrowly focused recruiting. And as go the recruiting sites, so go your resumes. I don't even want to guess how many specialty sites sit on the Net waiting to welcome computer-loveable resumes, but they number in the thousands!

Guides to online resources

Online job resources come and go too frequently to stay current. Fully a third of the dot.coms I referenced in the third edition (which was prepared in late 1999) are now dot.gones. So much is happening in recruiting today that a general sampling is no longer adequate. That's why I refer you to specialists.

1. **Gerry Crispin** and **Mark Mehler** are two recruiting industry consultants and workshop leaders who do an outstanding job of staying current with the employment marketplace. Each year, Crispin and Mehler publish a new edition of *CareerXroads: The Directory to Job, Resume and Career Management Sites on the Web.* It's hands-down the definitive consumer directory of the recruiting industry.

   The book has thorough reviews of 500 sites, with each review containing a cogent description of what the site offers. The authors cross-reference those 500 sites with hundreds of additional sites indexed for jobs and resumes. Additionally, if you sign up on their Web site, the authors will send you free quarterly bulletins with the latest scoop. That's a pretty good deal for a book that costs under $30. The directory is available through Crispin and Mehler's Web site (careerxroads.com) and at bookstores.

2. **Margaret Riley Dikel** and **Frances E. Roehm** are co-authors of the renowned bi-annual book, *The Guide to Internet Job Searching.* Too many people still don't have a clue about how to do an online job hunt. Dikel and Roehm have created the fourth edition of a chapter-and-verse-perfect book that tells you how online job searches flow and what you must know to keep from going under. Dikel and Roehm also describe hundreds of specialty Web sites grouped into a dozen career fields. The book, under $15, is published by VGM Career Books/ McGraw-Hill.

   Dikel also is the author of *The Riley Guide* (rileyguide.com), the Internet's number one site to find updated information about online recruiting resources and articles. It's free. A former librarian and online pioneer, Dikel is famous as the nation's foremost private consultant specializing in the use of the Internet for employment and career information.

   Roehm is a much-admired career librarian at the Skokie, Ill., Public Library, where she specializes in all things online and is in great demand by job hunters.

Every profession, locality, industry, and lifestyle is joined by networking hubs and entrepreneurial watering holes in catering to the select Web communities they target.

A free directory of 6,000-plus job sites, the largest collection the wired world has yet seen, is up and running as a service of AIRS, a training company that teaches online recruiters how to buff their performance. The AIRS Job Boards Directory (`airsdirectory.com/directories/job_boards`) is a technology sonnet to niche job boards with links that make access easy and fast.

You can search the AIRS directory by keywords that match the skill or profession you're in, or you can drill down through a directory of industries, functions, skills, and such specialty areas as diversity, new college graduates and executive search. You can also search and sort by country, region, state, and metro areas.

But if you want qualitative comments on hundreds of sites, you need the print guides, *CareerXroads* and *The Guide to Internet Job Searching,* which are mentioned in the nearby sidebar "Guides to online resources."

When specialty sites shine

The reasons to customize your job hunt by posting your resume on small sites are the following:

- More focused job listings for your purposes.
- Fewer cumbersome procedures to post a resume.
- More control over what your resume looks like. Big general job boards tend to insist on a chronological job history format when it may be to your advantage to use a project-oriented or functional approach. (See profiles of these different resumes in Chapter 16.)
- May limit listings by headhunters, which make up a heavy percentage of ads on super sites. Headhunters often don't name the potential employer, which could be a problem if it's your own company.
- Appear to have a higher percentage of mid- and upper-management jobs than the general super sites.
- Many job seekers say they like the smaller specialty sites' manageable size, better quality listings, and community feel.

Hail the corporate Web site

In the days before computers and the Internet, when you went directly to companies to apply for a job — without knowing if there were openings — the job search method was called "direct application."

Today, you can still use the direct application method, but you do it online at corporate Web sites that recruit through their *career portals* (gateways).

Among the nation's largest corporations — trendsetters for smaller employers — virtually all are recruiting new staff on their corporate Web sites. Here are things to bear in mind about submitting your resume through a corporate Web site.

Target your search

Although major commercial job sites, such as Monster.com, are centralized, the universe of corporate Web sites is decentralized. Exploring that universe is time consuming. You can easily spend two hours taking the measure of just one or two corporate career portals, picking up details of what you should know to maximize opportunity.

Begin by compiling a list of prospective employers. To prioritize the list, you can use company briefs on Plunkett's (plunkettresearch.com), Hoovers (hoovers.com) and other online company directories mentioned in Chapter 8, as well as information from newspapers and business magazines.

Another way to compile your list is to search large job sites — job boards, such as Career Builder or America's Job Bank — to sort opportunities by location, by job function, or by industry. Verify appealing job ads on the corporate Web site.

Notice company interests

As you scan a corporate career portal, back up to the company home page and click to press releases, annual report, and general areas for any edge you can use to enhance your application when you move to the careers area.

Job seeker connects through specialty site

According to *BusinessWeek*, David, a San Francisco Bay-area consultant, spent more than 30 minutes building his resume on a super job site, filling out multiple screens of information and check-off boxes. David wasn't a happy camper because he already had a resume he liked, but he went along with the drill. Nothing happened.

David finally tried the craigslist (www.craigslist.org) San Francisco job board, a community site. Happily, it let David cut and paste his own resume. Within a day, David got two calls for interviews that fit his requirements while his mandated super job site resume slept the sleep of the dead.

Why two-for-one doesn't add up

To make doubly sure that your resume is in a database for a job you really want, should you postal mail a duplicate hard copy as a backup in case a clerk messes up the electronic file?

No. When the company's career page directs you to e-mail your resume or to submit it via the company's online resume builder, do not send in a hard copy to the human resources department because the hard copy would more than likely be scanned, found to be a duplicate, and deleted. This unnecessary extra work causes a scowl on the poor scanning operator's face and

doesn't buy you a thing. The only time to send in a hard copy is to a hiring manager.

If company managers wanted duplicates to clog their files with paper, they wouldn't have installed the more efficient electronic recruiting systems.

As technical reviewer Jim Lemke says, "With any system, once you submit your resume, you are in the pond. There is no need to send another resume through the system at the same time."

Understand procedure

About the only standard advice for sending your resume to corporate Web sites is to submit information in a digital version only. Skip postal mail and fax.

Pay attention to specific instructions on each corporation's site. Some corporate Web sites ask you to attach your resume. Others require that you cut and paste it into a standard form, or use the site's resume builder.

If you attach your formatted resume (my preference if it's an option) and can't decide whether to lead off with an objective and or skills summary (see Chapter 10), try both, like this.

Objective: Position at (name or type of company) in (general locale) requiring a stand-out performer with the following skills and characteristics: (insert your keyword profile, as discussed in Chapters 9 and 10).

Additionally, don't be surprised if you're asked to take online employment tests. Be ready to provide good information on your skills and interests.

Some corporate sites won't accept anonymous candidates who cloak their identity.

Use paper resumes to rescue your career

Remember that the Web is just one more pebble on the employment beach. A big pebble to be sure, but, let's face it, some job hunters are never going to get past the E-Gatekeeping Godzilla (Internet recruiting systems) because they are too old, too young, have the wrong skills, whatever.

Evaluate why your online search isn't working

Is your online job search in trouble? Review this checklist and see which reason(s) could be at fault. Some job hunters

- ❏ Strike out in e-job search because they refuse to invest the effort to learn the ropes.

- ❏ Come up zero online because they just don't get this Internet thing, never did, never will and no longer care.

- ❏ Never lift off with their searches because their resumes lack the right keywords and accomplishment content.

- ❏ Bump into a wall of silence because their skills are not in demand and possibly are obsolete.

- ❏ Are ignored in today's youth culture because they're older ("overqualified") than employers want to hire.

- ❏ Are shut out because they're on the other end of the age discrimination spectrum — too young. Employers say they want a minimum of several years of current experience.

- ❏ Don't make it past the online screening programs because they lack the knowledge, competencies, skills, or ability to respond correctly to programmed questions.

- ❏ Never hear back because employers just aren't on a hiring spree.

Could this be you? Before cursing the darkness of a failed job search, decide whether you want to (A) improve your online search techniques or (B) decide the computer is rotting your mind and junk the whole cyberslimey thing.

Go back to finding jobs the classic way

If you have reason to think you belong in the Internet expatriate class and your chances of finding a job by e-efforts (even if the "e" stands for excellence) are nil, my best suggestion is head back to job hunting the way it was before the Web arrived and wasted your time.

E-mail, postal mail, or fax

A reader's letter to Joyce: "A very simple, but important question: If you are asked to e-mail, fax, or postal mail a resume to a prospective employer, what is the best way to send it?"

When a delivery mode preference isn't specified, I'd start with e-mail because it's easier to inventory in a database and send downstream to hiring managers. Next choice, I'd send postal mail (making sure it is scannable, see Chapter 15) and, as a last resort, fax.

Use your paper resume as your marketing tool of choice when you turn to newspapers and trade publications to find out who's hiring. Use your paper resume as your calling card while networking person to person and finding employment thanks to human intervention. Use your paper resume as your ace when cold-calling hiring managers, many of whom dislike reading computer screens and like the feel of a piece of paper in their hands.

As I often say, when the machines seem to be beating you, use people to beat the machines. Some good opportunities will always be captured the old-fashioned way.

Take Online Issues into Account

As you submit your resumes electronically here, there, and everywhere, you need to be aware that there are tricks and tips specific to using the Web. These sections address those related to sharing your resume.

Respect the difference between resume posting and resume blasting

Just as the Marines look "for a few good men and women," resume posters strategically place their resumes on selected job sites.

By contrast, resume blasters indiscriminately toss their resumes like confetti all over the Internet.

Ed's attachment etiquette

"If you are attaching something, consider the following guidelines when doing so," says Ed Struzik, president of BEKS Data Services, Inc. (beks@beksdata.com). Struzik speaks from a dozen-years' vantage point in providing outsourced resume processing services and applicant tracking system consulting to numerous Fortune 100 companies.

Do Not attach EXE files. An EXEcutable file could contain a virus, and no one will chance having the hard drive or network infected.

Do Not attach ZIP files. Who's to say the ZIP file doesn't contain an infected EXEcutable. And besides, can your resume be so large that you have to ZIP it?

Do Not attach password-protected documents. How would you expect someone or something to open it without the password?

Do Not attach documents with contact info in headers or footers. This one seems innocent enough. But the fact is, doing a "Select All" to copy/paste your resume may not capture your name, address, etc. if they are in header or footer data.

Do Not attach documents with text boxes. Another seemingly innocent situation. But again, doing a "Select All" to copy/paste your resume may not get the text box.

Do Not attach forwarded messages. In most mail systems, you have the option to "attach" a forwarded message or "include" the text of a forwarded message. For a number of reasons, choose "include" the text.

Resume posting

Resume posting should be an exercise in thoughtful placement. If you do it yourself, you exercise 95 percent control. The other 5 percent is a wild card — despite privacy statements, job sites and corporate Web sites have been known to "migrate" resumes to databases you don't know about. (Read about privacy protection issues later in this chapter.)

If you decide to post to a limited number of sites, heed these tips:

- Choose sites where you need not register first to search for jobs.

- Determine the control you have over your resume. On a case-by-case basis, what you want is the ability to choose when to release your resume to an employer listing a job you may want. The ability to say "yes" or "no" really shouldn't be negotiable if you want to control your own information.

- Determine the access you have to your resume. You want to be able to edit it (adding new facts or targeting it each time you apply for a different job), delete it entirely, and if your resume is expunged after a certain time period, you want to be able to easily renew it.

If you do want to post with caution but also want to save hours and hours, consider a resume-posting service that allows you to choose which sites receive your resume, give login information for each site, and allow you to apply directly to each site. In the resume-posting category, About.com Job Hunting Guide Allison Doyle likes ResumeRabbit (`resumerabbit.com`) and Career Soar (`careersoar.com`).

Resume blasting

You've probably received an e-mail pitch urging you to reach thousands of America's top search, recruitment, and placement firms. At least a half-dozen resume distribution services ask you to let their firms blitzkrieg your resume with abandon.

At first blush, that kind of resume blasting may seem like a smashing idea, an easy way to make your resume turn up as a face in every crowd. But after you think it through, you'll probably change your mind.

Indiscriminate posting of your personal information can trigger a wave of career failures and personal problems, which are intertwined with privacy issues. See the "Resume confidential: Protect your privacy" section later in this chapter to find out how these disasters can happen.

One irate hiring manager told Susan Joyce, who manages the excellent Web site Job-Hunt.org (`www.job-hunt.org`), that a resume blaster for IT (information technology) and other technical specialists began bombarding her with forwarded and unsolicited resumes even though she didn't have open jobs at that time. When the resume load proved to be too burdensome to comply with the company policy on replying to each job seeker, the hiring manager told the resume distribution service to stop. The hiring manager was frustrated not only because a large number of the forwarded resumes lacked contact or name information but also because she felt sorry for the job searchers who'd paid money for the resume blasting services and were actively on the market looking for work.

The hiring manager's parting comment: "These job seekers should know that (A) they are paying to reach recruiters without jobs or (B) to have their resumes forwarded in a way that cannot be responded to. They should use their money for something else."

As About.com's Allison Doyle points out, however, "Some resume blasting services will let you target only recruiters who asked to be put on a list to receive resumes in specific industries and geographic regions and will send you a list of the recruiters your resume was sent to."

There are other reasons to avoid services that send out a tornado of resumes, which I cover in the following sections.

Resume blasting equals spamming

I do not recommend resume blasting for a number of reasons, including the following:

- ✔ Negative perceptions of resume "spamming" (junk mail)
- ✔ Recruiter distaste for shopworn resumes
- ✔ Loss of control over your own resume

Gerry Crispin and Mark Mehler (CareerXroads consultants and experts on the recruiting industry) agree that resume blasting is ill-advised:

> *We are absolutely not in favor of sites that promise to distribute job seekers' resumes to "hundreds of subscribing recruiters and employers." Most charge a fee within the $20–$100 range, and it's a waste of money. Privacy and disclosure is too important, and while you may not care today, you certainly will tomorrow.*

Realize that resumes live forever

After your resume leaves earth to live in the stratospheric reaches of the Web, you can't control it. It may turn up anywhere, anytime — including on your boss's desk.

But what if you've been cagey — wink, nudge — and only listed events prior to your current job? Can't you just tell your boss that the resume is old, posted before you took your present position, and you have no idea how or why it's still alive? Sure you can, but the missing information describing your present employment is probably your best selling strength if you're on the market.

What to do when you're all alone by the telephone

No matter how picky-picky you were about the job sites where you posted your resume — including big national job boards and small specialty sites alike — if you're getting no action after a month to six weeks, whisk back your resumes from their current locations and post them elsewhere.

What about corporation Web sites you haven't heard from? Leave your resume in these databases. Consider them lifers unless you decide they need refreshing or the company's policy requires deletion of unused resumes after a specified time period — usually six months to a year.

By the way, repeated postings of the same resume won't make a positive difference, and may, in fact, make you look like a loser.

If you don't think resumes live forever, read this

Jim Lemke, this book's technical reviewer, received a spam e-mail from a resume distribution service that offered to "get his resume out and about where he would be seen by millions of employers and recruiters daily!" The marketing pitch opened with "Hi There! I just found an old copy of your resume (which Jim had posted six years earlier when the Web was just a gleam in dreamers' eyes) . . . you don't even need a current resume. There's a quick and easy resume builder on our Web site." Jim showed it to me and then tossed it.

Moreover, employers are realizing that as soon as your resume is up in Web lights, you'll continually be contacted if you seem to have what's wanted somewhere. And if you're having a bad day, you might just be tempted to say, "I'm gone."

Marked for life

Individuals who put their resumes on the big national job boards two years ago are still hearing from recruiters and companies even though they have accepted other employment. Not only do the resumes live on eternally, they may find their way to unintended databases.

Even job seekers who report that they de-activated their resumes on the boards where they originally posted them hear from places they never knew received their resumes. "Marked for life" is the way one job seeker put it.

The chances that your resume will escape from its designated space are multiplying.

Resume scraping

Job ads have long been openly "scraped" — a term for what happens when robots/spiders scour the Web looking for job listings and collect them on a second and unrelated site.

Now, resumes are being scraped, too. Ethical scrapers send you an e-mail and ask if you'd like to be included in the second database and are guided by your response. But most scrapers treat resumes like a commodity, don't get your permission, and take your resume to places unknown. When you don't know where your resume is, how can you call it back to make changes? Or withdraw it entirely?

Remember, online resumes may never die. They just fade away into the timeless Deep Web.

Be stingy with your resume

In addition to losing control of your resume, its wide availability can cause squabbles among contingency recruiters over who should be paid for finding you. An employer caught in the conflict of receiving a resume from multiple sources, including internal resume databases, will often pass over a potential employee rather than become involved in deciding which source, if any, should be paid.

Recruiters keep their distance

One more reason not to spread your resume all over the map: When you're targeting the fast track to the best jobs, nothing beats being brought to an employer's notice by an important third person — and an independent recruiter qualifies as an important third person.

Employers are becoming resistant to paying independent recruiters big fees to search the Web when they theoretically can save money by hiring in-house corporate recruiters to do it. That's why recruiting agencies need fresh inventory that employers can't find elsewhere. If you want a third-party recruiter to present you, think carefully before pinning cyber wings on your resume.

Resume confidential: Protect your privacy

Identity theft may be the worst-case scenario, but it isn't the only life-altering problem that can arise when you put your business on e-street.

You can lose your current job, if you have one. "Many employers do search for their employees' resumes in job site resume databases and search engines," explains Susan Joyce, CEO of Job-Hunt.org, who tracks the privacy issue. "When employees' resumes are found grazing in someone else's pasture before noon," says CareerXroads' Mark Mehler, who consults with countless company managers, "they may be on the street by the end of that same day."

At least one-third of U.S. employers, according to the Privacy Foundation (www.privacyfoundation.org), say they monitor employee e-mail traffic. Sometimes, employers tell employees that their e-mails are scrutinized; sometimes, they don't.

Who can you trust?

Larry Ponemon is founder and chairman of the Ponemon Institute, Inc., a privacy consulting group. Before that, he was an auditor of corporate privacy policies for PricewaterhouseCoopers, the international accounting and consulting firm. He's been on the inside of the privacy protection issue.

Speaking to a San Diego newspaper reporter, Ponemon said "Almost anything you buy, almost anything you do, leaves an electronic trail of data about you, from your name to your shoe size to the medications you take."

All too often, Ponemon said, that information is ending up in the wrong hands and as much as "85 percent of that information is grossly inaccurate. You don't find out because, as a consumer or job hunter, you don't have access to most of the widely distributed bad information." Among Ponemon's horror stories from the trenches, here are two:

- ✒ A medical diagnostics lab processing blood and other medical tests sold patient profiles, rating patients' health based on their tests — a 9 or 10, for instance, signified a terminal illness — then sold the information (by name) to other healthcare companies. (What if you had sent your resume to one of those healthcare companies that bought the data. Do you suppose anyone would tell you, "We're sorry but we can't hire you because you're dying of lung cancer"?)

- ✒ A pharmaceutical company shared the identities of patients taking a psychiatric medication with a call center. Just for sport, call center employees looked up the names of people they knew. When one employee recognized the name of her child's babysitter, she panicked and had her husband confront the babysitter. Lawsuits were discussed.

But these aren't resumes, you say. They're health records and not necessarily transmitted online. True, but these examples illustrate a contemporary culture that doesn't adequately respect the concept of privacy protection, as well as the character of people who are willing to bend the rules as an expediency of business. A resume and social security number are perfect building blocks for identity theft or harassment.

Privacy expert Pam Dixon, author of *Job Searching Online For Dummies* (Wiley), says privacy violations occur in job searches too frequently. In an investigative report that she wrote as a research fellow for the Privacy Foundation, "Click, You're Hired. Or Tracked," which you can read on the Foundation's Web site (www.privacyfoundation.org), Dixon reports evidence of substantial resume migration.

Recruiters verify her finding. As Plano, Texas, recruiter Steven Gatz recently told me: "Many recruiters in my industry will take a resume off the Net and send it out to many companies without the candidates ever knowing about it. Some staffing firms spam resumes."

Many job sites swear their programs guarantee confidentiality. As *Knock 'Em Dead* author Martin Yate warns: Don't count on that happening.

You can decide if you want to be a victim of your resume's lack of privacy protection. It could happen tomorrow or years from now because online resumes live eternally on the Internet.

Safeguard your identity

In some recruitment circles, job seekers who protect their identity are more desirable than those who don't, notes Susan Joyce. Employers assume you're employed and have an existing job you are protecting.

The downside in cloaking your identity is that some recruiters and potential employers won't accept anonymous resumes.

I suggest you take that chance.

Privacy protection doesn't rely on assurances from job sites that they're doing it for you. Here's how to look out for yourself: *Transform all identifying information into generic information.* But won't going generic hurt your chances of being hired? Maybe. Maybe not. There's a trade-off.

Combining suggestions by job hunt authority Susan Joyce, career expert and author Martin Yate, recruiter Steven Gatz, and myself, here's a roundup of techniques to help you avoid colliding with your boss, identity thieves, criminals, and other problems on the information highway:

- ✔ **Your name:** Replace your true name with an e-mail alias. Use a serious e-mail name, such as MEngineer. Or make up a name followed parenthetically by the words "screen name" — Able Smith (Screen Name). Or refer to yourself as someone like "Confidential Candidate" or "Confidential Systems Analyst." Or, using a special e-mail address that you maintain for just this purpose, just enter seven nine's — 9999999 — for each field requiring name, address, and phone number. Even if the original site sends your resume on to other sites, your personal information is never revealed.

- ✔ **Your contact information:** After obtaining a free e-mail account with Yahoo!, Hotmail, or the like, train yourself to check it daily. Use this address as your chief point of contact. If you feel you need to flesh out your contact information, for a street address, rent a post office box and use an unlisted telephone connected to a message recorder. Again, check regularly. One good tip: Recruiters often search by area and zip codes, so you may want to use the real ones in those spots, followed by fake numbers — 760-999-9999.

  Another good tip: Under pain of torture, never use your business e-mail address as your resume contact point: You risk being flayed alive when your boss finds out.

- **Your current employer:** Omit the name and replace it with a generic, but accurate, description. "Nuts 'n' Bolts Distributors, Inc." becomes "small construction supplies distribution company." Microsoft becomes "multinational information technology company." For company location, Pepsi-Cola in Chicago becomes "Fortune 500 beverage company in the Midwestern United States."

- **Your job title:** If your job title is uncommon (like "head geek") or, in combination with other facts, would identify you, use a generic title. However, if the title you choose could be misleading in any way, indicate that you've switched it — Network Engineer (position-equivalent title). New England regional gadget marketing director becomes "multi-state marketing manager of gadget-class products." If your job title is common, such as "Editor" or "Sales Representative," just go ahead and use it.

- **Prior employers:** You probably won't need to sanitize information about earlier employers unless you're in a small industry where everyone knows everyone else and can figure out who you are by your work history. In that case, continue to camouflage yourself with the use of generic terms for the past 10 years. Instead of "Five years with Jackson Plastics as a research design engineer," substitute "respected plastics company" for Jackson Plastics.

  Listing previous employers by name, title, and dates of employment (research design engineer, 1992–1997, Jackson Plastics) can strip you of stealth options. A suspicious boss can check personnel files for your old resume.

- **Education:** Use either your degree and institution (ChE, Rensselaer Polytechnic Institute) or your degree and date (ChE, 1987). Using all three makes you identifiable through alumni associations. A determined, suspicious manager can also track you down if you use both your undergraduate and advanced degrees by cross-checking lists of alumni.

  If one or both of your degrees are from a prestigious institution, ride on those coattails, leaving off dates. Or just list your advanced degree and decide whether the school or a recent graduation date is most important in qualifying you.

  The age factor as a potential discriminator plays a role in deciding which identifiers to include; if you're over 40, consider sticking to institutions and degrees. On the other hand, if you're under 40 and using your youth as a marketing tool, include dates.

- **Accomplishments:** Veil defining accomplishments with generic language. No to: "Lead design engineer on development of DayNight onboard navigation component — headed a team of eight design engineers with a project budget of $10 million." Yes to: "Led a large task force in a multi-million dollar automotive technology launch."

✔ **Certifications and licenses:** Showing national or local certification isn't high risk, but virtually all professional associations sell their member lists, and state governments open their licensing rosters to inspection. That's why you generally should not list the date or state certifying your professional designation or granting your license. Exception: When state recognition (like a lawyer admitted to the New York bar) would be a job requirement in that state.

✔ **Memberships:** Be careful which organizations you include. The Carlsbad, California, Chamber of Commerce has few, if any, design engineers specializing in plastics. But the Society of Plastics Engineers has 37,000 members, and you can hide in a crowd.

If taking all these precautions seems a little paranoid, choose only the stealth strategies you think you need to protect your privacy. Admittedly, too much of a masquerade-ball environment can be off-putting to recruiters and employers.

But to those people who kid themselves that privacy can be traded for profitable exposure, rationalizing "I need a job, and protecting my privacy is a luxury I can't afford right now," think again. In the words of the great English statesman, Winston Churchill: "Nourish your hopes, but do not overlook realities."

Target the best lists for your e-mail resume campaign

A targeted e-mail resume campaign is a sophisticated and often highly effective strategy for a job search campaign, and it's best used for senior-level jobs. The formula is simple: You use a commercial list of selected independent recruiters and companies that logically could hire you, and you contact them with e-mail — or a combination of e-mail and postal mail.

Let me play mind-reader for a minute and answer the questions that I think you might have.

Q: But isn't a targeted mailing campaign just an updated version of the old broadcast letter that most experts say doesn't work and that they'd rather drink bleach than recommend?

A: They do share a reaching-out commonality, but these methods have substantial differences. The broadcast letter typically is sent indiscriminately to all addresses on direct-mail lists. The targeted e-mail campaign depends on careful matching of potential employers to the requirements of the job seeker. The quality of the list is a make-or-break factor.

Q: Are these e-lists new?

A: They're not new, but the e-databases that create the lists became a stand-alone tool only within the past several years. E-databases have the power to customize a list of recruiters by specialty — both by industry (energy companies) and functional field (quality control). The way they're being used is very different than the old vendor lists of the last century.

Yesteryear's recruitment e-databases were like the original television show, "Charlie's Angels," featuring soft plots and good manners. Today's powerful e-databases are like the new hyper-action feature film of the same title that blows its heroines through skyscraper glass windows.

The old e-databases were offered on disk or CD-ROM and updated periodically; new versions are on the Web, and the premier products are updated daily.

Earlier versions were produced by information vendors and resold by outplacement, executive marketing, and resume writing firms as an optional service; today's renditions are directly accessible to individual consumers.

The best lists are not free, but they include a mail-merge feature allowing you to send your cover letter and resume yourself. You can hire it done if you're not comfortable with computers.

Q: Is a targeted e-mail campaign a good bet if you don't have a college degree?

A: Yes, if you use a resume letter instead of a resume; a letter doesn't flag your missing degree and gives you a chance to explain if a recruiter or employer calls you.

Q: What else is needed to find a good job by a targeted mail campaign?

A: You need good credentials and employers that are hiring your bundle of skills. Additionally, the following factors make the difference:

- ✔ You must address your mail campaign to a hiring decision-maker by name, not "Marketing Manager" or "President."

- ✔ Excellent marketing materials help attract employer interest. If you lack writing skills, hire a specialist to prepare them. The mailing package can consist of your resume and cover letter or note — or a combination resume letter.

- ✔ In the best targeted mail campaigns, you or your agent follow up with telephone calls to recipients within a week of the transmission. Anyone can be your agent for this purpose, paid or unpaid.

Q: Which is best — e-mail resumes or postal mail resumes?

A: Bob Bronstein, president of ProFile Research (`profileresearch.com`), a specialized resume distribution and lead development firm in Flourtown, Pennsylvania, has a dozen years' experience in targeted mail campaigns, and he says that recruiters prefer e-mail. E-mail is easy to inventory in databases and to forward resumes to clients. Send two e-mail versions — your formatted attachment and also an ASCII text within the body (see Chapter 15) of your e-mail.

By contrast, Bronstein advises you to send paper cover letters and resumes through postal mail to corporate America because they have no useful e-database mailing lists. You can find some e-mail addresses that will transport your resume to a specific decision-maker but, in essence, you have to e-mail to one address at a time.

Q: Can you give an example of a real-life successful targeted e-mail campaign?

A: Bronstein's recent success stories include a generational example I especially like. This one involves a father in top management and his son in sales. The father's search cost $2,000; his son's $400.

The father, Craig (not his real name), is a 50ish senior telecommunications executive earning in the mid six figures. In his previous position, Craig had turned a "fallen dot.com" into a positive cash-flow business. After the flood of red ink was cauterized, the owners of the business decided to step back in, and Craig was out.

On Craig's behalf, Bronstein focused on retained executive recruiters and on venture capital firms specializing in the telecommunications industry. More than 1,600 e-mails were sent with Craig's cover letter and resume.

After five days, Craig had four major hits for executive jobs through recruiting firms in various parts of the country. Delighted, Craig began to proactively work those four leads. Craig's job search continued for 12 weeks, during which he reached final-interview status for all four positions. Two didn't pan out. The third company put him through 12 interviews in various parts of the nation before selecting the other short-listed candidate. As this book went to press, the fourth and favorite opportunity remains viable.

At the same time, Craig's son David (also not his real name) was looking for a better sales job in New York. David's e-mail campaign went to 400 selected potential employers. Results were quick, and David began his new and much superior job within six weeks of the campaign.

Q: If targeted e-mail campaigns are so powerful, why doesn't everyone use them?

A: Targeted e-mail campaigns can be pricey, and they don't always work. You should be earning in the $75,000 and up range if you pay for a turnkey campaign. And they aren't for everyone. You can do them yourself at a substantial time cost until you learn the ropes. Or you can hire a specialist if you have the money to pay for services. E-mail resume campaigns work best when you are contacting executive recruiters and when companies are hiring in your field.

Q: In addition to Bob Bronstein, where else can I find resources to conduct such a campaign?

A: This question is a tough one because unethical operators with old or inappropriate lists or a poor grasp of the target process are out there fleecing honest job searchers at a vulnerable time in their lives. Dave Theobald, CEO of Netshare.com, a subscription national online job board for $100,000 and up executives, recommends only a few such services — Bronstein is one of those Theobald recommends. (Full disclosure: I have mentioned Bob Bronstein in my newspaper column twice over the past decade; every Christmas, he sends me a tin of chocolate pretzels.)

If you want to do your own targeted e-mail resume campaign but need a list, Theobald recommends Custom Databanks, Inc. (customdatabanks.com), which provides lists of targeted search firms, companies, and venture capital firms.

Or, you can build your own list from scratch, using other tips in this chapter.

Branch Out to Make Use of All Your Job-Finding Options

Networking (read *human interaction that includes employee referrals*) is rated number one in hiring results. That said, put the following tools to use.

Seek endorsement through employee referral programs

If you want fast action and special interest in your candidacy for a job, book your resume for the *employee referral program* (ERP) tour.

That is, identify companies where you'd like to work. Start with ten and then move on to a second batch of ten. And so on.

At each target company, network your way to an employee. You may already know some of the people inside a few companies. When you don't know a soul, keep asking someone who knows someone who knows someone. After you identify a contact, enlist that employee's aid in forwarding your name for employment.

The building of a corporate insiders network sounds like heavy-lifting, and it is. But this is a gift to yourself that keeps on giving — your efforts could pay off big, not only for your next job but for a number of ever more responsible positions in coming years.

At many American companies, large and small, employee referrals are the *number one source for new hires*. ERPs are used by 74 percent of *Fortune* magazine's "100 Fastest Growing Companies." A recent survey by the Society for Human Resource Management found that 66 percent of nearly 600 organizations polled have either a formal or informal employee referral program.

Companies pay special attention to ERP candidates because, according to human resource professionals, candidates hired through employee referrals stay longer and assimilate faster than those hired through other methods, including the Internet and headhunters.

Sometimes, employees cruise available openings and forward them to friends with the click of a mouse. But you can't sit back and wait for the call to come. To remain on the ERP tour, stay in touch with your employee contacts regularly.

What's in it for an employee who refers you? Dollars! Sometimes, big dollars — starting at $1,000 up to thousands of dollars per referral. And for most of us, that's not chump change.

Take a dip in talent pool programs

Swimming in a company talent pool isn't the same as trying to capitalize on an employee referral program, which I describe in the previous section. Building a network of employees ready to refer you to their companies could result in a fast job hunt, at least theoretically, while managing to get yourself in company talent pools could stretch out your search, or produce future jobs.

The talent pool concept is a new idea — except perhaps to professional sports teams where emerging talent pools are called "farm teams." But just as a farm team player isn't guaranteed a shot at the pro roster, a company talent pool member isn't guaranteed a job, now or someday, with that company.

What exactly is a company talent pool? Some recruiting industry consultants describe the talent pool function as a kind of customer service to woo potential future employees.

Corporate use of online screening and communication tools (see Chapter 1) is used to identify well-qualified applicants who could fill a variety of positions in a given company. Once tapped for the talent team-in-waiting, recruiters and candidates are supposed to maintain two-way communication (chiefly e-mail and e-newsletters), staying in touch as needed.

The rules for maximizing your resume's residency in a talent pool aren't ready for prime time, but if you believe in the proverb, "Out of sight, out of mind," find interesting or pertinent (job change) messages to send to the recruiter who reported that you made the talent-pool cut.

Ask job agents to stand guard

Many millions of Americans change jobs each year, voluntarily or involuntarily. Because of diminishing job security, increased ambition, and new technologies, many people are locked into a perpetual job search. Sounds like a grind. A job agent lightens the load and notifies you when a job you want comes along.

The basics are, well, basic

The nitty-gritty of engaging a *personal job agent* is simple but varies slightly among job sites. Most personal job agents are free to job seekers, but some come with membership in fee-based sites. On the job sites of your choice, you fill out a template to produce a profile of the job you want: your desired occupation, job title, industry, locale, and salary range. You may have to provide a profile or use the site's resume builder to provide a profile of your qualifications. You supply your e-mail address and go on with your life.

Now, for the part about the cyberbutler who tells you, "Employment is served." When a fresh job ad comes to a chosen career site that's a pretty good match for your profile, the site's personal job agent sends you a circumspect e-mailed message. The employer is identified in the message. If you're interested, you say "Yes, release my resume to this employer," and if not, "No, don't release my resume to this employer."

If you're mobile and have high-demand skills, personal job agents are the best thing since headhunters to add zest to your career management fortunes. In fact, personal job agents prove that the old admonition, "If you snooze, you lose," is no longer universally true.

Let the job come to you

You may have a way out of interminable job hunt pressure. If you're not in a hurry, you can post your career-move preferences on each of your chosen job sites and then sit back and wait for employers to find you — perhaps even being offered opportunities you would never have found on your own initiative.

We are witnessing the rise of what recruiters call "the passive job seeker" and the job search tools that serve them. A *passive job seeker* is employed and is not actively on the market, but is always interested in exploring the "right offer." It is good to be king, and it is good to be a passive job seeker. A passive job seeker isn't too easy to get, so he or she is valued above all others. After all, if a passive job seeker is employed doing a particular job, someone must think that person is good at it, right?

Are you a passive job seeker? Congratulations! You can use any of hundreds of personal job agents that will keep their ears tuned to the job market, and when a promising position you might like comes to their attention, they'll tip you off with an e-mail alert.

 Just as the devil is usually found in details, the downside is in the ratios: Each personal job agent has a gazillion more registered job seekers than job vacancies. Like 250,000 job hunters and 4,000 job openings. So don't count on personal job agents to come through if you're in a time-sensitive situation (read: *need to get a job fast*).

Follow-Up — An Act of Job Finding

The vast majority of employers — as many as eight of ten according to some surveys — that use digital recruiting systems (applicant management systems) send out an automatic receipt of your application, commenting that if they want to talk to you, they'll make contact. (To the two of ten who don't — boo!) The response rate of third-party recruiters is unclear, but if you are a potential candidate for a job opening they're trying to fill, you'll hear back fairly quickly; if not, you may get an auto response or none.

Even when an auto response is sent, job searchers say they're underwhelmed, considering the boilerplate e-mails next to meaningless. Canned response or not, you don't look like a quiz-show winner if you call to ask a transparent question, "Did you receive my resume?" Instead, say some version of:

I've had another job offer, which prompts me to ask if you had planned to contact me within the week.

I suggest other ways to make contact later in this section.

Bear in mind, however, that in these transitional times, the majority of smaller employers still don't use a digital recruiting system. If you send a resume to a workplace without a digital system (you know because you called first to check), calling later to ask, "Did you get my resume?" *is* a good question.

Reach out when you don't "have mail"

The reasons that employers ignore applicants who send their resumes are many. They range from too few staffers to handle the clerical response task to uncertainty about whether the position actually will be filled. No matter. For your purposes, you must take the offensive and follow up.

If you've had previous contact with the recipient of your resume, the nature of that experience (stranger, referral, friend, telephone call, personal meeting) will suggest whether your follow-up is a thank-you letter or some other kind of communication, such as carrying out the employer's direction: "At your suggestion, I forwarded my resume . . . "

If you've had no earlier contact with your resume's recipient, e-mail or telephone your follow-up. Which is best — e-mail or telephone? I recommend you use the medium that makes you feel most confident and comfortable.

If you've had an auto response and know your resume is in the database, you can ask what happened to it:

> *Was my resume a match for an open position? Was my resume passed onto a hiring manager? Can you tell me which manager?*

After you know your resume has been routed to a hiring manager — or you have personally sent your resume to that hiring manager — don't call the human resource department because HR will automatically consider you for all open job requisitions.

Try to contact the hiring manager, who is the one who will quarterback the decision to hire you or not hire you. If your resume was passed onto a departmental hiring manager and you can uncover the manager's name, try calling that manager early in the morning or late in the day. Lunch is not a good time.

Beat that frustrating voicemail

What should you do when you try to reach the manager but can't break through voicemail? Leave a short message showing upbeat interest, not desperation:

> *My name is Joyce Lain Kennedy, and I'm calling you because I've successfully outgrown my job, and you have a reputation for running a progressive department. I think you have my resume. If you like what you see, we should talk — 760-431-9999. The best time to reach me today is between 2 and 6 p.m. I look forward to hearing from you.*

Pronounce your name clearly and say your telephone number at a moderate pace. Give the hiring manager a chance to write it down without replaying the message. Otherwise, the manager hears a "garbledrushofwords" and decides "Idon'thavetimeforthis" and moves on.

How often should you call? Some very smart experts suggest calling every ten days until you're threatened with arrest if you call again. But busy employers insist that — unless you're in sales or another field requiring a demonstration of persistence — after you're certain your resume was received, call two weeks later, and then no more than once every six weeks.

An excessive number of telephone calls brands you as a pest. Instead, send notes or e-mail with additional facts about your qualifications, ideas to solve a problem you know the company is facing, or just an expression of your continuing interest in working for the company and the manager.

Everyone agrees that, in this increasingly impersonal world, effectively following-up on the resumes you send out is becoming harder and harder. But the challenge of getting your resumes into the right hands means going beyond transmission to connection with as many recruiters and employers as you reasonably can manage.

Part II
StandOut Resumes for Affinity Groups

The 5th Wave   By Rich Tennant

"You did a good job of converting your military experience into civilian terms on your resume. But you need to fix the typo that says you were a '...tanked operator'."

In this part . . .

You find special tips and targeted resume guidance to use if you're laid off, a bit older, an information technology professional, a transitioning military member, or a new college graduate. You also get tips for resumes when you want to change your career field or occupation.

Chapter 3

When You Lose Your Job and It's Not Your Fault

*A*bout the last thing you feel like doing when you lose your job is jumping into your charred psyche and writing a resume. If that's where you are as you read these words, you have company. More than 2.8 million Americans have been downsized during the twenty-first century (January 2000 to July 2002), according to published layoff summaries tallied by AIRS, a leading New England recruitment training firm that publishes weekly outplacement reports.

Job loss, first felt as a combination of depression and anxiety, is seasoned with nervousness, anger, and a sense of betrayal, as these two statements illustrate:

✔ A laid-off person explains, "Words I normally think of will not cover the feeling. It's as if I am going crazy, or having a bad dream, and am unable to wake up. My attitude to everything is negative."

✔ Another discarded individual elaborates on the feeling of betrayal: "You can accept it if a company has done everything possible and just isn't financially capable of keeping you on. But when it costs you your livelihood because someone high on the corporate ladder, who doesn't even know your name, was too slow to get new business, you feel angry, bitter, and empty."

Add to those feelings the rage provoked by early-twenty-first-century corporate abuse, and you quickly understand why a job loss that wasn't your fault can affect your physical and mental health.

No wonder writing a resume seems a dreary chore.

Facing Facts about Job Loss

Unless you were miserable in your lost job, there really isn't any good thing about losing it, so I won't babble nonsensical rationales akin to "Isn't it wonderful that I fell down and broke my legs because that gave me the chance to learn to use crutches." Your legs were knocked out from under you.

But if there is one "least worst" factor about losing your job, it's that today you're far less likely to be viewed as a failed performer, or as unable to get along with others and therefore unhirable than if you'd been cut loose in an earlier time when most employers tended to assume your joblessness was your fault. In this downsizing-happy era, you're far more likely to be presumed innocent, unless proven otherwise. So many people have worn the badge of joblessness that it has almost become a designer sportswear label.

Fighting back — starting NOW!

So you think the hurt is too raw, the sting too acidic, and the anger too lingering. Today is not a good day for resume writing. You just don't feel like writing your resume, and you'll wait until you feel better.

That attitude is easily understood, but it's not in your best interests. When a job loss lays you out, the number one action for putting your troubles behind you and landing new employment is moving on! The first six months are critical; after that, the odds of your being hired at comparable or better pay begin to head south.

Rethinking, retraining, and relocating

When large-scale layoffs occur, entire occupations and industries may be thinned out. Reestablishing yourself in the workplace may depend on becoming competent in another line of work or relocating to a more prosperous job market. A number of studies insist that flexibility in deciding what you'll accept, including a change of career, is the way to go when you've been pink-slipped.

But there's a time-honored counter caveat as well: Don't go overboard on changing your line of work if you don't have to or if you don't want to. **It is much easier for laid-off job hunters to find new jobs in their field than it is for laid-off career changers to start over.**

Two schools of thought surround another issue. Should you accept temporary work, related or unrelated to what you hope to be doing soon? I can argue that issue either way, depending on the circumstances.

✔ **School 1:** Accept temp work when you've been jobless for a while and prospects are bleak. The money helps, and the good feelings of acceptance and the momentum you derive from the work are equally valuable. (When you explain the detours from your career track in future job interviews, say that you experienced and overcame a rough patch of life, but now you're again ready to fight dragons.)

✔ **School 2:** Stick to your career track. If you don't, your resume will lose focus and, to some degree, you'll lose rising-star quality. Recruiters will want to know why a promising professional seemingly lost his or her footing.

Writing a Successful Layoff Resume

Have you ever wondered why so much is written for the downsized job hunter about the wider issues of job search and survival, and so little about the narrower issue of resumes?

The reason is simple. With a few exceptions, the same basic resume guidelines apply for the employed and unemployed: **Don't use your resume to explain why you left a job; save explanations for job interviews.**

There are exceptions. They are outlined in the following sections.

Overcoming a job-hopping image

Even when it wasn't at your initiative, holding five or more jobs in ten years can brand you as a job hopper. The fact that you're out of work now underscores that impression. Even employers who are guilty of round after round of employee dismissals instinctively flinch at candidates they perceive to be hopping around.

Take pains to reverse that disapproval. When you draft your resume, post a list of negative perceptions on your desk; when you're finished writing, compare your resume with the list. Offer information that changes negative perceptions of you as a job hopper. The following table lists the perceptions employers often have of a job hopper and ways to counter them.

Perception	*Counter*
Is disloyal and self-focused	Perfect attendance, volunteer office gift collector
Will split in a blink for a better offer and take company secrets along	Competition of projects
Doesn't know what he/she wants and is never satisfied	Diverse background that promoted impressive results

After checking for damage control, go back and review your resume for accomplishments that enhance your image as

- ✔ **A fast learner:** Give examples of how your skills aren't company-specific and you rapidly adjust to new environments.

- ✔ **A high achiever:** Show favored skills much courted by headhunters, and at end of each job mention, put "Recruited for advanced position."

- ✔ **A quick adapter:** Mention examples of agreeable flexibility in adjusting to new ideas, technology, and position requirements.

- ✔ **A relationship builder:** List praise from coworkers for commitment to team success.

If your current joblessness comes after a background that a quick-change artist would admire, use your resume to prepare the way to acceptance. Emphasize project completion and career progression, using years not months. If you still have trouble landing interviews, use positive statements in your cover letter to tackle your history.

When a departure wasn't your fault, but you look like a job hopper if you don't explain, do reveal the reasons.

Giving focus to a patchwork career

When a laid-off job searcher says she has too much in her background, and her resume is a scenic tour of the world of work, the solution is resume *focus*. Every creative cell in your brain will be challenged, but give it a go. Here's a case in point:

A woman in her early 50s wants to make a career move that's back to the future. Her career brief is as follows: master's degree in education; MBA studies; educating for six years as a teacher, counselor, and dean (left because pay was low); working in human resources for a major corporation for 20 years (downsized); operating a part-time fitness counseling and training center for women for 10 years (still going); writing for an online dot.com for two years (dot.com went bust); and substitute teacher (now wants regular teaching position to improve cash flow).

What, she asks, should she call all her diversified experience — human resources, fitness, journalism?

My answer: Build a *theme* (focus) and call everything *educational.* Relate the human resource experience to training and instructional experience, the fitness experience to guidance and knowledge-building, and the journalism to educational writing.

Although the educator in this example is older than many downsized job searchers, the same unifying technique works for much younger people with short tenures in various career fields.

Dealing with multiple layoffs

Hard to believe, but good workers sometimes experience one layoff after another. One of my readers wrote that he'd experienced four no-fault severances within seven years.

When you've been to the chopping block a few too many times, explain the circumstances after each listing of the company name:

> Carol Interiors (company closed doors) . . . Salamander Furnishings (multi-rounds of downsizings) . . . Brandon Fine Furniture (company relocated out of town) . . . Kelly Fixture Co. (plant sold and moved overseas).

Offering brief explanations takes the blame from your shoulders — but I suppose that a cynic could think that you're a jinx.

Explaining mergers and acquisitions

Another of my readers writes: "Upon graduating from college, I went to work for Company A. Several years later, Company A was acquired by Company B. More years passed, and Company B was acquired by Company C. Eventually, Company C merged with Company D, and as a result, after 10 years with the four companies, I was laid off.

"My question is how best to handle this work history on my resume? I worked for four different corporate entities, with four different names, without ever changing jobs. Do I list all four on my resume? Or just the last one?"

Always try to show an upward track record (that you acquired new knowledge and skills, and just didn't just do the same thing over and over each year). And, you don't want the reader to assume that you worked for only one company that laid you off after a decade.

Taking these two factors into consideration, can you show correlation between your job titles and responsibilities with the changes in ownership? If yes, identify all four owners:

> Job title, Company D (formerly Company C), years

> Job title, Company C (formerly Company B), years

> Job title, Company B (formerly Company A), years

> Job title, Company A, years

If no, you can't show an upward track record that correlates with changes in ownership, just use the current owner name with a short explanation:

> Job title, Company D, years
> (Through a series of mergers and acquisitions, the entities for which I have worked since college graduation were known as Company A, Company B, and Company C.)

The reason for naming every entity is perception. Background and credit checks will turn up those company names, and if your resume doesn't mention them, it sends up a red flag for your potential employer!

Rising through the ranks without a degree

Laid-off workers who rose through the ranks without a college degree and now can't find a comparable position in another large company have a problem. The educational shortfall can easily do them in.

Everyone knows about Bill Gates of Microsoft, a college dropout, and Dave Thomas of Wendy's, who left high school to work. But that knowledge really doesn't help you much when you can't even get interviews because you lack a college degree.

What can help is using the resume letter (combination cover letter and resume) instead of a resume. In it, refer to your "experience-based" knowledge, and "skills-building" experience. Emphasize that you enjoy learning and give examples. Mention that you've taken courses as you've found a need for them. And although you don't bring up the fact that you lack a degree, you do mention that you continue to be eager to get on with "real work," as opposed to theorizing about it.

Another tip: Target smaller companies because they may have fewer formal educational requirements and may be more willing to zero in on your knowledge and skills rather than where you acquired them.

Writing a Retainer Resume

A *retainer resume* is an internal, self-marketing document that you give to new management when rumors of mergers and acquisitions surface. It can also be used to resell you to current management when rumors of layoffs grapevine through your company.

A retainer resume differs from an *internal resume,* which points out qualifications that fit you for a different job where you work. A retainer resume proclaims to the acquiring or dominant company management why you're an invaluable asset to the company and should be kept on when staffs are combined. Or to your existing management, it provides reasons why they should sell off land before letting you go.

When your company is bought out or merged, the new owners usually take an oath that they have no plans to make personnel changes. View those assurances with a healthy dose of skepticism. The mergers and acquisitions (M&A) market has never been known to burn the candor at both ends. While they're denying that cuts will be made, stacks of pink slips are being spit out by a computer. M&A business guru Stanley Foster Reed, who has a half century of M&A experience, says layoffs will occur 70 percent of the time.

Although it's usually safer to be on a buyer's workforce than a seller's, exceptions arise because of the tax posture of the merging entities.

Here's your best move, says Reed: "While you should never believe your job is safe just because you have a good track record, do the best you can to assay the company's productivity and your seniority, tempered by your cost and age before assuming you're history.

"Rarely do employees gird up their loins and confront the new owners or their representatives with a statement like this: 'I love my job and I want to keep it. What can I do, or learn, that will make me more productive, more useful to the new combined companies?' Do it, then hand the owners a copy of your newly created retainer resume."

Pack Up All Your Skills and Go!

Just when you thought getting laid off was *your* fault, you took a step back and remembered it was *their* inability to manage well that put you on the bricks.

To reinforce your inner pep talk, glance over the transferable skills checklist in Figure 3-1. This checklist is far from being comprehensive or scientifically organized. I offer it merely as an illustration of the skills that you can tuck into your resume and take with you to a new workplace. Add any other skills that you think are important. Try to identify 20 skills.

Skills and competencies (see Chapter 10) are part of the same bolt of cloth. Skills have been discussed for many years, and that concept is better known than the relatively new *competencies.* Both address positive factors you bring to the employer.

The reason skills and competencies are presented separately in this book is because of wide recognition that everyone needs skills to work, but competencies as a concept hasn't hit Main Street yet and is chiefly used in technology that screens applicants online (see Chapter 1 for more on the most current HR practices).

A Bevy of StandOut Resume Tips

The following tips help you work up a StandOut resume at any time — jobless or employed.

- ✔ **Discuss teamwork in job descriptions, giving specific examples and results.** Employers love the word *teamwork.* They like *team building,* too. Talk about participating in tough tasks that help focus teams. Speak of trust as being essential to teamwork. Say that you were part of a team that succeeded in reaching a unified goal. The difficulty comes in making clear for which portion of the team's production you can take a bow. You must separate your contribution from the group's. If you don't, you chance being looked upon as one who falsely claims credit for work you didn't do. If you do find room for hobbies, be sure they're related to your job objective. Team-player sports such as volleyball, softball, and touch football are ideal for hobbies related to work in a group. (Building ships in bottles would better suit work as a lighthouse keeper.)

- ✔ **Give examples of leadership.** Even as organizational structures flatten by the sunlight hour, every team needs a leader — unless you're headed for a support job where leadership is a liability. In the same vein, vision and drive are desirable characteristics. What did you originate, initiate, spearhead, or propose? What have coworkers praised about you? What suggestions have employers accepted from you?

✔ **Discuss an upward track record.** Without mentioning dollar amounts, style yourself as a winner by mentioning that you received raises, promotions, and bonuses.

✔ **Answer the "So What?" question.** This question is hidden and lying in ambush in every employer's mind. Forget about sticking to the old name-your-previous-responsibilities routine. Every single time you mention a duty or achievement, pretend someone fires back: So what? Who cares? What does it all mean? Imagining these questions isn't really pretending — these are employer responses.

Don't just relay what you did — spell out the consequences and implications. A medical technologist may say:

- Organize daily work distribution for effective teamwork of 12 lab workers; absorb and solve workload issues from previous shift — backlog cut from 3 days to 3 hours.

- Monitor quality control; identify problems, find solutions; lab insurance rates, related to mistakes, lowered this year by 3 percent.

- Perform preventive maintenance on 14 machines on daily basis; reduced repair costs 8 percent over previous year.

✔ **Showcase anything that you did in the top 5 percent of company performance ratings.** Employers are impressed with the cream of the crop.

✔ **Don't apologize on your resume for any weakness that you may observe in your professional self.** Until you can do something about it, like get additional education or experience, don't even think about shortcomings, and they certainly don't belong on your resume.

✔ **Show how and whom you trained.** Employers appreciate the knowledge base suggested by the ability to teach. A smaller company in particular may be run by an entrepreneur whose nightmare is being forced to take time away from running the company to hire and train new people.

✔ **Don't try to explain a lifetime of disasters on a resume.** Save your explanations for an interview. Use your friends and acquaintances to help you obtain interviews. Make the resume as brief and as adversity-free as you legitimately can. At the interview, be prepared to justify your moves, without becoming defensive, and be sure to provide good references.

✔ **Ask a business-savvy friend to read your resume before you send it out.** Prepare a list of questions regarding the comprehensiveness of your resume's explanations and job victories for your friend to answer. Examples: *Does this resume show my mastery of bookkeeping skills? Does this resume adequately relate the prestige of my awards and recognitions for design skills?* It's better to know sooner than later when you're rowing with one oar.

Transferable Skills Checklist

This checklist is a simple tool to use in highlighting skills that you can pack up and take with you to a new job or career field. Check your winners. Add any other skills you're good at that you want to use again.

Work Skills

supervising		problem solving	
managing budget		meeting deadlines	
public speaking		planning	
scheduling		structuring	
systematizing		program designing	

Organizational/Interpersonal Skills

reporting		generalizing	
managing		networking	
leading		implementing	
teaching		consulting	
reviewing		assessing	
time-managing		advising	
organizing		negotiating	
conceptualizing		interpreting	
achieving		judging	
delegating		extracting information	
serving customers		administering	

Dealing with Things Skills

assembling		building	
constructing		operating	
inspecting		purchasing	
repairing		innovating	
certifying		designing	
delivering		selling	
using tools		using complex equipment	
lifting		remodeling	

Dealing with People Skills

building relationships	showing cultural sensitivity
interviewing	role-playing
empathizing	putting people at ease
coaching	motivating
cooperating	coordinating
promoting	listening
persuading	showing diversity awareness

Dealing with Words/Ideas Skills

outlining	creating
synthesizing	programming
inventing	researching
articulating	visualizing
remembering	calculating
reasoning	quantifying
recognizing patterns	editing
deciphering	thinking critically
explaining	comparing
analyzing	communicating

Behavioral Attributes/Behavioral Skills

diplomatic	flexible
loyal	versatile
warm	open
frank	cooperative
tenacious	discrete
initiator	efficient
diplomatic	orderly
expressive	enterprising
sophisticated	candid
adventuresome	decisive
responsible	self-confident
risk-taking	result-oriented

Making a Comeback

Hold this thought: *I will recover from this setback and I will rise again.* Lee Iacocca saved Chrysler after being bounced from Ford. Quarterback Trent Dilfer was dumped by the Seattle Seahawks in 2000, only to lead the Baltimore Ravens to a Super Bowl victory in 2001. And pop diva Mariah Carey — whom Virgin records paid $28 million to end her contract following the flop of her album *Glitter* — came back strong with a $20 million contract to cut three albums for Universal Music Group. But wait — isn't Mariah $8 million short? Yes, but I don't think she'll miss it.

Believe in yourself. This too shall pass. Trash your old resume and start fresh with the insights you're gaining.

Chapter 4

Beat Baby Boomer Bias

● ●

In This Chapter

▶ Fight-back resume tactics

▶ Jack Chapman's special reports

▶ Career-change resume tips

▶ Stepping down to lower-level jobs

● ●

Former U.S. Senator John Glenn handled space like a young man when he became the world's oldest astronaut at age 77. Scientists effectively exclaimed, "You go, Glenn!" — there's no reason why healthy older people can't fly in space.

Contrast that endorsement of age to letters I receive nearly every day, like these two:

> I am a 59-year-old involuntarily "retired" electrical/electronic engineer with lots of varied experience. I was replaced by two recent grads from my alma mater. I've been out of work before but never at age 59. How do I find a job that uses my experience or must, as some suggest, I take a counter job at Home Depot?

> I write concerning what to put and what not to put on a resume at age 48. I was laid-off four years ago and have not had a full-time permanent position since. I am feeling age discrimination — how does one tone down a resume for work I've done, just to get my foot in the door for an interview and hopefully find they are not discriminating against older adults?

Older but Not Golder

Age bias is shoving high numbers of America's bright, high-performing baby boomers (and pre-baby boomers) into unemployment and under-employment — picture professionals over 50 replaced with cheaper and younger talent, and PhDs working on computer help desks.

As if the normal wear-and-tear that an older worker racks up in the workplace weren't enough, recent looting and other criminal misdeeds by corporate officers have destroyed the retirement funds of many thousands of these workers. Now, like it or not, older workers and retirees are having to deal with the stress of remaining or returning to the workplace just to make ends meet.

This chapter looks at ways to combat biases an older job hunter faces, including a new resume-alternative idea. It also raises points to consider if you're a baby boomer who may want to change careers.

Fight-Back Tactics for Seasoned Aces

To forestall age discrimination, tailor your resume to make yourself look like a well-qualified candidate — not a well-preserved one — by using these tips:

Shorten your resume

The general guideline is, "Go back no more than 15 years." But if that doesn't work for the job you seek, one answer is to create a functional resume where you blow up your relevant skills in detail toward the top of the resume and give overly impressive titles little play by dropping them down to the bottom.

Focus your resume

For emphasis, I'll repeat that: **Focus your resume.** Concentrate on highlighting your two most recent or most relevant jobs. Do not attempt to give equal attention to each of your past jobs. If your job experience has been diverse, your resume may look like a job-hopping tale of unrelated job after unrelated job.

Show that you are a tower of strength

Give examples of how you solved problems, recovered expenses, and learned to compensate for weaknesses in your working environment. Emphasize how quickly such adjustments occurred. Gray heads who have survived a few fallen skies are valuable assets in difficult times.

Demonstrate political correctness

This is especially important for positions that have contact with the public. Show that you are familiar with contemporary values by using politically correct terms wherever appropriate. Examples include *diversity, cross-cultural, mainstream, multiethnic,* and *people with disabilities* (never handicapped).

Try shipping your resume online

You'll help dispel any ideas that you're over the hill. See Part IV for more on digital resumes.

Annihilate ancient education dates

Of course, the absence of dates sends a signal: *This is an old geezer who read a resume book.* But at least it shows that you have sufficient faculties left to play the game.

Trim your resume to fighting weight

For very experienced professionals, sorting out the most powerful resume points can be difficult. It's like being a gifted child — so many choices, and you're good at them all! You know what they say, though: *The longer the cruise, the older the passengers.*

Jack Chapman's Special Reports: A Tool that Boosts Resume Response

The *special report technique* is the creation of Chicago-area career coaching superstar Jack Chapman (jkchapman@aol.com). It is primarily a networking tool. It says, "Notice me. Talk to me. Remember me."

Specifically, a *special report* is three to ten pages describing how to do a simple but essential task relevant to the job you're seeking. The resume is added as the back page to a special report, so it does not replace a resume. A special report can be distributed online or delivered by postal mail or courier.

Special reports are kindred to the e-newsletters described in Chapter 16, but they are one-shots rather than ongoing publications.

Chapman has used the report technique more than 70 times, pointing out that it almost always (nothing is bulletproof) works better than a resume. I asked Chapman what "better" means, and here's his response:

> "Did your contact know who you were? Was your contact receptive to meeting with you? That's what I mean by 'better,'" Chapman explains. "Special reports are remembered ten times as often as resumes."

Ideal for baby boomers

Because you've been around for a while, you've got the know-how and the credibility to do a special report. (Exception: Don't use this resume tool if you're trying to change careers. If you were trying to change careers from teaching to sales, it would be presumptuous for you to issue a special report called "Ten Top Sales Techniques.")

Describing the value of a special report, Chapman says: "As a baby boomer, whatever your profession, you have some wisdom about how to make things run smoother, better, easier, more profitably, and so forth. Your special report would contain practical tips and techniques that can be easily applied in the daily work life of the reader.

"You may recall the book, *Seven Habits of Highly Successful People* by Steven Covey. The book is powerful, but how much rocket science is required to tell people to (1) be proactive, (2) begin with the end in mind, (3) put first things first, (4) think win/win, (5) seek first to understand, then to be understood, (6) synergize, and (7) sharpen the saw. YOU could have written that book, couldn't you? The ideas in its pages are simple, and they are as old as Napoleon Hill's *Think and Grow Rich*. Yet this book was a multimillion-copies bestseller. That's the power of a special report — simple ideas that work," explains Chapman.

Examples of special report topics

Jack Chapman gives the following examples of special reports his clients have written:

> *54 Ways to Market Career Services* (a college career counselor illustrates methods of attracting more students to the campus career center).

Ten Ways to Make Your Property Make Money (a residential property manager shows simple things to do to make renting apartments easier, retain more tenants, and reduce pesky maintenance calls).

An International Trade Trend Opens Brief Window of Opportunity to Double Your Margins and Underprice Your Competition (a purchasing manager reveals how to source certain cast-iron parts from China at a ridiculously cheap price).

Six Money Tips for Self-Employed and Small Business Professionals (an accountant building a private practice gives tips on taking more tax deductions, protecting your business from an IRS audit, and managing your own expenses).

A Simple Low-Tech Manufacturing Solution that Saved Hundreds of Thousands of Dollars with No Increase in Staff or Overhead (an oil refinery plant manager gives seven examples of challenging 'TWWADI' — That's the Way We've Always Done It — and saving $300,000). Figure 4-1 shows excerpts from this report.

Why sample reports are effective

If the strategy appeals to you, here's why Chapman says a special report puts a routine resume in the shade:

- Speaks immediately of the contributions you can make, a good opening in a networking conversation in a company where no opening has been announced.

- Positions you as an expert by providing substance and depth to your competence.

- Provides interesting reading.

- Offers value to the reader. Special reports give money-making or time-saving information. They don't need to be highly original, just offer good information.

You have enough information to start using special reports on your own. But if you want more coaching or examples, Jack Chapman has published a book titled, *Ten Best: A Variety Pack of Special Reports.* You can get more information and order the book on Chapman's Web site salarynegotiations.com.

SPECIAL REPORT: A SIMPLE LOW-TECH MANUFACTURING SOLUTION THAT SAVED $863,000/YR WITH <u>NO</u> INCREASE IN STAFF OR OVERHEAD.

Most managers today look for high tech, computerized solutions to keep pace and stay competitive. While technology can produce savings, that's not the only place to look. My experience has shown that paying attention to one simple low-tech principle can save 10 times as much as the high-tech solution, and do it with virtually no increase in costs or staff.

I call this low-tech solution: Challenge the "TTWWADI" method of business. Here are ten examples of what I term "ANTI – TTWWADI" and the savings of each. TTWWADI stands for "That's The Way We've Always Done It." I illustrate each principle with a short story from plants I've worked in: but remember, my experience is not unique. Old solutions linger, even when the problems no longer exist. "That's The Way We've Always Done It" can keep them in place for a long time, sometimes imbedded in written SOPs, maybe even [horrors!] in your plant!

I hope you enjoy and profit from this report. As you ponder the question after each example, you may find some of my strategies will apply right now to your situation.

1) <u>Special Work Assignments</u>

Two mechanics were called out on overtime each weekend during the winter months to perform preventative maintenance inspection of a steam system. For safety and quality sake, they made sure no pipes were frozen.

I noticed the overtime on the payroll and questioned it. I asked "Why do we do it on days when the temperature is above 32 degrees?" The reply was, "That's the way we've always done it." (TTWWADI).

By limiting the call outs to days with below freezing weather, we saved over $16,000 in overtime costs and <u>still</u> made sure no freeze damage would occur.

QUESTION: Are there tasks still regularly done by employees that no longer serve a purpose?

2) <u>Let's Replace It with the Same Thing</u>

When it was time to replace a piece of malfunctioning equipment with something new, the first thing the engineering and maintenance people would consider was replacing it "like-kind," i.e. equipment essentially like the existing equipment.

Figure 4-1: An abbreviated two-page illustration of a special report. Source: Jack Chapman.

What was the cause of the delays? It was those pumps that were to be replaced like-kind. The pumps were undersized for our current loading needs. We had paid the demurrage for delaying trucks for many years. No one questioned it, because "That's the way we've always done it." (TTWWADI)

By replacing the equipment with adequate equipment to get the job done on time, the demurrage was eliminated, saving over $50,000/year.

QUESTION: Is your plant engineering or maintenance personnel just replacing without investigating?

[Ed. Note: To give you the idea of the whole report, here are the titles of the next 8 TTWWADI lessons, and the cost savings Mark attributed to each. Note that the ideas here are not "rocket science," they're just things that demonstrate wisdom and experience on the job. Perfect for baby boomers... or anyone experienced in his or her field.]

3)	Double Work	$15,000
4)	Doing a Study and then Not Implementing the Recommendations	$30,000
5)	Waiting for Breakdowns to Maintain Equipment	$25,000
6)	Cleaning Up after Yourself	$50,000
7)	Cost of Renting Equipment	$12,000
8)	Not Meeting New Regulations	$200,000
9)	Costs of Not Calibrating Equipment	$400,000
10)	Spending More than You Make	$65,000
	Total:	$797,000/year

If you wish to discuss ways this report can be applied to your operation, please call **Mark A.** at (314) 555-4951. By the way, this report is not copyrighted. Feel free to pass it along to your friends – just keep my name and number on it.

Thanks, Mark.

Concepts for Career-Changing Boomers

Some 72 percent of out-of-work professionals change industries, with 16 percent starting their own businesses, says a survey of 14,000 people from 35 countries by DBM, a leading human resource consulting and outplacement firm.

DBM offers three salient points to bear in mind about how to use your resume in a career-change effort.

- ✔ **Forget about ads and search firms.** With the exception of entry-level positions, companies run ads to recruit prospects with specific experience. The same is true of search firms — they are paid to find highly experienced talent that matches the job description exactly.

- ✔ **Network, network, network.** Networking is especially the key in the case of career change to a successful outcome. The most effective way to transfer skills to a new field or career is by using your contacts. Companies are more willing to take risks on people who are referred to them by individuals who can account for the candidates' abilities and potential.

- ✔ **Find a mentor.** Mentors provide guidance, facilitate introductions, and endorse your capabilities.

Additionally, I offer these suggestions when new directions beckon.

Turning your life around with portable skills

Skills, not preferences, entitle you to be employed. (Tough, but the money doesn't always follow when you do what you love.)

The molecules of self-discovery are elusive. Self-discovery in a group setting is more fun than sitting alone scratching your head. Enroll in a career workshop and get help. The group dynamics are similar to those that motivate members in a weight-control organization: "How many pounds did you lose?" equates to "How many skills did you come up with?"

Start trolling for transferable skills as you review abbreviated lists in Chapters 3 and 11. Plan to spend as many as 20 hours over the next few weeks in putting a name to each of your marketable skills.

What if you don't have the transferable skills you need to ply a new trade? Maybe you can use volunteerism as a stepping stone to a new career. Volunteer for a brief period of time through a volunteer referral service to make sure that you're legally working without pay.

Choosing your best format

Choose the functional format or its hybrid offspring. This class of formats emphasizes the transferable skills in your pocket. Your presentation must help the employer see what you can do, not merely what you have done. A lockstep reverse chronological format doesn't give you the flexibility to change your image.

Starting with pertinent skills

Place the skills relevant to your intended change up front in your resume. If you don't have any, start the analysis process again or get a night job to cover your bills while you gain relevant experience or education. Relevant skills are what employers must hit on immediately.

Acquiring more skills

Figure on two indispensable skills for most career changers:

- ✔ **Computer literacy.** You need the ability to use word processing and spreadsheet programs at minimum.
- ✔ **Internet literacy.** You need the ability to use e-mail and search engines at minimum.

If you didn't grow up digital, take seminars and find a tutor (a neighborhood teenager may be perfect), or enroll in community college courses or adult education classes at a high school. Possessing computer and Internet skills makes you seem not old and rigid, but young and flexible, which encourages employers to look at you and see reduced training costs along with a new source of technological support.

Matching your target job description

When you've firmly labeled your mobile marketable skills and found more than you expected (thank you, God), what's next? Here's a practical idea to begin your career shift:

Find or write job descriptions of your target occupations. If you like your current field and are leaving involuntarily because it's disappearing from under your feet, start with job descriptions in closely related jobs. Compare requirements of related jobs with your transferable skills profile. If you don't like your current field, forget I mentioned it.

To identify occupations closely related to your current field, check a library copy of the *Occupational Outlook Handbook* published by the U.S. Department of Labor. Or, see it online at `bls.gov/oco`.

Knowing the name of what you have to offer gets you up off your knees, out of the past, and into the future. You no longer have to say, "This is what I have done; can you use me?"

Now you can write a resume that readers will respect, by saying, "This is what I can do for you that will add to your productivity, efficiency, or effectiveness. Not to mention a little bump on the bottom line."

Using appropriate headings

If you are using freelance, hobby, or volunteer experience, use the heading *Work Experience* and list it first, unless you have changed your focus through education. Then, begin with the heading *Education*. To refine this heading, substitute target-job-related education, such as *Accounting Education* or *Healthcare Education*. Your employment history follows.

What do you do with all the experience that was great in your old job but means zero where you want to go? Lump it together at the end of your resume under *Other Experience* or *Earlier Experience*. Shrink it to positions, titles, employers, and/or degrees and educational institutions. If extraneous experience is older than five years, squash it entirely.

Taking a lower-level job

When you are willing to step down from your previous level of work, the first thing to know is don't try to do it with a resume. Do it by a personal first contact where you get a chance to color your positioning in the best hue, and to defuse intuitive rejection. You tell your story before recruiters and employers can say they don't want to hear it.

You are not a manager lowering yourself by looking for a much less responsible job. You are a career changer exploring new fields:

In the past decade, I've put in very long hours and exceeded expectations in jobs in the same industry. I realized I'm a doer who needs new mountains to climb. I have too much to give to the business world to ride on autopilot the rest of my life. I want to check out other ways I can make a contribution in a different career field, hopefully at your company.

Go directly to the hiring manager and explain why, and from the manager's point of view, WIIFM (What's in it for me?):

> *What's in it for you? I have a great work attitude and excellent judgment. Show me a new task, and I get it right away. I understand, of course, that the trade-off in looking into your industry is less pay and responsibility.*

When you've opened the door, hand over your resume. Write a hybrid resume (detailed in Chapter 9) with heavy emphasis on the functional part. You need breathing room to shape your resume in a way that spotlights your transferable skills as they pertain to the job you seek, such as talent for working with numbers, reliability, and good attendance record, as well as fast-learning ability.

When you are a major seeking a minor position, emphasize that, sometimes, good people need new challenges.

And don't forget WIIFM. WIIFM may not prove to be the answer every time, but that's the way to bet.

Hitting pay dirt on career changing

From the very first moment a reader sets eyes on your resume, the answers to these questions must be apparent:

> *Why are you qualified for the position in my company?*

> *Why doesn't your last position relate to this one?*

Answer these on your resume, and you're on your way to the career change you seek.

Show skills as they apply to new position

In a career change, as you list your skills, education, and experience, lead with the information relevant to the new position and then list the other data. You have to quickly convince the employer that you have the ability to handle the position.

Assume an engineer wants to move into sales. The resume should mention things like "client liaison," "preparing presentations for meetings," and "strong communications skills."

In an asset statement (see Chapter 13), you may begin by writing: "Used a strong technical background and excellent communications skills in a sales role." Then continue to speak of your ability to provide good technical advice in a business relationship. But writing that you "enjoy learning" is a coin with two sides; the employer may see you as flexible in your desire to further your education, or, conversely, make a negative judgment that you don't have the skills right now to hit the ground running.

TIP

Presenting short-term work on your resume

Baby boomers may find that they're doing work for a specific company but are being paid through a temporary staffing firm or other intermediary and ask how to report the information on their resumes. Don't list the middle-man firm. Note only the companies for which the work was performed. Here's a brief template:

Company A, Company B, Company C   20xx to present

For **Company A,** Name of Department/Division

As **job title,** performed:

✔ achievement

✔ achievement

✔ achievement

For **Company B,** Name of Department/Division

As **job title,** implemented:

✔ achievement

✔ achievement

✔ achievement

For **Company C,** Name of Department/Division

As **job title,** credited with:

✔ achievement

✔ achievement

✔ achievement

P.S. If your job titles are extreme — insignificant or overly exalted — don't bold them.

Gaffes Common to Seasoned Aces

When you've a long job history, you're more likely to need updates on the following issues.

Using old resume standards

Many baby boomers, still working on last decade's calendar, have an outdated concept of what a resume should be. An office neighbor recently expressed surprise when I told him to leave out his personal information, which once was standard fare on resumes. "Oh, I thought personal information was supposed to humanize you," the ace said. Busy employers and job computers don't care that you are a par golfer or play tennis; this kind of personal bonding information comes out at the interview.

Revealing age negatively

Don't blurt out your age. Your mindset should be: Start with ageless — you can always move to senior. Do not put old education first on your resume (unless you are a professional educator). Avoid listing jobs with dates older than 10 or 15 years. If you must include dusty jobs, de-emphasize the dates or omit them. You can summarize old jobs under a heading of "Prior to 20XX" and avoid being too specific. Alternatively, you can include all jobs under functional headings. Try not to describe older jobs in detail.

Choosing the wrong focus

Choosing the wrong focus is a problem shared with new graduates who fail to elaborate on those jobs that best address the hoped-for next job.

Try this approach: Use the worksheets in Chapter 13 to draft an encyclopedic master resume. The number of pages doesn't matter — you'll never use it in its entirety. Each time that you're tailoring a resume for a specific job opening, review your master resume and choose those jobs most directly related to your new goal.

Lacking a summary

Because of the extensiveness of your experience, your resume may be unwieldy without a summary. Usually, using both an objective and a summary is superfluous, but exceptions occur. Suppose you're fed up living as a city slicker and want to move to a small town where agribusiness is dominant. Your objective may take only one line — "Wish to work as internal auditor in the farm equipment industry." Follow that statement with a one- or two-paragraph summary of why you are qualified. Think of a summary as a salesperson's hook. It describes some of your special skills, your familiarity with the target industry, and your top achievements. For examples of summaries, see Chapter 13.

A guide: If your objective and summary are two ways of saying the same thing, dispense with one of them.

Appearing low-tech

Seasoned aces who do not have computers still type resumes; others with computers have old-fashioned dot matrix printers. Their resumes are often stopped at the door. Today's readers like crisp, attractive layouts that only a computer and laser printer can create. Trade a dinner for resume services from a friend, use a computer free at a library, rent a computer by the hour at a copy center, or pay a professional to do your resume.

Not supplementing a high school education

If your highest education attainment is high school, don't forget to mention any continuing education, including seminars and workshops related to your work — if it applies to what you want to do next.

Smiling Beats Frowning

No one is silly enough to claim that for mature workers the rejection experience in job hunting is fun. But a smile a day helps keep your morale from sagging. Here's one to start you out:

Oh Lord, give me patience — and give it to me NOW!

Chapter 5

Info Tech Resumes: Write Them Right

In This Chapter

▶ Getting across your skills and experience

▶ Looking at your resume through recruiters' eyes

▶ Finding the right formula

nformation technology (IT) professionals were the golden boys and girls of the job market until the downturn in the early twenty-first century. Now, they're the market's gladiators, battling for every job opening. If you're one of these tech-savvy job hunters, this chapter is for you.

Give Your Job Search Your Best Shot Right Now

If you've been laid off or you just want a better IT job, get cracking without delay. That's the word from experts who track IT careers. This isn't the time to kick back or take time off to go adventuring through a rain forest.

First, Janet Ruhl speaks. Ruhl is CEO of RealRates.com. She says:

"Working is always better than not working. A couple of years ago, you might have been able to turn down a couple of jobs while you held out for $100 an hour, but in the current down market, you'd be wise to take any contract or job that keeps your skills current. A gap of more than six months on your resume may make it much harder to find any new position."

Dr. Norman Matloff, professor of computer science at the University of California, Davis and operator of the number-one mailing list for IT professionals (matloff¢.ucdavis.edu) also has some advice. He says that you shouldn't let grass grow under your feet and warns against age discrimination fall-out:

"If a programmer goes, say, more than a year without programming work, he or she is considered 'out of the field,' and is generally shunned by employers and headhunters. The programmer is told, 'Sorry, the field is changing extremely rapidly, and you are just not up to date.' Actually, the situation is somewhat similar to the one in which a programmer stays in a job that uses an old technology and then gets laid off and tries with poor luck to find other programming work. But the out-of-the-field people have it even worse. They are presumed to have even forgotten how to program altogether during that year of absence."

You've got the message. Pour it on!

Components of a StandOut IT Resume

No one can predict when the IT job market will reignite, so I won't even try. Instead, what I can do for you human technical powerhouses is describe in this section the important fundamentals in making a StandOut IT resume (in addition to general advice given throughout this book).

For that discussion, I talked with the West Coast recruiting manager for a well-known defense contractor, Adrian Barbour. Barbour says that he spends 90 percent of his time at a computer screen reading resumes. How many does he review each year? I wondered. "Thousands!" the very experienced resume reader replied.

I asked Barbour a series of questions. Here are his responses.

JLK: Which is more important on a resume: technical or people skills?

AB: On the IT side, technical skills weigh more heavily than personality. On the management side, the reverse is true. People skills are an area in which techies are very, very weak.

JLK: What kind of resume makes HR people warm to you?

AB: HR professionals like resumes that center on a focus statement. A resume that says "I'm a networking administrator," for example, immediately clues HR professionals what to look for. The HR person can say, "Does this person have enough years of experience? Okay, that's what we want." And we go from there. Contrast that direct connection with a resume that's all over the place. When job seekers have a multiplicity of skills, they need to split those up into different resumes. You'd be surprised how many people fail to spell out their skills and talents in relationship to the job they want. In effect, they're saying, "Do you think I can fit anything you do? Let me know." I don't have time to guess.

JLK: So the main problem is a lack of specificity?

AB: That's correct. A resume that lacks a specific objective receives scant attention. Is it software? Is it engineering? I don't want to think for an applicant.

JLK: Anything else that causes a resume to be passed over?

AB: A problem I see over and over is the failure to relate functions to the positions you've held. A resume will mention a long list of applications or operating systems, but they're never explained — never fleshed out — in the body of the positions held. It's a kind of disconnect. The resume claims abilities in Java, C++, and says in a cursory manner, 'I programmed this and did a database' — but gives no details to back up the claims."

JLK: Thanks, Adrian Barbour. Can you now show us a couple of IT resumes that you like?

AB: Absolutely. One is at an executive level; the other a technician.

The IT Resume Explained

This section contains two IT resumes from Adrian Barbour's electronic cellars. They illustrate both ends of the experience spectrum. Dates, job searcher names, and some company names are fictional on both. Figure 5-1 markets a senior candidate, and Figure 5-2 is a resume for a junior candidate.

Seth Luther

The Seth Luther resume in Figure 5-1 is heavily muscled, highlighting the candidate's seniority. Luther opens with a strong summary of qualifications, so the reader quickly gains an overview of his experience, skills, and abilities.

Notice that Luther's heading includes immediate credential identification. Additionally, it offers multiple means of contact to interested employers. This feature is very important because each hiring manager has a preference for contacting applicants: Some prefer e-mail, and others take the traditional approach of using the phone.

IT Executive

Seth Luther
MBA, MCSE+I
seth@ciomagazine.com

(760) 555-0443 (home) ❖ 2546 Washington Ave Oceanside, CA 92057 ❖ (760) 555-8450 (cell)

EXECUTIVE SUMMARY

A leader. A Self-motivated, results-driven senior information technology (IT) professional with hands-on experience in company operations, and all aspects of IT. Have business background in manufacturing processes. Experienced with Lawson, JD Edwards One-World, and many other ERP software platforms.

Possess an in-depth understanding of emerging technologies. Seeking a position in a dynamic environment, with extensive experience developing, managing, analyzing infrastructures with NT, Sun Solaris, SQL, JDE, VPN, TCP/IP, AS400, SAP, Oracle, PeopleSoft Financials, e-business, EDI, IP telephony designs, software development and customer service solutions.

Responsible for P/L's, multi-million dollar network deployments and product launches, budgets, policies, business analysis, risk assessment, auditing and cross-functional operations, domestic, global and tactical planning. A seasoned professional with senior management planning, international and domestic business operations experience.

AREAS OF EXPERTISE

• SQL Server	• ERP/MRP/Globally
• VOIP/ unified messaging	• MS NT Exchange/Citrix
• Software Programming	• International Development
• Data/Internet Security	• Sales Order Processing
• JDE One-World	• Disaster Recovery Planning
• HMTL, ASP	• Supply Chain Management
• Network System Engineering	• Data Warehousing
• TDMA/CDMAWireless	• Buying/Purchasing
• Web Development.	• Financial systems
• Visual Basic	• Product Management
• Unix, AS400, Sun	• Risk Management
• ASIC Design	• Project Management

EDUCATION

• MBA, Barbour Center for International Business, University of California at Oceanside, CA.
• BSCS Degree, Institute for Engineering & Information Technology, Los Angeles, CA.
• MCSE+I, Institute for Engineering & Information Technology, Los Angeles, CA.

EMPLOYMENT HISTORY

10/04- Present
PeopleVu International Corporation, Oceanside, CA.
Executive Manager Information Technology
• Establish goals, objectives, and policies. Develop and implement programs to ensure attainment of business plan for growth, profit and branding. Implement cost-savings, cost avoidance exceeding four hundred thousand within two months. Responsible for daily operations of IT department. Develop

(1 of 2)

Figure 5-1: Resume of a senior professional.

organizational structure, strategic growth plans and all operational policies and procedures. Create business processes and flows for revenue and initiated data/Internet security, auditing, implementing best practices.

- Manage and implement Oracle platform, Unix, IBM AS400 IT-related projects to supply chain management and operations, program Lawson software and EDI Platform. Responsibilities include three WAN/LAN networks and a lab using management methodology for "IT", budget analysis, user requirements, and communication of project status, schedule development and tracking.

10/99 - 9/04
WonderWerks, Irvine, CA.
Chief Information Director of Operations
- Developed and implemented the JDE One-World experience technology for Star Trac and all operations in every department on a Unix platform. Implemented over five million dollars in cost savings, and cost-avoidance procedures within two years on several initiated programs. Initiated all IT budgets, manufacturing supply chain management, recruitment and P/L.

- Initiated and developed the disaster procedures and methodologies appropriate for the information infrastructure, EDI, SQL, web site and telephony system to mitigate risks. Successfully created and deployed the infrastructure utilizing LAN/WAN globally for international and domestic projects, VPN solution, DHCP, SSL, Citrix, wireless solution and Microsoft globally. Developed and initiated data/Internet security, auditing, implementing best practices procedures. Initiated, designed the infrastructure and rollout for all desktop computers, NT processes.

- Successfully replaced the old "PBX phone system" and developed the new "IP telephone system" telecommunication from Cisco System VOIP unified messaging.

- Created a platform and published white papers for internal and external distribution.

- Led 11 project manager-teams globally on Cisco deployment remote access (RAS).

8/89 - 10/99
Lamb Enterprises, Santa Ana, CA.
IT Business Manager
- Implemented best practices on risk mitigation and emergency contingency with, manufacturing, ERP, MRP processes, IS departments and all phases of operations and finance. Managed product development life cycle and communication platforms. Developed business processes and flow for revenue, platform with JDE. Implemented cost savings, cost avoidance over two million dollars.

- Extensive hands-on experiences with MS Exchange, CICS, and IBM products, AS400, OS/390, RS/6000 and network server clustering. Initiated, "San" backup solution technology in the event of a catastrophic and developed and implemented numerous disaster recovery designs, defining and documenting new processes and interdepartmental relationships with contingency plan. Successfully developed and implemented network designs, SAP, e-business platforms, ERP/MRP, IP phone systems processes, EDI and supply chain management. Created platform and published white papers for internal and external distribution. Conducted seminars on catastrophic and contingency plans for customer service. Effectively directed, influenced, developed and motivated subordinates, obtaining positive team solutions.

(2 of 2)

The *areas of expertise* section allows for easy scanning into databases, yet the resume maintains an attractive professional appearance. The style is conservative and tasteful. If the candidate wrote his own resume, a reader could ascribe these characteristics to the candidate.

Short paragraphs and bullets in the *employment history* section make Luther's resume easier to read and comprehend.

The general rule in resume construction is to lead with the most important, relevant, and impressive information. Luther has already done that with his powerful executive summary and areas of expertise. That's why Luther has placed his education section before a formal description of his experience. When educational attainment is a firm requirement with no possibility of exception, a recruiter wants to know quickly that time isn't wasted reading through to the end only to find that the candidate has high achievement but a shortfall of educational credentials.

Note that Luther doesn't supply the years of his graduations. Although some employers still insist on knowing the year when a candidate graduated and received a degree, those details can easily lead to age discrimination. So Luther omits the years, wanting to be evaluated for the benefits he brings, not for the candles he blows out on his birthday cake.

Daniel Bessant

Daniel Bessant, a much younger and more junior candidate than Luther, also "gets it." He provides several forms of contact and clearly states his objective in Figure 5-2.

Bessant launches his self-marketing with a statement of what he has to sell. The skills list incorporates personal characteristic statements (*positive attitude, dependable, accountable, and work under minimal supervision*) as well as an itemizing of his abilities. The certification information validates his claims of competence and is very important.

Bessant's work experience is scant, but he makes the most of it by listing functions and adding a statement about his self-employed moonlighting activities repairing computers, a clue that he truly enjoys technical work.

The young technician's formal education rounds out a straightforward resume of a job searcher who's not yet able to report a history of measurable achievements similar to that of Seth Luther's resume but who clearly has the qualifications to work in a position a step or two above entry-level employment.

IT Technician

Daniel Bessant

2525 Garfield Street, Vista, CA 92084
Home: (760) 555-0169 ~ Mobile: (760) 555-3627 ~ E-mail: dandan@peoplevu.com

Objective

Computer Technician/Network Support

Skills

- ➤ Proficient in assembling, diagnosing, repairing, and rolling out new computer systems
- ➤ Effective helpdesk trouble-ticketing system and remote desktop connection experience
- ➤ Able to resolve network connectivity, security, e-mail, and protocol issues
- ➤ Experience with Novell, Linux, Windows 9x, XP, NT, 2000 server and workstation
- ➤ Knowledgeable in MS Word, Excel, Outlook, PowerPoint, and Access applications
- ➤ Qualified to create, update, and deploy Symantec Ghost System Images
- ➤ Able to fabricate, test, and install UTP or Fiber-optic cables
- ➤ Possess strong written and oral communications skills along with a positive attitude
- ➤ Reputation as dependable, accountable, and able to work under minimal supervision

Certifications

- ➤ **MCP** — Windows 2000 Professional
- ➤ **Network+, CompTIA** — Networking Technologies
- ➤ **A+, CompTIA** — Software and Hardware Technician
- ➤ **Network Architect/Telecom Cable Installation** — Network Design

Experience

Helpdesk I – Oceanside Harbor Police — 2004 - Present
Successfully used a helpdesk trouble-ticket system to document event-calls and remotely connect to customer computers. Involved with Symantec Ghost System Imaging, transferring user preferences, data integrity, and insured domain user connectivity associated with a new computer rollout. Performed PC service calls to troubleshoot and replace hardware, install applications, and upgrade memory. Performed printer maintenance, upgrades, and resolved network connectivity issues.

PC Repair – Self Employed — 1997 - 2005
Repaired, upgraded, and built PC's.

Education

Miracosta College — 2004
- ➤ **Associate of Science in Computer Science Information Systems and LAN Support Specialist**
Emphasis in PC troubleshooting skills, network security, connectivity, structured cabling design, and Microsoft Office applications. Continually achieved the President's List for outstanding academic performance.

Figure 5-2: An IT resume that makes the most of limited experience.

Security clearances help IT hiring

Security clearances may be required in any defense-related industry.

Technical reviewer Jim Lemke recounts the story of a recent IT candidate who applied to a defense contractor for a position. The candidate later called the company to complain that he was not contacted for a job for which he was confident he was a match. Lemke looked at his resume and, indeed, he was a match — except that the candidate omitted the fact that he holds a secret clearance. Because the position he applied for required a clearance, he never came up in a search of the database.

If you currently have or qualify for a clearance, add that fact to your resume. Here are a few tips about security clearances:

- Some jobs in government require a security clearance. "An agency will hire you on a tentative basis and then apply for the clearance for you," explains Kathryn Troutman (resumeplace.com), an expert in the federal hiring process and applications. "It may take six months to receive your clearance, and you can't start the job until the clearance is complete. Many people keep another job until then."

- As for a security clearance to work for a defense contractor, Troutman says you also have to be hired tentatively, based on having a clearance process performed.

- New terminology is emerging. The 'full lifestyle polygraph' is the same as a security clearance. Follow the security clearance issue on the Web site of the Defense Security Services (www.dss.mil).

Chapter 6

Out of Uniform and into Civilian Resumes

*T*he military recruiter told you that service in the Armed Forces — with its training programs and real-life experience — would make the civilian world do flip flops over you when you finished serving your country. Now that the moment for leaving is near, you're wondering: Was that just marketing hype?

Okay, soldier . . . Okay, sailor . . . Okay, marine . . . you're about to find out the truth as you transition to a workplace where you no longer salute. In this chapter, we help you get your bearings and show how your military experience is transferable to a civilian job. "We" is Bill Gaul and myself. Gaul, himself an Army veteran, is president and CEO of The Destiny Group (destinygrp.com), a "Have You Hired a Vet Today?" job board based in San Diego and San Francisco. The following section is a transcript of my interview with Gaul.

Turning Your Resume into a Civilian Must-Read

Veterans are highly trained, exceptionally skilled and remarkably disciplined. They have a strong work ethic and try to get it right the first time. Many military members move ahead much faster than their civilian counterparts.

JLK: Is it true that the civilian world views vets as highly qualified?

BG: While many private sector employers will not immediately understand the value of your military training and experience, you can bridge the gap by communicating in language they relate to. "Milspeak" won't do it. If you can convert your experience into private industry terminology and use current buzzwords to demonstrate your transferable expertise, you'll be well on your way to the interview.

JLK: Can you give an example of what you call "Milspeak"?

BG: An Army colonel's resume we were recently sent read: "As commanding officer of a 500-person organization, I was responsible for the health, morale and welfare of all personnel." Health, morale and welfare? Just think of the incredible range of skills and experience completely overlooked in that Milspeak phrase. Far-reaching accomplishments and important responsibilities are whitewashed into noneffective boilerplate terms that mean nothing to a civilian hiring manager.

For example, digging into "health, morale, and welfare," we found "policy development, human resource management, budget planning and administration, process improvement, operations management, and staff development."

JLK: What are the places where Milspeak is most likely to turn up in a resume?

BG: Job titles, responsibilities, and education and training sections.

JLK: Please tell us about job titles.

BG: Many military job titles are ambiguous. Some are downright misleading. For example, a Navy fire control technician does not put out fires but operates and maintains electronic weapons targeting systems.

JLK: What should you do about that on a resume?

BG: If there is a simple way to translate your job title without misleading a reader, do so:

- ✔ Mess cook (food service specialist)
- ✔ Fire control technician (electronic weapons systems technician)
- ✔ Motor pool specialist (automotive maintenance technician)
- ✔ Provost marshal (law enforcement officer)
- ✔ Quartermaster (supply clerk)

JLK: What about when your specific work experience doesn't closely relate to the job you're applying for?

BG: You can list your organizational position instead of your job title. An E-5 Marine Corps embassy guard applying for a management position in the security industry listed his job title as "facility supervisor." He then added the details of his experience within the body of his resume. This drew readers further into his resume because it represented more of a fit than someone who kept people in proper lines applying for visas.

JLK: Aren't most military members in combat-related jobs?

BG: Yes, and that can be a problem, trying to relate the job you've had to the job you want, unless you're applying for law enforcement positions. But for the straight combat MOS (military occupational specialty) — infantry, tank gunner, reconnaissance Marine, and the like — there are several options to choose from:

Select a functional resume format (Chapter 9) that emphasizes skills first and lists work history and job titles last.

List your relative position in an organization — "unit supervisor" instead of "platoon sergeant" as your title.

Your work in collateral duties may be the key. A platoon sergeant seeking a position in staff development and training, based on duty as a training NCO, could list training supervisor as her title. The dates listed must accurately reflect the time you spent in the specific collateral duties, of course. As you know, it is often the case that you will have more than one collateral duty while performing a key role for an organization.

JLK: You just used the word "officer." Even though the civilian world uses terms like "bank officer," and "trust officer," do you recommend its use in transitional resumes?

BG: It's fine. The word "officer" is used in civilian employment and is a term human resource professionals understand. But omit references to rank or grade like "NCO" (noncommissioned officer), "petty officer," and "sergeant." Unless an employer has military experience, these terms won't communicate your relative position within an organization. Instead, list civilianized equivalents appropriate to your level of authority:

- ✔ Safety Warrant Officer OSHA (coordinator)
- ✔ Training NCO (training supervisor)
- ✔ Barracks sergeant (property manager)

One more resume tip for officers: If you intend to work with third-party recruiters, check with several to determine their resume format preferences. Many will want a description of your responsibilities by job title, almost like a chronological format but without the years spent at individual posts. This format works well for any officer selling management experience because it highlights important assignments and allows you to select only those that support your objective.

JLK: What about the second problem area, responsibilities?

BG: Take nothing for granted. Explain, detail, describe. Suppose you're a technician; what specific technical aspects of your job are transferable to the civilian sector? Do you read blueprints, schematics, and technical drawings? Have you utilized specific diagnostic equipment? Your objective is to let an employer know just how much training she would not have to provide if she hired you.

If you're short on equivalency facts, research (see Chapters 8 and 13) can mean the difference between a trip for your resume to the "No" pile and a trip to the interview room.

JLK: And the third problem area — education and training?

BG: The United States military is always training and educating, and they know how to do it effectively. Military graduates are highly desirable in the civilian world. But many courses and schools leave experienced human resource professionals wondering exactly what you trained for because the course titles can be esoteric and arcane. The rule is this: List your training in a way that will provide immediately apparent support for your job objective.

If the name of a school or course doesn't communicate exactly what was taught there, modify it because you are trying to inform, not mystify. You are trying to de-militarize the language to help resume reviewers understand the nature of your military training.

These examples illustrate:

- SNAP II Maintenance School (Honeywell Mainframe Computer Maintenance School)
- NALCOMIS Training (Automated Maintenance and Material Control System Training)
- Mess Management School (Food Service Management School)
- NCO Leadership Training (Leadership and Management Training)

JLK: Is that all there is to civilianizing a military background?

BG: Not quite. To help resume reviewers understand the depth of your training, list the number of classroom hours you studied. To determine the number of hours, multiply the number of course days by 8, or the number of weeks by 40. If you completed the course within the last 10 years, list the competition date. If the course is older, leave off the date.

  ✔ Leadership and Management Training, 3/95 (160 hours)

  or

  ✔ Leadership and Management Training (160 hours)

JLK: You've sent us two sample resumes (see Figures 6-1 and 6-2). Can you make a few comments on each one?

BG: The first resume, Christopher Hart (not his real name), shows through his experiences that he offers a great deal more competencies and skills than may be associated with a NCO (non-commissioned officer). He does it by using civilian equivalent job titles followed by his actual title in parenthesis and itemizing his background to highlight his role in training, employee retention, and accountability for property. By defining his demonstrated skills, Hart increases his universe of potential employers. He has stayed away from the overused term "Responsible for" and instead used action verbs to do his talking.

JLK: Translating military titles really does alter images and increase possibilities, doesn't it?

BG: You bet it does! The second resume, Scott C. Summers (not his real name), also shows a good understanding of the need to write resumes in "civilianese," not Milspeak. Although Summers's military title, Marine Aircraft Logistics Support Equipment Asset Manager, is impressive, it's more than a mouthful when applied to the type of managerial position he seeks. By using the civilian term, "Inventory Manager," an employer quickly sees that Summers is not limited to the aircraft or military sectors, but can be considered for any type of industry.

JLK: Thanks, Bill Gaul of The Destiny Group for spelling out the benefits of making sure the civilian world knows how your experience qualifies you for the world outside the military.

Military Transition

Christopher Hart, Jr.
9544 Valley Dr.
Jonesboro, Georgia 30236
chris.hart1@earthlink.net
(770) 555-9911

EDUCATION   **Webster University**, St. Louis, MO   **Saint Leo University**, St. Leo, FL
             Master of Arts: March, 2002   Bachelor of Arts: January, 2001
             Concentration: Human Resource   Major: Business Management
                             Development   Cum Laude

EXPERIENCE   **United States Army**
             43d Adjutant General Battalion, Fort Leonard Wood, Missouri

January 2000 –   **Senior Administrative Manager (Company First Sergeant)**
March 2002
                 • Personally directed the organization of a newly activated company consisting of 400
employees
                 • Improved the company's training program which greatly increased morale, discipline,
and motivation
                 • Flawlessly executed Fort Leonard Wood's holdover mission for years 2000 and
2001, encompassing more than 6700 enlistees
                     • Maintained prudent care of a $6 million facility housing a maximum of 672 employees
                     • Recognized as mastering the Army's complex personnel management system
                     • Cited as a Master Trainer for exceptional ability to motivate and train

                 United States Army
                 Criminal Investigation Command, Fort Gillem, Georgia

Nov 1997 –   **Senior Personnel Supervisor (Senior Personnel Sergeant)**
Jan 2000
                 • Designed and developed automated tracking procedures for individual awards and
outstanding personnel actions
                 • Conducted individual counseling and professional development programs for over 200
employees daily
                 • Provided training and supervision of employees on the proper operation and
maintenance of the Army's personnel database
                     • Lead research initiatives designed to improve personnel services for remote employees
                     • Advised superiors on equal opportunity matters

                 United States Army
                 Recruiting Command, Minneapolis, Minnesota and Fort Knox, Kentucky

Apr 1991 –   **Personnel Specialist (Personnel Sergeant)**
Sep 1996
                 • Served as the personnel manager for a regional organization represented throughout
five states in the upper Midwest
                     • Provided short- and long-range personnel requirements
                     • Expeditiously coordinated hiring actions
                     • Provided training and professional mentorship to seven district personnel managers

AFFILIATIONS   **Member**
                Delta Epsilon Sigma - National Scholastic Honor

SKILLS   Security clearance, facilitator and motivator, Microsoft Office, equal opportunity advisor,
advanced leadership and management development courses

Figure 6-1: A military career translated into equivalent civilian job positions.

Military Transition

Scott C. Summers
8450 Blackbird Rd.
Baltimore, MD 21214
(410)-555-9125
scsummers@aol.com

Objective: Seeking a career in the logistics industry as an Asset Manager Coordinator.

Professional Summary

- Four years' experience as an asset management coordinator.
- Supervisory management level experience.
- Understand total supply chain management and familiar with current logistics solutions.
- Software skills using Access, Excel, Word, PowerPoint, Fedlog, Nalcomis, G Link, and local asset management databases.
- Ability to work in a fast-paced operations environment and be a team player.
- Understanding of materials management.
- Proven strong organizational, analytical, communications and presentation skills.

Experience

United States Marine Corps – June 1998 to June 2002, Honorable Discharge

Inventory Manager (Marine Aircraft Logistics Support Equipment Asset Manager)
- Managed 37,000 aircraft maintenance items valued at $6.5 million.
- Insured that order entry/order control inventory management was correctly maintained on a daily basis.
- Developed and initiated preparation of handbooks, bulletins, and information systems to provide and supply logistics support.
- Compiled and coordinated data from multiple sources; such as contracts, purchase orders, invoices, requisitions, and accounting reports.
- Entered information into a computer to maintain inventory, purchasing, shipping, and other records.
- Verified accuracy of requisitions and shipping orders by comparing nomenclature, stock numbers, authorized substitutes, and other listed information with catalogs, manuals, parts lists, and similar references.
- Reviewed files to determine unused items and recommended disposal of excess stock.

Education

1999 – Present   Cherry Point, NC
  Craven Community College

2001   Cherry Point, NC
  Leadership School, U.S. Marine Corps

1998   Cherry Point, NC
  Material Readiness Managers Course

1998-1999   Cherry Point, NC
  Support Equipment Asset Managers Course

Figure 6-2: Showing broad applications for military experience.

Focusing on the Fed: Jobs with Staying Power

Vets: Listen up! Baby boomers retiring from the 1.8 million-person federal workforce are leaving lots of shoes to fill. You may like the size of those shoes — federal jobs pay an average of more than $52,000 nationally, and offer attractive benefits, pensions, good healthcare and flexible work hours. After you're hired by "the fed," you usually stay hired because federal jobs aren't as shaky as economic shifts in the private sector. With these attractions, Uncle Sam is the employer of choice for many across the United States.

This section shows you what a StandOut federal resume looks like, thanks to the stand-out Kathryn Kraemer Troutman, president of The Resume Place (`resumeplace.com`), a resume-writing firm specializing in federal employment. The Baltimore resident is the federal job expert's expert, having trained workers to successfully apply for federal jobs for nearly three decades. Troutman also has a soft spot for vets.

Good deal for vets

"Veterans should pay particular attention to federal employment opportunities," Troutman explains, "because their military experience entitles them to an extra 5 or 10 points on their applications." The point preference system is a benefit Troutman says is explained "pretty nicely" on these two Web sites: www.usajobs.opm.gov/EI52.htm and www.usajobs.opm.gov/EI53.htm.

Troutman is the author of six federal job books, including *Ten Steps to a Federal Job* (The Resume Place), and she created the three-page information technology resume of Marvin McClovsky (not a real person) with fictional dates shown in Figure 6-3.

Highlights of a federal IT resume

Federal job expert Kathryn Kraemer Troutman explains why the resume in Figure 6-3 is a StandOut resume:

Marvin McClovsky, Petty Officer 2nd Class, seeks a civilian position as an information technology professional, GS 9–11 grade level. To match his resume to the federal positions and use the right keywords (see Chapter 11),

I researched the federal occupational standards (position descriptions) for GS 2210 Information Technology Management Series. McClovsky is especially interested in the IT positions of systems administrator, Windows administrator, and customer support. McClovsky shows the specific required 'compliance' details for 10 years of his career, which include: Social Security number, veteran's information (including the 5 points' preference), citizenship, employer addresses, supervisor names and phones. The previous 10 years' experience is listed without the extra compliance details to demonstrate his entire career in a concise presentation.

This reverse chronological format is easy to read because of the formatting and design. It clearly presents McClovsky's diverse IT positions: supervisory, senior operator, network controller, and Windows systems administrator. McClovsky's technical skills, combined with skills in communications and teamwork, make him stand out as a candidate for a government IT position.

I chose information technology to illustrate a StandOut federal resume because of the enormous interest in the topic. But do remember that career fields in the federal government virtually match career fields in the private sector. Survey opportunities and write the resume most likely to land you an interview.

For more information about the IT classification series, refer to opm.gov/fedclass/html/gsseries.htm.

Clasping More Helping Hands for Military Members

Service women and men in civilian conversion mode may be interested in two free Web sites. Both sites lead to additional resources: resumes, career articles, job fairs, former military member organizations, and job-hunting books:

- ✔ Carl Savino's site (greentogray.com)
- ✔ Impact Publications's site (veteransworld.com)

If you didn't take advantage of transition services offered to departing military members and find the civilian job market disappoints you, don't overlook the fact that the military is a family and that networking is natural among family members.

Military to Federal

Marvin McClovsky
72 Sandalwood Lane / Alexandria, VA 22409 / (703) 555-2324
mmclov48@aol.com

Social Security Number: 222-22-2222   Veteran's Preference: 5 points, Honorably Discharged
U.S. Navy, 1986-2005
Citizenship: United States   Highest Federal Civilian Position: N/A

OBJECTIVE: SYSTEMS ADMINISTRATOR / CUSTOMER SUPPORT, GS-2210 9/11

SKILLS SUMMARY:

Over 17 years of Desktop Support, User and Customer Support, Help Desk and Computer Operations experience while serving in the United States Navy. Five years' experience as Windows Systems Administrator.

♦ **Customer Support** - Supervised, managed and trained personnel for Desktop/PC and LAN Support, Help Desk, and Computer Operations; time management and production scheduling.
♦ **Top Level Customer Satisfaction to all commands** - Achieved 98+% satisfaction rate at the Naval Computer and Telecommunications Area Master Station.
♦ **IT Equipment Manager** - Managed over $7,000,000 of equipment and software, as well as liaison with Operations and Maintenance Division personnel.
♦ **Team Leader** - Effective team-builder with strong leadership skills and proven track record at setting and achieving realistic goals for self and others. Maintained mission of command and division in perspective at all times.
♦ **EEO Leader and Trainer** - Proactive EEO leader meeting all command EEO objectives. Effectively motivated and trained junior personnel contributing to unit cohesiveness.

EMPLOYMENT HISTORY:
UNITED STATES NAVY
Jan. 1986 – Aug. 2005

Naval Computer and Telecommunications Area Master Station   9/98 – 8/05
52 Lieutenant Way, Virginia Beach, VA 22832   45+ hours/week
Petty Officer 2nd Class, Systems Administrator
Supervisor: CDR Kris Vanderweit; (804) 555-4000; contact may be made

     Systems Administrator / Microsoft Windows
     Help Desk and Customer Support Supervisor   48 hours/week
     Supervised five personnel providing desktop and user support to 5,000 users for MS Word for Windows 8.0, Windows 2000 and NT in a Novell NetWare 3.x LAN environment. As Help Desk Supervisor personally handled 20-50 trouble calls on a daily basis.

     Provided Level I and II customer support for communications and COTS issues to seven sites on a global basis including Puerto Rico, Alaska, Italy and U. S. Naval vessels afloat. Help Desk handled over 300 trouble calls daily and was in operation 24 hours a day, 7 days a week.

     Prepared and presented training lectures to station personnel on hardware, COTS software and proprietary software such as GATEGUARD, PCMT, NOW and NOWNET.

Figure 6-3: Three pages of military experience applied to the federal work place.

Marvin McClovsky

VQ-2 Reconnaissance Squadron   10/96 – 9/98
Electronic Warfare Department - ADP Maintenance Division
Naval Air Station Madrid, Spain
Petty Officer 2nd Class, Data Processing Technician
Supervisor: LTC Michael Runnestrand

   Automated Data Processing Technician   48 hours/week
      Provided desktop and user support to 250 users. Installed, upgraded, repaired and
      maintained PC's, software, printers, scanners, projectors, and associated peripherals.
      Assisted in installation and maintenance of a 1 server, 250 node Novell NetWare 3.1x
      network. Server was used as a repository of files and e-mail using cc:Mail.

      Prepared lectures and trained personnel in automated data processing (ADP) security as well
      as use of computer applications and utilities.

USS Orion (AS-18) – Submarine Tender   5/94 – 10/96
Supply Department – Automated Processing Division
La Mena, Manata, Spain
Petty Officer 2nd Class, Data Processing Technician
Supervisor: CDR Bradford Hill

Shift Supervisor   56 hours/week
Supervised the operation and monitoring of the Honeywell DPS-6 System and the AN/UYK 65
Tape Drive Unit. Provided technical assistance and software support to end-users.

Managed the daily work activities of four personnel including data entry, production control and
production scheduling. Developed technical documentation for functional descriptions,
maintenance and operation of equipment. Prepared training lectures for technical personnel and
end user on proper operating procedures.

Naval Headquarters Europe   2/92 – 5/94
Naval Operations Support Atlantic Command, London, England
Petty Officer 2nd Class, Data Processing Technician

   Senior Computer Operator   48 hours/week
      Operated and monitored the Honeywell DPS8/70 with an AUTODIN interface and
      associated peripherals for the WWMCCS (World Wide Military Communications Command
      System). Provided technical assistance to end users and taught proper operating procedures.
      Supervised shift personnel and also had role as media librarian.

National Security Agency   9/90 – 4/91
Central Security Service, Fort Meade, MD
Petty Officer 3rd Class, Data Processing Technician

   Network Controller   40 hours/week
      Monitored and controlled local and worldwide packet switching networks for the worldwide
      Signal Intelligence Generator Network Technology (SIGNT) system. Documented all
      outages and occurrences affecting network operations and maintained system software
      databases. Performed fault isolation and initiated corrective measures such as alternate
      routing of communication trunk lines, reconfiguring network nodes or executing emergency
      backup and restoration procedures.

      Scheduled and coordinated maintenance activities for both local and remote sites and
      provided technical and software assistance to end users and network support personnel.

Marvin McClovsky

National Security Agency   3/89 – 9/90
Central Security Service, Fort Meade, MD
Petty Officer 3rd Class, Data Processing Technician
   Computer Operator

USS Sierra (AD-18)   6/86 – 2/89
Supply Department – Automated Data Processing Division, Charleston, SC
Seaman (Undesignated)
   Data Entry Clerk/Computer Operator

EDUCATION:

2000   B.S., Information Technology, University of Maryland, University College: European
         Division, Rota, Spain
        Hardware and Software, Desktop Publishing, Networks and Communications
        Advance Operating Systems

TRAINING:

2004   Microsoft Certified Software Engineer (MCSE) Old Dominion University/ ICTS,
         Alexandria, VA 22314.

2001   Harvard Graphics Human Resources Office Naval Air Station, Rota, Spain.

2000   SNAP 1 (Shipboard Naval Automated Processing) ADP System Enlisted
         Operator/Supervisor Fleet Training Center Naval Base, Norfolk, VA.

1998   WWMCCS (World Wide Military Computer Communications Systems) Computer
         Operator 3300 Technical Training Wing Air Force Base Keesler, MS/London, England.

HONORS AND AWARDS:

1999   Good Conduct Medal – Third Award (previously awarded 1990 and 1994)

1997   Letter of Commendation for the Successful Installation of the Fleet Air Reconnaissance
         VQ-2 Local Area Network

CLEARANCE:

        Successfully completed an SSBI for access to classified material. Clearance granted active
        May 2001.

Chapter 7

Good Advice for Graduates

. . . .

In This Chapter

▶ Implementing hot tips

▶ Writing with little or no experience

▶ Handling advanced degrees on resumes

▶ Avoiding self-defeating errors

. . . .

*Y*our first job after graduation is a pivotal point in your life because it sets the stage for what follows. Whether you're writing your first resume in anticipation of putting work clothes on your bachelor's degree or updating your resume as a graduate who went back to school for an advanced degree, this chapter can help you master the resume-writing course.

Tips for New Graduates

Any recent graduate can benefit from using the resume tips in these sections.

Getting educated about resumes

The number one tip for new graduates: Attend resume workshops. Resume workshops are offered at your campus career center or vocational-technical school placement office. Whether you're an undergraduate, graduate student, or an alumnus, nothing beats a classroom setting for focusing on the knowledge presented.

Seek advice from your school's career counselors. They can help you understand the prerequisites individual recruiters look for in their specific career fields.

Compensating for shortcomings

If you can't qualify for a hiring prerequisite, try to figure out a compensatory benefit you offer. For example, if your GPA is a little below the prerequisite, use an opening summary that focuses on knowing the value of hard work — especially if you learned that value by holding a series of demanding student jobs while working your way through school.

Beefing up a sales pitch

Thicken your work experience by including all unpaid positions — internships, special projects, and volunteer jobs. List them in chronological order in your Work Experience section. Statements like these are powerful agents on your resume:

Sales: Sold $1,200 worth of tickets to college arts festival

Counseling: Advised 16 freshman students as peer counselor

Public Policy Coordination: Coordinator for student petition drive to save California Cougar from sports hunting, gaining 2,000 signatures in 35 days

Highlight the work experience most relevant to your intended future. If you have more than two years of full-time professional experience, place education at the bottom.

Clarifying your aim

Make your objective clear if you use an objective statement. Don't use a lofty statement of the absurd, like this one:

I'm seeking a challenging position that will allow me to actualize my talents in saving the world, with good potential for professional growth and pay commensurate with my ability.

Including positive information

List awards, honors, and citations. Such items as scholarships, appointments, elections, chairs, and university faculty who hold you in esteem belong in your extracurricular activities or highlights section. Use reverse chronological order.

Include your GPA if it's at least 3.0 or high enough for employer prerequisites. You can limit your GPA to the courses in your major, if necessary, but make it clear that's what you did.

Omitting unhelpful information

Do not enclose your resume in a report cover or bulky package or attach school transcripts or letters of recommendation, unless they are requested.

Include an activity only if it reveals skills, accomplishments, results, or the qualifications to support your intended job. Omit high school data unless it adds a unique fact to the total impression that you're creating.

What about the laundry list of your college courses — do they earn their keep on your resume? No, unless the course work is unusual or you have little to say without them. Many graduates struggle to fill one page, so use the worksheets in Chapter 13 to get rolling. The quick reminder list in the "Data-Mine Your College Experience" section later in this chapter may nudge the memory banks.

Being open-minded

When you're batting zero in a slow job market, look for alternatives. For example, if private industry is ignoring you, take a look at opportunities in the public sector. The federal government, in particular, will be receptive in immediate years because a big chunk of the federal workforce is nearing retirement age. Use a search engine to find an abundant site stash of double-eagle jobs and directions on how to get them.

Other back-up plans students use include finding temporary jobs, joining the Peace Corps, relocating to another part of the country, and enrolling in graduate school.

When you graduate at the wrong time

If you find yourself graduating into in a tepid job market, make up your mind that your paste-click-send resume won't pull the interviews you need. Instead, research companies and rewrite your resume to address the companies' needs. Highlight your experience that most applies to the company you're interested in and get it to a hiring manager. Your competition is writing targeted resumes — should you do less?

Even when the job market is flying high, you can soar above the crowd by writing a targeted resume for each job you really want.

Data-Mine Your College Experience

Consider the following factors in identifying the experience and skills you garnered in college and matching the information with the job you hope to land:

✔ **Work:** Internships, summer jobs, part-time jobs, campus jobs, entrepreneurial jobs, temporary work, volunteer work, and so on

✔ **Sports:** Proven ability to achieve goals in a team environment

✔ **Awards and honors**

✔ **Research papers and projects**

✔ **Campus leadership**

✔ **Grade Point Average (GPA):** If it's 3.0 or above; otherwise, omit it

✔ **Technical skills and software facility**

Before you vault in and write, read the reminders in the rest of this chapter to be sure the results are StandOut style.

New graduate with laudable experience

Figure 7-1 shows the resume of a new graduate who has good experience. Knowing that he may face an apathetic job market armed only with a liberal arts degree, the graduate makes certain that he highlights his impressive work experience to beef up his self-marketing document.

New graduate with some experience

Internships and student jobs are the ticket to the job market. Many students are getting the work-experience message, as this question from a reader of my newspaper column suggests:

> *My school's career center is holding resume workshops for graduating seniors. I can't go because I'm doing as I was told — getting work experience. Do employers really believe that a student job produces valuable real-life experience?*

Absolutely yes. And a StandOut resume shows every shred of work experience, paid and unpaid, through internships, student jobs, co-op education, and extracurricular activities. Figure 7-2 presents a student with some experience.

New Graduate — Good Experience

Dominic Preisendorfer

123 45th Way
Washington, OR 67891
(011) 121-3141

Muhlenberg College
Box 321
Allentown, PA 18104
(141) 312-1110

EDUCATION

Muhlenberg College, Allentown, Pennsylvania
BA, Art, June 20XX. Chair, Campus Arts Festival

INTERNSHIPS

Drury Design, Green Mills, Oregon
Fall 20XX
- Contributed to all aspects of a cutting-edge, multifaceted design firm.
- Researched trends as part of "Genie for the New Century" campaign. Drew sketches for new Genie: resulted as subject of article in New Yorker magazine.
- Developed mechanicals for *U.S. Museum of Film Profiles* magazine.
- Transformed BMX Bicycle Company's logo to evoke 21st Century image for racing jersey.
- Assisted with layout for the first Dark Horse style guide to be used by comics firms for licensing.

Washington Magazine, Washington, Oregon
Summer 20XX
- Assisted in day-to-day operations of the art department and in each aspect of production schedule.
- Helped evaluate and provide solutions for layouts in well of book.
- Contributed to redesign of book front. Recommended changes in typefaces, colors, and sizes.

Net Line Design, Allentown, Pennsylvania
Spring 20XX
- Provided extensive clerical support for office, including billing, data entry, filing.
- Prepared samples for presentation.

WORK EXPERIENCE

Freelance, Cafe Paradise, Green Mills, Oregon
Summer 20XX
- Graphic Design: Designed logo, letterhead, business cards, and brochure.
- Advertising: Developed, implemented ad campaign including media purchasing.
- Interior Design: Worked with architect to design funky, eclectic bar, interior environment.

R.R. Manning, Washington, Oregon
Sales, Fall 20XX-Present. High-end country furnishing and accessories store.
- Create windows and furniture displays, developing visual marketing skills and strategies.
- Servicing clients based on customer satisfaction and responses to marketing strategies.
- Train and supervise new hires in stocking and inventory.

COMPUTER SKILLS

- Macintosh Programs: Macwrite, QuarkXPress, Photoshop, Aldus Freehand, Pagemaker, Type Styler, Super Paint, and Illustrator.
- PC Programs: Microsoft Publisher and Works for Windows XP.

Figure 7-1: With a little work and strategy, new graduates can have impressive resumes, too.

New Graduate — Some Experience

MARTINA RABINOVICH
#543-B College Drive, Boston, Massachusetts 45678, (910) 111-2131

OBJECTIVE
Position with environmentally and socially conscious public relations firm. Proven skills in public relations, research, and organization; demonstrated leadership qualities throughout university activities and professional experience. Computer skills.

HIGHLIGHTS OF PUBLIC RELATIONS EXPERIENCE

- **House of Representatives Intern,** Renee H. Glamer's District Office, Elvin, MA.
  Summers 20XX – 20XX
  Assisted Representative Glamer to resolve consituents' issues. Communicated with legislative committees, researched legislation through the House computer system, and attended town meetings. Accumulated invaluable public relations skills using interpersonal abilities effectively in high-pressure, deadline-oriented situations. Major project: Veteran's Festival, 50th Anniversary.

- **Student Body Vice-President,** Boston University, Boston MA. 20XX – 20XX
  Chaired Council Operations Committee. Conducted all student body elections, using strong leadership and public speaking skills to accrue 1,600 votes.

- **Medford Municipal Pool Lifeguard,** Medford, MA. Summers 20XX – 20XX
  Began as snack bar employee, earned certificate, promoted to lifeguard, and then to head lifeguard with managerial responsibilities. Supervised 11 employees.

- **OTHER PUBLIC RELATIONS ACTIVITIES:**
  Student advisor, tour guide, campus delegate, student ambassador for alumni, peer tutor for critical thinking.

RESEARCH EXPERIENCE

- **Republican Party Pollster,** Medford District, Medford, MA. May 20XX – Nov. 20XX
  Distributed more than 50,000 sample ballots. Tabulated results, using math skills. Developed effective organizational skills, communicating with the general public and responding to their interests diplomatically.

- **Medford County Historical Society Intern,** Medford County Historical Society, Medford, MA. Fall 20XX
  Using practiced research skills, researched and designed an exhibit focusing on elections of Progressive party candidates. Exhibit is on display at Medford County Museum, visited by more than 200 individuals a day.

ORGANIZATIONAL SKILLS

- **Alpha Kappa Omega Sorority Leader,** Boston University, Boston, MA. 20XX – 20XX
  Chaired Assault-Risk Management meetings, 20XX – 20XX. Organized events to minimize individual and group risks of physical assault on campus. Assistant Bursar, 20XX – 20XX. Used strong prioritizing and math skills to assist Treasurer in distribution of funds.

Figure 7-2: Turning student work experience to good account.

One technique is to separate your jobs into fragments and explain them. For example, don't say that your job title was "office help" or "office clerk" and stop there. Divide the job into such functions as telephone reception, telephone sales, contract negotiations, purchasing, inventory, staff training, computer application training, public speaking, and written communications. Describe each one in terms of your accomplishments and their outcomes (see Chapter 10). Your inventory of worksheets (see Chapter 13) is invaluable to pump up your experience without fibbing about it.

Stretching your experience is the spin, although you can't get away with claiming that you spent your summers as vice president of Microsoft.

Don't rely on the function-inflation technique if you have other good information such as the lifeguard experience in Figure 7-2.

Too little or no experience

Need a job? Get experience! Need experience? Get a job! This predicament has frustrated new graduates since the continents broke apart.

A few graduates get the message almost too late. Frequently, a marginal new graduate not only drags along a low GPA (grade point average), but also has invested four or five years developing skills as a television watcher, shopper, or socializer. The new graduate not only has no career-related internship or job experience, but also didn't bother to get a job on restaurant row to fund such frivolities as kegs before finals and skiing afterward. There were no co-op assignments, no volunteer stints — zilch!! This reader writes with a challenging query:

> *I'm just a college brat — I have no experience, plus I didn't exactly distinguish myself with grades. How do I write a resume from thin air?*

Having nothing but education to work with makes for a difficult resume scenario. Only dedicated job research and customizing each resume gives you a chance of producing a StandOut product. Perhaps you overlooked something; even child-sitting or pet-sitting offers experience in accepting responsibility and demonstrates reliability.

If an exhaustive search of your hobbies, campus activities, or community service turns up nothing worth putting on your resume, your education must carry the entire weight of candidacy for employment. Milk it dry, as the example in Figure 7-3 suggests.

New Graduate — Little Experience

Deanna R. McNealy
(111) 213-1415

1234 University Drive,#56B
Irvine, California 78910

Seek entry-level retail sales position. Offer more than three years' intensive study of public communication. Completed Bachelor's degree, developing strong research, language, interpersonal, computer, and disciplinary skills. Proven interactive skills with groups and individuals. Energetic, adaptive, fast learner.

BACKGROUND & EDUCATION

- **Bachelor of Arts, University of California at Irvine (UCI), May, 20##, Literature & Social Studies**

Self-Directed Studies   20## - Present
Focusing on mainstream culture and trends, study merchandising and population demographics of individuals between the ages of 18 and 49. Browse media and advertising extensively, developing an in-depth understanding of material consumption in U.S. culture.

University Studies
8/1 – 12/29, 20##   Literary Philosophy, Graduate, UCI, Irvine, California
Accumulated skills in prioritizing, self-management and discipline, accomplishing over 90 pages of commentary on the subject of philosophical thought.

1/23 – 5/25, 20##   Social Text and Context, UCI, Irvine, California
Developed in-depth understanding of public consensus and modern value systems.Concentration: the relationship between ideals and historical and economic patterns.

1/23 – 5/25, 20##   Critical Thinking, UCI, Irvine, California
60 hours of self-directed research and lecture attendance, studying essential elements of critical thought. Developed skills in argumentative dialogue, logic, analysis, and approaching perception from an educated and diverse persepctive. Focus: anatomy of critical thought.

1/23 - 5/25, 20##   Public Communication, UCI, Irvine, California
Intensive study of the psychological and social techniques of speech and communication. Developed comprehensive understanding of debate, physical language, formal and informal delivery, subliminal communication, and advertising. Focus: written and visual advertising techniques.

Other Experience   20## - Present, UCI, Irvine, California
15th and 16th Century Rhetoric, French Poetry, Literature in Music, Women, Words & Wisdom, FilmTheory, Shakespeare, British Fiction, U.S. Fiction, World Literature.

SKILLS
Computer: All word processing applications on Macintosh and PC, Internet savvy.
Interpersonal: Experienced in working with groups and individuals using teamwork and collaboration, setting goals, delegating and communicating effectively.

Figure 7-3: The resume of a graduate with little experience but marketable skills.

Starting Over with a Master's Degree

An advanced degree represents another kind of "too-little experience" when you use it as a door-opener to a new career instead of continuing in your current field.

After career mishaps, many people see a master's degree as a born-again employment credential for a well-planned career change. And new beginnings often are the happy outcome. By contrast, if your goals are murky as a master's degree graduate, you're likely to be disappointed. You may be better educated but you probably will fail to get what you want. The resume takes the brunt of the blame, as this question from a reader of my column suggests:

> *I am seeking a job with a new master's degree — obtained at age 47 — and experiencing a lot of difficulty. I have mailed out at least 500 resumes and received only one response — from a telephone company suggesting that I install telephone equipment. What is wrong with my resume?*

The resume isn't the real problem here. If the reader sent the same resume to 500 potential employers, he's clearly not focused on what he's best fit to do. When it comes to resumes, one size does not fit all. This individual should learn a great deal more about job hunting and then write a career plan to be reviewed monthly. If your master's degree upgrades your credentials in the same field in which you now work, begin your resume by reporting your work experience. Follow up with the education section, leading off this section with your newly minted master's degree. Make use of a resume-ending section titled *Other Information* to say that you view learning as a life skill, as evidenced by the master's degree.

A PhD Can Be a Liability

A doctorate traditionally has been reserved for research or teaching, but those job prospects aren't living up to expectations. Doctorate-holding job hunters return home day after day with heads hung low because they are rejected for being "overqualified."

Although it's disheartening, unless you are certain that a PhD is required for the positions you seek, I suggest that you omit the Piled High and Deep degree from your resume. If asked in an interview, claim it but don't go out of your way to bring it up. As for the application form, when asked for "highest educational attainment," assume they mean as related to the job you seek.

Gaffes Common to New Graduates

New graduates are more likely than experienced job seekers to make these mistakes.

Not meeting image standards

If you present your resume personalized with little printing errors, such as off-centered or crooked placement, ink blotches, or flaws in the paper itself, you flunk.

Aiming too high too soon

An imperfect understanding of the world off campus may cause you to indicate in a job objective that the job you're seeking is over your head. You'll be dismissed as naive if you write such aims as becoming "an operations manager in a well-established organization." *Manager* isn't quite the word for an entry-level person, although graduates with several years of experience leading up to a managerial position could swing it. *Well-established organization* may exile you not only from dynamic start-up companies but cause a perception that you expect a lot — perhaps more than an employer can deliver.

Overcompensating with gimmicks

Don't tart up your resume to cover barren qualifications. Avoid using exotically original language, such as the "eyelinered genius," a term used by a business graduate applying for an entry-level marketing position in the cosmetics industry. The term may be colorful, but charm communicates better in the interview.

Making employers guess

Employers hate it when they are asked to decipher your intent. Merely presenting your declared major and transcript excerpts is not enough to kick off a wowser job search. Add either an objective to your resume or a skills summary directed at a specific career field. Show potential employers that you've thought about your next move.

Leveling the experience field

Your resume is no place to give every job equal billing. Many rookie resumes are little more than rote listings of previous jobs — subpoena server, TV satellite dish sales representative, waiter, landscape helper, and computer coach, for example. Separate your jobs into an A list and a B list. The A list contains the jobs that relate to what you want to do next, even if you have to stretch them to make a connection. Briefly mention jobs on the B list in a section called *Other Experience* or *Other Jobs*.

Stopping with bare bones

Some rookies look at a sheet of paper and then at their embarrassing, bedraggled collection of instant-rice jobs in their paid-experience stew. Desperate to get *anything* on paper, they settle for name, rank, and serial number (employer, job title, and dates of employment).

The solution is to pull in *all* experience, including volunteer and part-time gigs. Sit, think, think some more, and pull in all relevant skills pointing in the direction in which you hope to thumb a ride.

Hiding hot information

Data entombed is data forgotten. Employers remember best the information you give first in a resume, not the data smushed in the middle. Decide what your selling points are and pack that punch up front. Ask three friends to read your resume and tell you what they remember about it right afterwards.

Highlighting the immaterial

Featuring the wrong skills and knowledge acquired on each job is an error that many first-time resume writers make. Suppose you want to be a multimedia producer, and one of your work experience citations is your three years of effort for campus student theatrical productions. You painted scenery, sold tickets, and designed sets. It's the experience in designing sets that helps qualify you for multimedia producer, not painting scenery or selling tickets. Costume yourself in the skills that help employers imagine you playing a role in their company.

Ignoring employers' needs

Even the smartest new graduates, who may have survived research challenges as rigorous as uncovering the body language of ancient French cave dwellers, make this mistake. They forget to find out what employers want from new hires. In addition to following the standard research techniques mentioned in Chapter 8, if you can find former or present employees willing to share company culture information *from the inside,* go to the head of the StandOut class.

Writing boastfully

Appearing too arrogant about your talents can cause employers to question your ability to learn as a junior team member. As one recent graduate says, "It's hard to work in a team structure when you're omniscient."

Even when you're just trying to compensate for your inexperience, avoid terminology that comes across as contrived or blatantly self-important. If you're not sure, ask older friends to describe the kind of person they think your resume represents.

Stay on Your Feet

If you're getting out of college in a year of plentiful jobs, congratulations, you lucky graduate. But if jobs are scarce and the going is tough, show that you know how to take a punch and come up swinging. Strategies scattered throughout this book can help you make a winner's case for jobs you want.

Part III

The Making of a StandOut Resume

The 5th Wave   By Rich Tennant

"I love the way MS Word justifies the text in my resume. Now if I can just get it to justify my asking salary..."

In this part . . .

You find out how to choose the best format for your resume, write the most effective content, choose keywords and action verbs that bring you to the top of an interview scheduler's pile, use worksheet tools, upgrade the appearance of your resume, and deal with job gaps and other dilemmas anyone can face — and some that fewer face.

Chapter 8

Market Yourself with a StandOut Resume

In This Chapter

▶ Using the StandOut resume to get a better job

▶ Doing your research to create StandOut resumes

▶ Deciding how many resumes you need

You say you're ready to step out and find a terrific job? You say you're tired of selling off a piece of your life in return for forgettable pay in going-nowhere jobs? Or you're fed up with starving as a student? You say you want a job that speaks fluent money with an interesting accent? Sounds good. But that's not *all* you want, you say?

You Want, Well, Everything!

You want a job that puts jingle in your pocket and paper in your bank account. Yes. But you also want *meaningful* work.

I understand. What you want is a job that you love to get up in the morning to do and that pays major money, has first-class benefits, provides self-actualizing challenges, doesn't disappear overnight, and maybe sends you off on pleasant travels periodically. In Hollywoodspeak, what you want is one of those above-the-line jobs that star you in Purposeful Endeavor.

Those StandOut jobs are going to people who, with StandOut resumes and self-discipline, have found out how to outrun the crowd. This chapter tells why you need a StandOut resume to make the new workplace work for you.

Help in discovering what you want to do

Does your career make you feel as if you're stuck in traffic? Then here are a few free Web sites that can help you start moving again. They offer many tips on career decision-making and management:

✔ **The Career Key** (www.careerkey.org) by Dr. Lawrence K. Jones and other academicians specializing in career development. Much of the work is based on legendary John Holland's six basic personality types. You're given a list of jobs that may be appropriate for each of the personality types.

✔ **Online Personality Tests** (www.2h.com) aren't scored but focus on you as a person who works. (When you get to the site, click on *Personality tests*.)

✔ **Queendom's Best Tests for Career Hunters** (www.queendom.com) doesn't pretend to be scientific, but it does offer a collection of career-focused quizzes, ranging from personality to owning a business. (When you reach the site, click on *Tests & Profiles*.)

✔ **Keirsey.com** (www.keirsey.com) contains links to understanding and taking the Keirsey Character/Temperament Sorter tests, a kissing cousin to the Myers Briggs test.

You can also use the **CACTI** (Core Adult Career Transition Inventory), which is a paper self test by Martin Elliot Jaffe. Order from Public Relations Division, Cuyahoga County Public Library, 2111 Snow Road, Parma, OH 44134. It's inexpensive — call 216-475-2225 for the cost. Adults can use the CACTI instrument at home, as can counselors working with adults in mid-life career transition and discouraged job seekers.

Keep in mind that a global knowledge revolution, as far-reaching as the Industrial Revolution, is changing business. And business is changing the job market. No one is immune to getting laid off as lifetime jobs become a memory. The good news is that more resources to help us find new work connections have appeared during the past decade than in all of previous history.

 What should you do when you want to change careers, and you don't know exactly to what? Sorry, but you're not ready to write a StandOut resume. First, you need to clarify your direction through either introspection or professional career counseling. For a jumpstart on mapping out your life's direction, see the sidebar in this chapter: "Help in discovering what you want to do."

Really, Must You Have a Resume?

Periodically, job guide writers, with gunslinging self-assurance, assert that resumes are unnecessary baggage. These critics insist that the best way to find a job is to network and talk your way inside. Put wax in your ears when you encounter these folks — they're shooting blanks. The only people for whom the no-resume advice is okay are those who can leave talk-show hosts struggling to get a word in edgewise. Very few people are extroverted and glib enough to carry the entire weight of their employment marketing presentations without supporting materials.

More importantly, you need a resume because most employers say that you need a resume. Employers don't have time to take oral histories when you call to "ask for a few minutes of time to discuss opportunities." Those days are gone. A StandOut resume that's easily read and absorbed saves employers' time and shows that you're aware of this new reality.

Even if — as a corporate executive's child, pal, or hairdresser — you land on a payroll by fiat, somewhere along the way you'll need a resume. At some point, people who make hiring decisions insist on seeing a piece of paper or a computer screen that spells out your qualifications. Resumes are an important first step on the road to the perfect job.

Resumes open doors to job interviews; interviews open doors to jobs.

Your Resume as a Sales Tool

A resume used to be a simple, low-key sheet or two of paper outlining your experience and education, with a list of references at the end. That kind of resume is now a museum piece.

By contrast, your StandOut resume is a specially prepared sales presentation. Created as a sales tool to persuade a potential employer that you're the best one to do the job you seek, your resume is a self-advertisement that showcases your skills. With a series of well-written statements that highlight your previous work experience, education, and other background information, your resume helps prove what you say about your achievements, accomplishments, and abilities. It tells an employer you have a positive work attitude and strong interpersonal skills.

As a sales tool, your resume outlines your strengths as a product:

- ✔ The skills you bring to the organization
- ✔ The reason you're worth the money you hope to earn
- ✔ Your capacity for doing the work better than other candidates
- ✔ Your ability to solve company or industry problems

In every statement, your resume strategically convinces employers that you can do the job, have positive work attitudes, and get along with others. Your resume — whether stored in the rapidly expanding electronic universe or on paper — helps employers see how they could benefit by interviewing you.

Tailor Your Resume to the Company and the Position

When do you need more than one version of your resume? Most of the time. Following the usual approach, you develop a core resume and then amend it to fit specific positions, career fields, or industries.

Nothing beats a perfect or near-perfect match. Suppose a company sports a job opening requiring A, B, and C experience or education. By designing your resume for the target position, you show that you're well endowed with A, B, and C experience or education — a very close match between the company's requirements and your qualifications.

Research is the key to tailoring your resume to the company your want to work for or the job you know you'd excel at.

By researching a company and industry to customize your resume and determine new job prospects, not only do you gain the firepower to create a StandOut resume, but you build an arsenal of data points to use in interviews.

You won't use every scrap of research, of course. Some data will be useful only for impressing your future coworkers at the next office holiday party. The problem is knowing which data will be surplus and which will be necessary; glean as much information as time and your study habits permit. In general, the higher the level of job you seek, the more research you need to do in order to be seen as the best candidate for the job. Certainly, if you're writing a resume for an above-the-line job that you really want, pull out all the stops.

Finding out about the company

What does your resume reveal about you? Right off the bat, your resume reveals whether you're willing to take the time to discover what a prospective employer wants done that you're well qualified to do. It shows the health of your judgment and the depth of your commitment to work. Your impulse may be to assume that you can write a resume out of your own head and history — that dogged, time-eating research makes a nice add-on but is not essential. Don't kid yourself. At the core of a StandOut resume is research, research, and more research.

For a comprehensive approach, educate yourself about the company's history, growth and acquisition record, products and services, corporate philosophy on outsourcing, sales volume, annual budget, number of employees, division structure and types of people it hires, market share, profitability, location of physical facilities, and how recently and deeply it has downsized personnel.

Research into your prospective company — in this usage, *company* means non-profit organizations and government agencies as well as private companies — lets you glimpse how you may fit into the company and what you can offer it. Research gives you a sound basis for selecting those areas to include in your resume that demonstrate good judgment and commitment to the goals of your prospective company.

When you know what an employer is willing to employ someone to do, you can tell the employer why you should be the one to do it. *In a tight job race, the candidate who knows most about the employer has the edge.*

Resources for company research

Pulling together the information to write StandOut resumes used to be such a chore that resume writers could spend weeks running down all the facts they needed, visiting libraries for books and newspapers and stock brokerages for annual reports. Mercifully, research is far easier today with a multitude of tools at your beck and mouse-call. To be comprehensive:

✔ Line up the usual suspects in printed form — directories, annual reports, newspapers, magazines, and trade journals.

✔ Scout the Internet, then use these sites:

- **American Journalism Review** (www.newslink.org): Useful for researching small companies, this resource allows searching Web news sites including hometown newspapers across the nation.

- **Bizjournals.com** (www.bizjournals.com): Another resource to check out small companies, with links to local business.

- **CEO Express** (ceoexpress.com): This site covers fewer industries than you might expect but the wealth of research and information about each industry is impressive. The site offers a large number of links to business magazines and business news Web sites.

- **CorporateInformation** (corporateinformation.com): Type in the name of a company, and get a list of sites that report on that company. Or, select an industry, and get a list of companies in that industry, plus news, overviews, and a short write-up about the industry.

- **FreeEDGAR** (www.freeedgar.com): View Security Exchange Commission Edgar filings for any company.

- **Hoover's Online** (hoovers.com): A business information database with a ton of information about companies, contact information, key officers, competitors, business locations, and industry news.

- **Plunkett Research** (www.plunkettresearch.com): An encyclopedic provider of business and industry information, specializing in market analysis, and in coverage of market trends, statistics, technology, and leading companies in many fields. View the full database at your library.

- **PR Newswire** (prnewswire.com): View full-text news releases and multimedia from public and private companies and organizations worldwide.

- **Superpages** (superpages.com): Comprehensive business information for over 11 million businesses in virtually every city in the United States.

✔ Employee message boards are forums where employees candidly comment on what life is like at their companies. They talk about pay raises, the names of scrappy managers to avoid, impending downsizings and other items of interest that can help you decide if you really want to saddle up with certain companies.

Finding out about the position

The ultimate StandOut resume, like a custom-made suit, is tailored to the job you want. After researching the target company and position, you can make your resume fit the job description as closely as your work and education history allow.

At minimum, find out the scope of the position and the skills the company is looking for. The next section, "Resources for position research," gives you more information about how to research your next job.

Resources for position research

Many companies develop what is called a *candidate specification,* which describes the competencies, skills, experience, knowledge, education, and other characteristics believed to be necessary for the job.

When a friend touts your resume

What should you do when a friend wishes to float your resume among clients and colleagues, and you don't know where it will land? If you value the friendship and can't persuade your friend that you'd appreciate an interview instead, create a general resume reflecting what you most want to do. Complete the worksheets in Part III and then write a resume based on what you'd most like to do, listing the qualifications that support your goal.

Grab this idea and turn it around. Prepare a counterpart — your own *position analysis.*

The content you're looking for to put in your position analysis includes the major responsibilities, technical problems to be solved, and objectives for the position as well as competencies and skills, education required, and so forth. Find the data for your position analysis in a number of places:

- **Commercial job descriptions:** Buying job descriptions is pricey but try libraries or friends who work in HR offices. A limited number of free job descriptions are available on the Web; find them with search engines by typing in "job descriptions."

- **Recruitment advertising** (print and online): Find online recruitment job sites on AIRS Job Boards Directory (airsdirectory.com/directories/job_boards). Look for job ads for the career field and occupation you want. On the print side, newspaper help-wanted ads are happy hunting grounds for the data you need to write your position analysis.

- **Occupational career guides:** The U.S. Department of Labor's *Occupational Outlook Handbook* (www.bls.gov/oco) contains career briefs that describe the nature of the work for popular occupations.

After writing your position analysis, you are ready to roll in composing a StandOut resume.

When One Resume Will Do — or Must Do

The trouble with creating a custom-tailored resume for every job opening is that many busy and beleaguered people feel as though they can barely manage to get to the dentist for a checkup, buy groceries, pick up the dry cleaning, ship the kids off to school on time, run over to fix Mom's furnace, and generally get through the day — much less write more than one version of an irresistible resume.

It may come down to this: one great resume or no great resume.

You can generally get by with a single version of your resume if you (A) are a new graduate or (B) have a fairly well-defined career path and intend to work exclusively within the lines of your experience.

Even when you allow yourself the luxury of fielding just one resume, you can't put your feet up, watch the sunset, and drink margaritas. With each resume that you distribute, you must attach a personalized cover letter that directly targets the specific job opening. If writing letters isn't your strong suit, *Cover Letters For Dummies, 2nd Edition,* written by yours truly and published by Wiley, tells you how.

Chapter 9

Format Means So Much: Choose Wisely

In This Chapter

▶ Selecting your best format

▶ Using handy templates

▶ Comparing format features

*R*esume format refers not to the design or look of your resume but to how you organize and emphasize your information. *Different format styles flatter different histories.* This chapter helps you choose a format that highlights your strengths and hides your shortcomings.

An extensive lineup of resume formats follows. A template that you can use for developing your own resume illustrates each of the formats in this chapter. Survey the lot of them before deciding which one best tells your story.

Resume Formats

At root, formats come in three family trees: The reverse chronological lists all employment and education, beginning with the most recent and working backward. The skills-based functional shouts what you can do instead of relaying what you've done and where you did it. The hybrid or combination is a marriage of both formats. Take a close look at each of these three progenitors before you examine their saplings, of which there are many.

Note: The narrative format is an outdated chronological format that starts with the oldest facts and works forward to the newest facts. A pretentious variation of the narrative format uses the third person as though you were writing a biography. I don't bother to even discuss them, and I strongly suggest that you don't use either one.

Here are the three basic resume styles:

- ✔ Reverse chronological
- ✔ Functional
- ✔ Hybrid (also called *combination*)

These basic styles have spawned a variety of other formats:

- ✔ Accomplishment
- ✔ Targeted
- ✔ Linear
- ✔ Professional
- ✔ Keyword
- ✔ Academic curriculum vitae
- ✔ International curriculum vitae

Table 9-1 gives you a breakdown of which format to use when.

Table 9-1	Your Best Resume Formats at a Glance
Your Situation	*Suggested Formats*
Perfect career pattern	Reverse Chronological, Targeted
Rookie or ex-military	Functional, Hybrid, Accomplishment, Targeted, Linear
Seasoned ace	Functional, Hybrid, Accomplishment, Keyword
Tech-savvy	Keyword
Business	Reverse Chronological, Accomplishment, Targeted
Technical	Keyword, Targeted, Accomplishment, Reverse Chronological
Professional	Professional, Academic Curriculum Vitae, Portfolio
Government	Reverse Chronological, Professional
Arts/teaching	Professional, Portfolio, Academic Curriculum Vitae
Job history gaps	Functional, Hybrid, Linear, Targeted
Multitrack job history	Functional, Hybrid, Targeted, Keyword
Career change	Functional, Keyword, Targeted
International job seeker	International Curriculum Vitae
Special issues	Functional, Hybrid, Targeted

The following sections explore each type of resume format so that you can choose the style best for you and your skills.

Reverse Chronological Format

The *reverse chronological* (RC) format, shown in Figure 9-1, is straightforward: It cites your employments from the most recent back, showing dates as well as employers and educational institutions (college, vocational-technical schools, and career-oriented programs and courses). You accent a steady work history with a clear pattern of upward or lateral mobility.

Strengths and weaknesses

Check to see whether the RC's strengths are yours:

- This up-front format is by far the most popular with employers and recruiters because it is so, well, up-front.
- RC links employment dates, underscoring continuity. The weight of your experience confirms that you're a specialist in a specific career field (social service or technology, for example).
- RC positions you for the next upward career step.
- As the most traditional of formats, RC fits traditional industries (such as banking, education, and accounting).

Take the weaknesses of the reverse chronological format into account:

- When previous job titles are at variance with the target position, this format does not support the objective. Without careful management, it reveals everything, including inconsequential jobs and negative factors.
- RC can spotlight periods of unemployment or brief job tenure.
- Without careful management, RC reveals your age.
- Without careful management, RC may suggest that you were plateaued in a job too long.

Reverse Chronological Format

YOUR NAME
Home Address
City, State, Zip Code
(###) ###-#### (Telephone)
###@###.### (E-mail)

Objective:
A position that uses your skills.

SUMMARY
- Number of years of work experience, paid and unpaid, relevant to target position
- Achievement that proves you can handle the target
- Another achievement that proves you can handle the target
- Skills, traits, characteristics — facts that further your ability to handle the target
- Education and training relating to the target (if unrelated, bury in resume body)

PROFESSIONAL EXPERIENCE AND ACCOMPLISHMENTS

20## - Present   Job Title   Employer, Employer's Location
A brief synopsis of your purpose in the company, detailing essential functions, products
and customer base you managed.
- An achievement in this position relevant to objective (do not repeat summary)
- A second achievement in this position relevant to current objective
- More accomplishments, i.e., awards, recognition, promotion, raise, praise, training

20## - 20## Job Title   Employer, Employer's Location
Detailed as above.

20## - 20## Job Title   Employer, Employer's Location
A briefer synopsis of your purpose in the company, overviewing functions, products,
customer base.
- An achievement made during this position relevant to current objective
- More accomplishments, i.e., awards, recognition, promotion, raise, praise, training

19## - 20## Job Title   Employer, Employer's Location
An even briefer synopsis of your purpose in the company, overviewing functions,
products, customer base.
- An achievement made during this position that's relevant to current objective

EDUCATION AND PROFESSIONAL TRAINING

Degree(s), classes, seminars, educational awards and honors
Credentials, clearances, licenses

Figure 9-1: The tried-and-true, basic reverse chronological format.

Who should use this format and who should think twice

Use the RC if you fall into any of these categories:

- ✔ You have a steady school and work record reflecting constant growth or lateral movement.

- ✔ Your most recent employer is a respected name in the industry, and the name may ease your entry into a new position.

- ✔ Your most recent job titles are impressive stepping-stones.

- ✔ You're a savvy writer who knows how to manage potential negative factors, such as inconsequential jobs, too few jobs, too many temporary jobs, too many years at the same job, or too many years of age.

Think twice about using the RC under these circumstances:

- ✔ You have a lean employment history. Listing a stray student job or two is not persuasive, even when you open with superb educational credentials enhanced with internships and co-op experiences.

  With careful attention, you can do a credible job on an RC by extracting from your extracurricular activities every shred of skills, which you present as abilities to do work with extraordinary commitment and a head for quick learning.

- ✔ You have work-history or employability problems — gaps, demotions, stagnation in a single position, job hopping (four jobs in three years, for example), reentering the workforce after a break to raise a family.

  Exercise very careful management to truthfully modify stark realities. However, you may find that other formats can serve you better.

Instructions

The StandOut way to create an RC is as follows:

- ✔ Focus on areas of specific relevance to your target position or career field.

- ✔ List all pertinent places worked, including for each the name of the employer and the city in which you worked, the years you were there, your title, your responsibilities, and your measurable achievements.

The RC template included in this chapter is generic and doesn't show how to handle problems such as unrelated experience. You can group unrelated jobs in a second work history section under a heading of Other Experience, or Previous Experience, or Related Experience.

Functional Format

The functional format, shown in Figure 9-2, is a resume of ability-focused topics — portable skills or functional areas. It ignores chronological order. In its purest form, the functional style omits dates, employers, and job titles. But, employers don't like it when you leave out the particulars, so contemporary functional resumes list employers, job titles, and sometimes even dates — but still downplay this information by briefly listing it at the bottom of the resume. The functional format is oriented toward what the job seeker *can* do for the employer instead of narrating history.

Strengths and weaknesses

The strengths of the functional format are

- A functional resume directs a reader's eyes to what you want him or her to notice. It helps a reader visualize what you can do instead of when and where you learned to do it. Functional resumes salute the future rather than embalm the past.

- The functional format — written after researching the target company — serves up the precise functions or skills that the employer wants. It's like saying, "You want budget control and turnaround skills — I have budget control and turnaround skills." The skills sell is a magnet to reader eyes!

- It uses unpaid and nonwork experience to your best advantage.

- It allows you to eliminate or subordinate work history that doesn't support your current objective.

The weaknesses are

- Because recruiters and employers are more accustomed to RC formats, departing from the norm may raise suspicion that you're not the cream of the crop of applicants. Readers may assume that you're trying to hide inadequate experience, educational deficits, or who knows what.

- Functional styles may leave unclear which skills grew from which jobs or experiences.

- A clear career path isn't obvious.

- This format doesn't maximize recent coups in the job market.

Functional Format

YOUR NAME
Address, City, State, Zip Code
(###) ###-#### (Telephone)
###@###.### (E-mail)

Job Title You Desire

More than (# years paid and unpaid) work experience, in target area, contributing to an (achievement/result/high ranking in industry/top 5% of performance reviews). Add accomplishments, strengths, proficiencies, characteristics, education, brief testimonial — anything that supports your target job title.

PROFESSIONAL EXPERIENCE AND ACCOMPLISHMENTS

A TOP SKILL (Pertinent to objective)
- An achievement illustrating this skill, and the location/employer of this skill*
- A second achievement illustrating this skill, and the location/employer of this skill*

A SECOND TOP SKILL (Pertinent to objective)
- An achievement illustrating this skill, and the location/employer of this skill*
- A second achievement illustrating this skill, and the location/employer of this skill*

A THIRD TOP SKILL (Pertinent to objective)
- An achievement illustrating this skill, and the location/employer of this skill*
- A second achievement illustrating this skill, and the location/employer of this skill*

A FOURTH SKILL (Optional — must relate to objective)
- Detailed as above

A UNIQUE AREA OF PROFICIENCY (Pertinent to objective)
- An achievement testifying to this proficiency, including the location/employer*
- A list of equipment, processes, software, or terms you know that reflect your familiarity with this area of proficiency
- A list of training experiences that document your proficiency

EMPLOYMENT HISTORY

20## - Present	**Job Title**	Employer, Location
20## - 20##	**Job Title**	Employer, Location
19## - 20##	**Job Title**	Employer, Location
19## - 19##	**Job Title**	Employer, Location

PROFESSIONAL TRAINING AND EDUCATION
Degrees, credentials, clearances, licenses, classes, seminars, training

* Omit locations/employers if your work history is obviously lacking in lockstep upward mobility

Figure 9-2: No experience? Use the functional resume format.

Who should use this format and who should think twice

This resume is heaven-sent for career changers, new graduates, ex-military personnel, seasoned aces, and individuals with multitrack job histories, work-history gaps, or special-issue problems.

Job seekers with blue-ribbon backgrounds and managers and professionals who are often tapped by executive recruiters should avoid this format.

Instructions

Choose areas of expertise acquired during the course of your career, including education and unpaid activities. These areas become skill and functional headings, which vary by the target position or career field. Note any achievements below each heading. A few examples of headings are: *Management, Sales, Budget Control, Cost Cutting, Project Implementation,* and *Turnaround Successes.*

List the headings in the order of importance and follow each heading with a series of short statements of your skills (refer to Figure 9-2). Turn your statements into power hitters with measurable achievements.

Hybrid Format

The hybrid, a combination of reverse chronological and functional formats, satisfies demands for timelines as well as showcases your marketable skills and impressive accomplishments. Many people find the hybrid — or one of its offspring — to be the most attractive of all formats.

Essentially, in a hybrid, a functional summary tops a reverse chronological presentation of dates, employers, and capsules of each position's duties. Figure 9-3 gives you a template for this format.

The hybrid style is similar to the contemporary functional format — so much so that making a case for distinction is sometimes difficult.

Hybrid Format

YOUR NAME
Address, City, State, Zip Code
(###) ###-#### (Telephone)
###@###.### (E-mail)

Objective: Position as_____using your___ (#) years of experience in skills key to target.

SUMMARY OF QUALIFICATIONS
Number of years in area of target position
Related education, training and accreditation
An achievement pertinent to objective
Traits that reinforce your candidacy for this position
Other accomplishments, characteristics, proficiencies

SUMMARY OF SKILLS
• Technical skills   • Processes   • Computer software

ACCOMPLISHMENTS AND EXPERIENCE

Job Title, Top Proficiencies Used   Employer, Location

A Top Skill (Pertinent to objective)
• Accomplishments made while in this position
• Several apt achievements from position, pertinent to this skill and the objective
Another Skill (Pertinent to objective)
• Several achievements pertinent to this skill and the objective
                                                    20## - Present

Job Title, Top Proficiencies Used   Employer, Location

A Top Skill (Pertinent to objective)
• Accomplishments made while in this position, even more detailed
• Several apt achievements from this position, similar to above
Another Skill (Pertinent to objective)
• Several achievements pertinent to this skill and the objective
                                                    20## - 20##

Job Title, Top Proficiencies Used   Employer, Location

A Top Skill (Pertinent to objective)
• Accomplishments made while in this position
• Several apt achievements from position, pertinent to this skill and the objective
Another Skill (Pertinent to objective)
• Several achievements pertinent to this skill and the objective
                                                    19## - 20##

PROFESSIONAL TRAINING AND EDUCATION
Degrees, accreditations, licenses, clearances, courses

Figure 9-3: The hybrid format — the best of both worlds.

Strengths and weaknesses

A hybrid format combines the strengths of both the reverse chronological and functional formats, so check out those earlier sections. Its weakness is that it contains more "frills" than a very conservative employer may prefer.

Who should use this format and who should think twice

The hybrid is a wise choice for rookies, ex-military personnel, seasoned aces, those with job history gaps or a multitrack job history, and individuals with special-issue problems.

Career changers or job seekers needing more appropriate formats, such as functional or portfolio, should skip the hybrid.

Instructions

Build a functional format of ability-focused topics and add employment documentation — employers, locations, dates, and duties.

Accomplishment Format

Definitely not a boring read, an accomplishment format immediately moves your strongest marketing points to center stage, grabs the reader's interest, and doesn't let go. If you want a rhyme to remember: Use flash and dash to go for cash.

A variation of the hybrid resume, the accomplishment format (shown in Figure 9-4) banners both qualifications *and* accomplishments. This is the format of choice for many executives — particularly in traditionally mobile industries, such as advertising, communications, and publishing.

Strengths and weaknesses

This format offers benefits similar to those of functional and hybrid styles noted earlier in this chapter. Readers who prefer a reverse chronological style may view the accomplishment format as too jazzed up.

Accomplishment Format

YOUR NAME

Address   Telephone Number: (###) ###-####
City, State, Zip Code   E-mail: #####@##.###

OBJECTIVE
Position as___using skills and experience accumulated over __(#) years.

QUALIFICATIONS
- Number of years of experience that is pertinent to objective
- Your record of improvement or reputation in the industry
- Specific skills and training apt to objective
- Areas of specialized proficiency
- Work ethic traits demonstrating candidacy and constructiveness

SKILLS

• Equipment familiarities	• Terminology familiarities
• Procedural familiarities	• Technological familiarities

ACCOMPLISHMENTS
In any order, list accomplishments (quantifying with numbers and percentages when appropriate) that elaborate such achievements as

-competitive skills, technological proficiency, professional aptness
-improvements, innovations
-revenue-saving strategies
-promotions, raises
-increasing responsibilities, management and troubleshooting functions
-praise from employers and/or coworkers
-training rendered, training received

PROFESSIONAL EXPERIENCE

• Job Title	Employer, Location	20## - Present
• Job Title	Employer, Location	20## - 20##
• Job Title	Employer, Location	19## - 20##
• Job Title	Employer, Location	19## - 19##

EDUCATION
Academic and professional accreditation(s), major(s), minor(s), emphasis
Universities, schools, and courses attended or in progress

Figure 9-4: The accomplishment format really lets you strut your stuff!

Formats to use when the executive recruiter calls

Executive recruiting is usually a response to an employer's known problem in a given business area. Accomplishment formats, along with reverse chronological and targeted styles, are well equipped to tell employers how you can solve their problems.

When an executive recruiter calls, ask for enough details about the position's problem areas to give you ammunition for whipping out a made-to-order resume. If you're a candidate, the recruiter may be happy to have as many as four readable pages about your background, as long as you grab his or her attention on the first page. Remember that most executive decision makers favor reverse chronological presentations, so use conservative language in drawing attention to your accomplishments on this format. See Chapter 11 for more information about the language of resumes.

Who should use this format and who should think twice

Use the accomplishment format when:

- ✔ You're considering using a functional or hybrid resume style: You're a career changer, new graduate, ex-military personnel, seasoned ace, or have a multitrack job history, work history gaps, or special-issue problems. The accomplishment presentation is especially effective for individuals whose work history may not have been smooth but was, at times, bright with great successes.

- ✔ You're returning to payroll status after a period of self-employment.

If you've climbed career steps without a stumble, use a reverse chronological format instead of the accomplishment format.

Instructions

List accomplishments in order of importance, making chronology a secondary factor. Close with a summarized reverse chronological work history.

Targeted Format

A targeted format, tailored to a given job, is VIP (very important person) treatment. Targeting is persuasive because everyone likes to be given the VIP treatment.

The targeted style is written to match point-for-point a specific job offered by a specific employer.

The template in Figure 9-5 is but one way to build a targeted resume. You can equally benefit with other format options springing from the functional or hybrid branches of the resume family. You choose.

Strengths and weaknesses

The strength of the targeted format is that it shows the employer that you're a good match for the position. Its weakness is that you may not be readily considered for other jobs.

Who should use this format and who should think twice

Pretty much everyone stands out with a targeted resume. Ex-military personnel can translate militaryspeak to civilianese, rookies can equate their non-paid experience to employer requirements, and seasoned aces can reach deep into their backgrounds to show, item for item, how they qualify. This format is a good choice for people with strong work histories but a few zits here and there.

When resumes and research are beyond reach

You say you're not sure you want to do enough research on a position to write a targeted resume? Definitely not a StandOut mind-set, but you're still ahead of an applicant who wrote the following query to the human resources department of a big company (I did not make this up):

Dear Sirs, I would very much like to send a resume to you, but I haven't the slightest idea how to fill out a resume, and I can't remember the dates or addresses for any of it anyway. So if that is going to keep me from being employed by your company, then to hell with it! Otherwise, call me in for an interview and a job.

Targeted Format

YOUR NAME
Address, City, State, Zip Code
Telephone (###) ###-####
E-mail ###@###.###

Objective: Position as_____(title of job employer offers) using your___ (#) years
of experience in skills essential and specialized to the position.

SUMMARY OF QUALIFICATIONS

• Number of years in area of target, explaining similarities to objective position/duties
• Related education, training, accreditation — specifically those employer appreciates
• An achievement directly related to target
• Traits reinforcing your candidacy for this position, specifically those employer wants
• Other accomplishments, characteristics, knowledge either rare or prized in the field

SUMMARY OF SKILLS

•Technical skills employer wants
•Processes employer uses
•Computer and software skills employer needs

ACCOMPLISHMENTS AND EXPERIENCE

Job Title   Employer, Location   20## - Present

   A Top Skill (Pertinent to objective)

   • Accomplishments made in this position targeting the employer's priorities or
     customer base

   • Several other apt achievements from position, pertinent to skill and objective

   Another Top Skill (Pertinent to objective)

   • Several apt achievements pertinent to this skill and the objective

Job Title   Employer, Location   20## - 20##
Details as above

Job Title   Employer, Location   19## - 20##
Details as above

PROFESSIONAL TRAINING AND EDUCATION
Degrees, accreditations, licenses, clearances, courses

Figure 9-5: Use the targeted format to hit the bull's-eye with a specific employer.

The targeted format isn't a great idea for anyone lazy about doing research — the success of the targeted resume depends on lining up data ducks in advance.

Instructions

Find out what the position demands and write — fact for fact — how you offer exactly those goods.

If you can meet better than 80 percent of the position's requirements, you've got a shot at an interview; if less than 80 percent, don't give up breathing while you wait for your telephone to ring.

Linear Format

A linear format (line by line — hence, *linear*) relates the benefits you offer in short spurts of achievements, winning moves, and the like. An offspring of the reverse chronological format, the linear doesn't get into great detail; it sparks curiosity to meet you and find out more. Check out the template in Figure 9-6.

This spaced-out variation of the reverse chronological format lacks a job objective section and opens with a skills summary instead. Plenty of white space is the hallmark of this achievement-highlighted document.

Career advisers pin a blue ribbon on this format.

Strengths and weaknesses

The pluses of linear resumes are

- ✔ Linear resumes are very easy to read quickly, particularly in a stack of resumes a foot high. Instant readability is increasingly important as harried recruiters struggle with the clock, and baby boomers become middle-aged readers whose eyes don't enjoy poring over pages sagging with text.

- ✔ Because the format presents your starring events in a line-by-line visual presentation, your achievements aren't likely to be overlooked as they would be if buried deep in a text paragraph.

The minus is that you can't pack as much information into a linear format (remember the white space), but, with careful planning and good writing, you can pack plenty of sell.

Linear Format

YOUR NAME
Address, City, State, Zip Code
(###) ###-#### (Telephone)
###@###.### (E-mail)

QUALIFICATIONS SUMMARY
- Number of years of work experience, paid and unpaid, pertinent to objective position
- Accomplishment(s) that prove your unique candidacy for this position
- Skills geared for the objective position or company
- Other things the employer will like to know — proficiencies, characteristics, achievements, training, credentials and education

PROFESSIONAL EXPERIENCE AND ACCOMPLISHMENTS

20## - Present   **Job Title**   Employer, Employer's Location

- An achievement made during this position that is pertinent to current objective, detailing job skills and responsibilities

- A second achievement made during this position also pertinent to current objective

- More accomplishments — that is, awards, recognition, promotion, raise, praise, training

* Divide description according to titles held with employer, listing titles as subheadings.

20## - 20##   **Job Title**   Employer, Employer's Location

Same details as above.

* Divide description according to titles held with employer, listing titles as subheadings.

19## - 20##   **Job Title**   Employer, Employer's Location

Same details as above.

* Divide description according to titles held with employer, listing titles as subheadings.

EDUCATION AND PROFESSIONAL TRAINING

Degree(s), university, year
Major
Top achievement

* Include other seminars, awards, honors, credentials, clearances, licenses.

COMMUNITY LEADERSHIP

Memberships and other offices in community organizations

Figure 9-6: The logical linear format appeals to many employers' eyes.

Who should use this format and who should think twice

This format works to showcase career progression — steady as you go. If that's you, use the linear.

Job seekers with gaps in employment, too many jobs, few advancements, or scant experience as well as those who've seen enough sunrises to be on the shady side of 50 should avoid the linear.

Instructions

Write down your achievements and other necessary data, look at the big lumps of text, and then divide and conquer. Think white space.

Professional Format

A professional format, also called a *professional vitae,* is slightly long-winded (say, three to five pages) but factual. It emphasizes professional qualifications and activities. This format, shown in Figure 9-7, is essentially a shortened academic curriculum vitae.

Strengths and weaknesses

The professional resume is mandatory for certain kinds of positions; your choice is whether to send this type or go all the way and send an academic curriculum vitae.

But be aware that professional resumes are reviewed under a microscope; every deficiency stands out. Adding a portfolio that shows your experience-based work skills may compensate for missing chunks of formal requirements. Just make sure that any unsolicited samples you send are high quality and need no explanation.

Professional Format

YOUR NAME
Address, City, State, Zip Code
(###) ###-#### (Telephone)
###@###.### (E-mail)

EDUCATION AND PROFESSIONAL TRAINING

Degrees, credentials, awards, achievements, honors, seminars, clearances, licenses.

OBJECTIVE: A position that uses your talents, with an emphasis on your special skills.

SUMMARY

• Number of years of work experience, paid and unpaid, relevant to target

• Accomplishment(s) that prove your unique candidacy for this position

• Strengths geared for the objective position or company

• Other things the employer will like to know — proficiencies, characteristics, achievements, training, credentials and education

PROFESSIONAL EXPERIENCE AND ACCOMPLISHMENTS

20## - Present   **Job Title**   Employer, Employer's Location

A brief synopsis of your purpose in the company, detailing essential functions and products you managed, and your customer base.

  • An achievement made during position pertinent to target

  • A second achievement made during position also pertinent to target

  • More achievements — awards, recognition, promotion, raise, praise, training

19## - 20##   **Job Title**   Employer, Employer's Location

An even briefer synopsis of your purpose in the company, overviewing functions, products, customer base.

  • An achievement made during this position that is applicable to target

  • More achievements — awards, recognition, promotion, raise, praise, training

* *List three previous jobs with the same detail as above; divide jobs according to job title, not employer.*

Figure 9-7: The long but effective professional format is perfect for certain careers.

Who should use this format and who should think twice

Professionals in medicine, science, and law should use this format. Also use it when common sense or convention makes it the logical choice.

For most nonprofessionals, especially managers, the professional format is tedious.

Instructions

Begin with education, professional training, and an objective. Follow with a summary of the main points you want the reader to absorb. Follow that information with details of your professional experience and accomplishments.

Follow the template in Figure 9-7, paying attention to accomplishments. Just because you present yourself in a low-key, authoritative manner doesn't mean that you can forget to say how good you are.

Keyword Format

Any resume can be a keyword resume. It becomes a keyword resume when you add a profile of *keywords* (nouns identifying your qualifications) anywhere on any type of format. I like front-loading a keyword preface at the top of the resume.

Keep in mind these keyword resume tip-top tips:

- ✔ Use as many valid keywords as possible in your resume, but if you place a keyword summary at the top of your online resume, 20 to 30 keywords are enough in one dose.

- ✔ Computers read keywords in any part of your resume, so if you use a summary, avoid redundancy.

If you use an acronym, such as UCSD, in your summary or opening profile, spell out University of California at San Diego later. If you mention that you have "four years of experience with three PC-based software programs," name the programs elsewhere: Excel, RoboHELP, QuickBooks.

The template shown in Figure 9-8 is a format that works well for computer scanning. Support your keywords with facts but don't repeat the exact phrasing in a keyword profile and in other parts of your resume — vary your language. Repetition must be handled with thought.

Strengths and weaknesses

Virtually everyone benefits from using a keyword profile — it functions like a skills summary. Job seekers sending resumes by e-mail or postings on the Internet should always include keywords.

A minority of recruiters dislike a keyword preface. Their objection: "It appears to be a check-box-oriented approach to doing a resume." This weakness isn't likely to get you rejected out-of-hand, however. If the body of the resume supports your keywords (which it should if it's StandOut quality), and you can do only one resume, it's worth the risk.

Who should use this format and who should think twice

Most job seekers should consider the keyword option. Technical people can't leave home without it.

However, top management executives (the $500,000-a-year-and-up kind) are unlikely to be recruited from resume databases. Executive recruiters do, however, construct their own in-house databases. In building these in-house databases, they may import from public-domain databases that input information from traditional resumes and other sources.

Instructions

As Figure 9-8 shows, you begin with your contact information, followed by a keyword profile, an objective, several strengths, and reverse chronological employment history.

You may choose not to use a front-loaded keyword profile but rather a one-paragraph qualifications summary or a skills section composed of brief (one- or two-line) statements. The more keywords (or skills) in your resume, the better your chances of being summoned for an interview.

Keyword Format

YOUR NAME
Address
City, State, Zip Code
(###) ###-#### (Telephone)
###@###.### (E-mail)

Keywords: General nouns, phrases, and terminology known to be valued in the position and industry; specific keywords descriptive of duties and proficiencies necessary to position; specific terms known to be priority to employer/company you're applying to, including credentials, years of experience, areas of familiarity, and equipment involved

Objective: Title of opening, using the following highlights of your background:
• Number of years of work experience, paid and unpaid, relevant to target
• Accomplishment(s) that prove your unique candidacy for this position
• Strengths geared for the objective position or company, education, credentials and training

PROFESSIONAL EXPERIENCE AND ACCOMPLISHMENTS

20## - Present Employer, Employer's Location
Present Job Title
A brief synopsis of your purpose in the company, detailing essential functions and products you rendered, and customer base.
• An achievement made during position appropriate to current objective
• A second achievement made during position also apt to objective
• More achievements, awards, recognition, promotion, raise, praise
• Equipment used, processes, procedures, in noun form

20## - 20##   Employer, Employer's Location
Job Title
* Same details as above.

19## - 20##   Employer, Employer's Location
Job Title
A briefer synopsis of your purpose, similar to previous job.
• An achievement made during position pertinent to current objective
• A second achievement made during position that's a priority in current objective
• Equipment used, processes, procedures, in noun form

19## - 19##   Employer, Employer's Location
Job Title
An even briefer synopsis of position, overviewing functions, products, customer base.
• An achievement made during position pertinent to current objective
• Equipment used, processes, procedures, in noun form

EDUCATION AND PROFESSIONAL TRAINING
Degrees, classes, seminars, awards, achievements, honors, credentials, clearances, licenses

Figure 9-8: The keyword resume is a great format to submit to resume databases.

Academic Curriculum Vitae

The academic *curriculum vitae* (CV) is a comprehensive biographical state-ment, typically three to ten pages, emphasizing professional qualifications and activities. A CV of six to eight pages, ten at the most, is recommended for a veteran professional; two to four pages is appropriate for a young profes-sional just starting out (see the "Professional Format" section earlier in this chapter).

If your CV is more than four pages long, show mercy and save eyesight by attaching an *executive summary* page to the top. An executive summary gives a brief overview of your qualifications and experience.

Among various possible organizations, the template in Figure 9-9 (a variation of the hybrid format but with exhaustive coverage) illustrates a lineup of your contact information, objective, qualifications summary, skills summary, and professional background.

Strengths and weaknesses

A CV presents all the best of you, which is good, but for people with aging eyes, a CV is reading-intensive. More important, weaknesses in any area of your professional credentials are relatively easy to spot.

To use or not to use

Anyone working in a PhD-driven environment, such as higher education, think tanks, science, and elite research and development groups, needs to use this format.

Anyone who can avoid using it should do so.

Instructions

Create a comprehensive summary of your professional employment and accomplishments: education, positions, affiliations, honors, memberships, credentials, dissertation title, fields in which comprehensive examinations were passed, full citations of publications and presentations, awards, discov-eries, inventions, patents, seminar leadership, foreign languages, courses taught — whatever is valued in your field.

Academic Curriculum Vitae Format

YOUR NAME
Curriculum Vitae
Address, City, State, Zip Code
(###) ###-#### (Telephone)
###@###.### (E-mail address)

Objective (optional): Position as_____(title of position employer offers) using ___ (#)
years of experience in _____ (skills essential and specialized to the position).

SUMMARY OF QUALIFICATIONS

- A summary of your education, proficiencies, and career pertinent to target
- Number of years in objective area, explaining similarities to job and its responsibilities
- Related education, training, and accreditation, reflecting employer's goals/priorities
- An achievement directly related to target
- Traits reinforcing your candidacy for this position, specifically those asked for by the
  employer and those generally in demand in the field
- Other accomplishments, characteristics, knowledge either rare or prized in the field

SUMMARY OF SKILLS

•Topics of specialty or innovation within field •Areas of particular familiarity
•Software equipment •Processes •Terminology relevant to target •Languages

PROFESSIONAL BACKGROUND

EDUCATION
Degrees:
    Ph.D., institution, date of degree (or anticipated date), specialization
    M.A./M.S., institution, date of degree, major, minor, emphasis, concentration
    B.A./B.S., institution, date of degree, major, minor
Courses: Those taken, honors, seminars, number of units, G.P.A. (if a recent graduate)
Other Accreditations: Licenses, clearances
Academic Achievements: Appointments, nominations, leaderships, scholarships, grants,
    awards, praise, scores, recognitions, accomplishments
Affiliations: Societies, associations, clubs, fraternities, sororities, leagues, memberships

PH.D. DISSERTATION
    Title, advisor, director
    Abstract summary (4-5 sentences) discussing content and methodology

HONORS, AWARDS, AND ACHIEVEMENTS
Appointments, nominations, leaderships, awards, praise, scores, recognitions,
accomplishments, high scores, grades, G.P.A.s, fellowships, scholarships, grants,
(including B.A./B.S.)

Figure 9-9: Brevity definitely isn't a feature of the academic CV (this continues on the next page).

TEACHING EXPERIENCE

Job Title, Top Proficiencies Used   Employer, Location   **20## - Present**

A Top Responsibility (Relevant to objective)
• Accomplishments made in this position targeting the employer's priorities/mission
• Several other achievements from this position, pertinent to objective
Another Skill (Appropriate to objective)
• Several achievements from this position, pertinent to objective

* *Repeat above pattern for each position.*

RESEARCH EXPERIENCE
Positions, locations, dates, descriptions of research in pertinence to target position

TEACHING INTERESTS
Discipline, certification

RESEARCH INTERESTS
Areas of inquiry

PUBLICATIONS
* List all those you are willing to show the search committee
* Include work in progress or pending
* Cite works as follows:

•**"Title of work,"** Name of publication/publisher (*Newsletter, Newspaper, Magazine, Journal, Book*), location of publisher (state & city or major city), date of publication, volume number (v.##), issue number (#.#), series number (#.#.#), page numbers (# - #) (type quotes around the title of your article).

PRESENTATIONS AND PUBLIC APPEARANCES
* Include conference papers and research reports
* List as follows:

•**"Title of presentation,"** location of presentation (City, State), Date (20## - 20##); optional synopsis of content and/or purpose of presentation, audience, results, etc.

PROFESSIONAL AFFILIATIONS
A society, association, league, or club with which you associate, position held, 19## - 20##
A society, association, league, or club with which you associate, position held, 19## - 20##
A society, association, league, or club with which you associate, position held, 19## - 20##

RECOMMENDATIONS
Names and contact information of 3-4 references willing to write recommendation letters

CREDENTIALS
Address where the recipient can access your career/placement file

International Curriculum Vitae Format

The international CV is *not* the same document as an academic CV. Think of an international CV as a six-to-eight-page excruciatingly detailed resume (Figure 9-10 gives you a template). Although it solicits private information that's outlawed in the United States, such as your health status, the international CV is favored in some nations as a kind of global ticket to employment.

The international CV is usually a reverse chronological format that includes your contact information, qualifications summary, professional background, education, and personal information. Some European countries prefer the chronological format, which lists education and work experience from the farthest back to the present.

Americans should remember that when working overseas for a native employer, they are not protected by Equal Employment Opportunity laws.

Strengths and weaknesses

International employment experts say that if you don't use this format, foreign recruiters may think you're hiding something. But keep in mind that the international CV format intrudes into private areas of your life.

Who should use this format and who should think twice

Use this format if you're seeking an overseas job and don't object to revealing information that may subject you to discriminatory hiring practices.

Individuals who feel strongly about invasions of privacy or who aren't willing to be rejected out of hand because of gender, religion, race, age, or marital status should avoid this format.

Of course, if you want an overseas job and you don't use this format, you may be out of luck unless you're working through an American recruiter. The recruiter can interpret your concerns and negotiate for a bare minimum of personal information. Nationals of countries other than the United States can also use this technique.

International Curriculum Vitae Format

YOUR NAME
Curriculum Vitae
Home Address, City, State, Country, Province, Zip Code
Include international codes:
(###) ###-#### (Telephone)
###@###.### (E-mail address)
Objective (optional): Position as_____(title of position employer offers) using
your___ (#) years of experience in _____ (skills essential and specialized to the position).

SUMMARY OF QUALIFICATIONS

• A summary of your education, proficiencies, and career pertinent to target
• Number of years in area of objective, explaining similarities to it/its responsibilities
• Related education, training, and accreditation, reflecting employer's goals/priorities
• An achievement directly related to target, that the employer needs
• Traits reinforcing your candidacy for this position, specifically those asked for by the
  employer and those generally in demand in the field
• Other accomplishments, characteristics, knowledge either rare or prized in the field
• Traveling in field, countries visited, improvements made, distinctions, and so forth

SUMMARY OF SKILLS
• Topics of specialty or innovation within field   • Areas of particular familiarity
• Software equipment   • Processes   • Terminology relevant to target   • Languages

PROFESSIONAL BACKGROUND

EMPLOYMENT

Job Title   Employer, Location   **20## -
Present**
A Top Responsibility (Relevant to objective)
     • Accomplishments made in this position targeting the employer's
       priorities/mission
     • Several other achievements from this position, pertinent to objective
Another Skill (Appropriate to objective)
     • Several achievements from this position, pertinent to objective

  * *Repeat above pattern for all jobs.*

PROFESSIONAL HONORS
All honorary positions, awards, recognitions, or titles, with locations, 19## - 20##

PUBLICATIONS
•**"Title of work,"** Name of publication/publisher (*Newsletter, Newspaper, Magazine,
    Journal*), location of publisher (country, languages, state & city or major city), date of
    publication, volume number (v.##), issue number (#.#), series number (#.#.#), page
    numbers (# - #)

  * *Repeat above citation for all publications.*

Figure 9-10: The international CV is an option when applying for jobs outside your home country. It's
continued on the next page.

PRESENTATIONS AND PUBLIC APPEARANCES
•**"Title of presentation,"** location of presentation (Country, City, State, Province, Language), Date (20## - 20##); optional synopsis of content and/or purpose of presentation, audience, results, etc.

  * *Repeat above citation for all presentations.*

PROFESSIONAL AFFILIATIONS
  All societies, associations, leagues, or clubs, positions held, locations, 19## - 20##

EDUCATION

Degrees: Ph.D., institution, date of degree (or anticipated date), specialization
        M.A./M.S., institution, date of degree, major, minor, concentration
        B.A./B.S., institution, date of degree, major, minor
        * *Give equivalents of these degrees in other countries*
Courses: Those taken, honors, seminars, number of units, G.P.A. (if a recent graduate)
Other Accreditations: Licenses, clearances
Academic Achievements: Appointments, nominations, leaderships, scholarships, grants, awards, praise, scores, recognitions, accomplishments
Affiliations: Societies, associations, clubs, fraternities, sororities, leagues, memberships

DOCTORAL DISSERTATION
Title, advisor, director
Abstract summary (4-5 sentences) discussing content and methodology

HONORS, AWARDS AND ACHIEVEMENTS
Appointments, nominations, leaderships, awards, praise, scores, recognitions, accomplishments, high scores, grades, G.P.A.s, fellowships, scholarships, grants, (including B.A./B.S/equivalents)

PERSONAL INFORMATION
• A sentence or so that describes personal attributes pertinent to employer's interests. Think positively, omit negatives, and highlight goal-oriented, functional characteristics that promise of a good worker-employer relationship and reliably good work product. Present specific work-related examples of these personality highlights and explain how they are significant to the employer. Without exaggerating, accentuate the positive, and include all favorable quotes from employers and co-workers, members of the clergy, and public service, volunteer organization, nonprofit organization and political officials
• Age, Marital Status (Single, Engaged, Married)
• Hobbies and leisure activities (travel, clubs, sports, athletics, collections, subscriptions)
• Volunteer service, public service

Instructions

Formality prevails with the international CV. In Japan, for example, job hunters still fill out standard forms, available at Japanese book shops. England has a suggested CV form, which is more like the American resume than not.

- ✔ If you're applying in a non-English-speaking country, have your CV translated into the appropriate foreign language. Send both the English and the native-language version.

- ✔ Unless it's untrue, mention in the personal section that you have excellent health.

- ✔ Suggest by appropriate hobbies and personal interests that you'll easily adapt to an overseas environment.

- ✔ Handwrite the cover letter that goes with your CV — Europeans use handwriting analysis as a screening device. If your handwriting is iffy, enclose a word-processed version as well.

In addition, make sure that your cover letter shows a sincere desire to be in the country of choice.

A Roundup of Other Formats and Styles

A few adventuresome job seekers are experimenting with (or soon will be) newer resume formats, developing distribution technology and imaginative styles of communication. Take a quick look at possibilities that can't be classified as mainstream methods, but may be just the vehicle you need to find the job you want.

Portfolios

Samples of your work, gathered in a portfolio, have long been valuable to fields, such as design, graphics, photography, architecture, advertising, public relations, marketing, and education.

Often, you deliver your portfolio as part of the job interview. Some highly motivated job seekers include a brief version of a career portfolio when sending their resumes, although recruiters say that they want less, not more, paper. Still others create online portfolios and try to entice recruiters and employers to review them.

A career portfolio is rarely used today but is a job-searching tool that may rise in future popularity charts as the work force moves more briskly among jobs, often working on short-term projects as contractors. The portfolio is a showcase for documenting a far more complete picture of what you offer employers than is possible with a resume of one or two pages.

Getting recruiters to read it is the problem.

If you believe that a portfolio is your best bet, put it in a three-ring binder with a table of contents and tabs separating its various parts. Mix and match the following categories:

- **Career goals** (if you're a new graduate or career changer): A brief statement of less than one page is plenty.

- **Your resume:** Use a fully formatted version in MS Word.

- **Samples of your work:** Include easily understandable examples of problem solving and competencies.

- **Proof of performance:** Insert awards, honors, testimonials and letters of commendation, and flattering performance reviews. Don't forget to add praise from employers, people who reported to you, and customers.

- **Proof of recognition:** Here's where you attach certifications, transcripts, degrees, licenses, and printed material listing you as the leader of seminars and workshops. Omit those that you merely attended unless the attendance proves something.

- **Military connections:** The U.S. military provides exceptionally good training, and many employers know it. List military records, awards, and badges.

Make at least two copies of your portfolio in case potential employers decide to hold on to your samples or fail to return them.

Your portfolio should document only the skills that you want to apply on a job. Begin by identifying those skills; then, determine what materials would prove your claims of competency.

Educator Martin Kimeldorf is responsible for the recent popularization of career portfolios. Browse a library of Kimeldorf's portfolio samples at amby.com/kimeldorf/portfolio. You can also look at Professional Employment Portfolios at the Web site of Ball State University's Career Center (www.bsu.edu/careers), and find various books about career portfolios at bookstores, both clicks and bricks.

Direct letters: A resume alternative

The broadcast direct letter — postal mailing or e-mailing to megalists of companies asking for a job — is an old strategy widely panned by career advisors. But in the hands of experts and sent to a targeted list, the strategy can work surprisingly well. I discuss the direct letter strategy in more detail in Chapter 3.

Special reports: A resume supplement

A special report, the creation of career counselor Jack Chapman (jkchapman@ aol.com) is a white paper of fewer than 10 pages describing your special wisdom to make things run cheaper, faster, better. I cover this highly creative document, which establishes you as an expert in a specific field or niche, in Chapter 4.

E-Mail networking newsletters: A resume supplement

Job seekers, usually over 50, who have special knowledge of a topic (such as classic cars or music) as well as computer savvy, are publishing free newsletters as a vehicle for reminding their network core that they're still between gigs. For more info on the newsletter approach, which is a fairly recent development, flip back to Chapter 4.

Web resumes: HTML

Turn to the chapters in Part IV for discussions of technical savvy resumes and developments related to the Internet.

Choose What Works for You

The big closing question to ask yourself when you've settled on a format is:

Does this format maximize my qualifications for the job I want?

If the format you've chosen doesn't promote your top qualifications, take another look at the choices in this chapter and select a format that helps you shine.

Chapter 10

Contents Make the StandOut Difference

In This Chapter

▶ Understanding the parts of your resume

▶ Making each part dazzle the reader

Deciding what information to put into your resume isn't difficult if you remember the basic purpose: You must show that you can and will provide benefits to an employer. A small lad whom author Robert Fulghum met understood that principle very well. Fulghum wrote about him in *All I Really Need to Know I Learned in Kindergarten.* The boy rapped on Fulghum's door and handed him this note: *My name is Donnie. I will rake your leaves. $1 a yard. I am deaf. You can write to me. I read. I rake good.*

Regardless of how many sophisticated bells and whistles you add, the content of your resume must tell employers just how well you will rake their leaves.

The Parts of Your Resume

To make your contents easy to access, organize the facts into various categories. Here are the essential parts that make up a resume:

- ✔ Contact information
- ✔ Objective or summary statement
- ✔ Education and training
- ✔ Experience
- ✔ Skills
- ✔ Competencies

✔ Activities

✔ Organizations

✔ Honors and awards

These other sections may also be included:

✔ Licenses, work samples

✔ Testimonials

To increase the likelihood that your resume will position you for an interview, take the time to understand the purpose of the different resume parts, which I explain in the following sections.

Contact Information

No matter which format you choose, place your name first on your resume, followed by contact information.

✔ **Name:** If your name isn't first, a job computer may mistake Excellent Sales Representative for your name and file you away as Ms. Representative. You may want to display your name in slightly larger type than the rest of the contact information and in boldface.

✔ **Mailing address:** Give a street name with the unit number, city, state, and zip code. If you're a college student or member of the military who will be returning home, give both addresses, labeled Current Address and Permanent Address. You can add operational dates for each address but don't forget to delete a date after it's passed. Otherwise, you will look like a product whose shelf life has expired.

✔ **Valid telephone number:** Use a personal number, including the area code, where you can be reached or where the recruiter can leave a message.

Don't allow children to answer this line. Don't record a clever message — play it straight. If you must share a telephone with kids, emphasize the need for them to answer the phone professionally and to keep their calls short.

✔ **Other contact media:** Use any or all of the following, if available to you: e-mail address, mobile phone number, telephone answering service number, and Web page address.

What about using company resources? Should you ever use your employer's e-mail address or letterhead? Many employers see an employee's use of company resources to find another job as small-time theft. In certain situations, however, you can use your company's help. For example, when a company is downsizing, it's expected to provide resource support for outplacement. Contract employment is another exception: When you're ending the project for which you were hired, your employer may encourage you to use company resources. Indicate permission to use them in your resume's cover letter: *The project for which I was hired is finishing ahead of schedule; my grateful employer is cooperating in my new search.*

Is it okay to list your work telephone number on your resume? In a decade when employers have been tossing workers out without remorse, it's a tough world, and you need speedy communications. The practical answer is to list your work number — if you have a direct line and voice mail or a mobile phone. To show that you're an ethical person, limit calls to a couple minutes — just long enough to arrange a meeting or an evening callback. Avoid the issue by packing your personal mobile phone and calling back on breaks.

Hooks: Objective or Summary?

Your StandOut resume needs a hook to grab the reader's attention. The hook follows your name and contact information and is expressed as a *job objective* or as an *asset statement* (also called a skills summary, see Chapter 13) — or some combination of the two.

A job objective can look like this:

> **Objective:** Assistant to Executive

A skills summary can look like this:

> **Summary:** Over 14 years of progressively responsible office support experience, including superior computer skills, with an earned reputation for priority-setting and teamwork.

Or a job objective can be linked to a skills summary:

> **Objective:** Assistant to Executive, to keep operations under firmer control, using computer skills, contemporary office procedures, and pleasant manner with people.

However fashioned, the hook tells the recruiter what you want to do and/or what you're qualified to do.

Debate rages among career pros over the topic of objective versus summary.

✔ Objective backers say that readers don't want to slog through a document, trying to guess the type of position you want and how you'd fit into the organization.

✔ Summary advocates argue that a thumbnail sketch of your skills and other competencies allows you to be evaluated for jobs you haven't identified in your job objective — a serious consideration in this age of resume database searches.

A quick guideline taken from a sampling of six recruiters, as reported in *Job Choices* magazine, is this: "Objective statements are essential for recent graduates, summary statements for seasoned professionals."

On balance, I agree with the recruiters: An objective may be a self-defeating force for seasoned aces with well-established career paths, whose insistence on a particular job objective may be seen as rigid and for those whose resumes will be stored in electronic databases. But an objective is nearly essential for job seekers who are short on experience or don't have a clear idea of what they'd like to do, but know the general direction.

What you really need on your resume is *focus,* whether you style it as a job objective or as a summary.

The job objective statement

Weigh these considerations when deciding how to help readers visualize what you could do in the future for them.

When to use an objective

Use a job objective when:

✔ You're a new graduate or a career changer exiting the military, the clergy, education, or full-time homemaking. A job objective says what you're looking for.

✔ You have a greatly diversified background that may perplex some employers.

✔ You know the job being offered; make that job title your job objective.

Being objective about objectives

The debate over job objective or a variant of a skills summary continues unabated. These snatches of recruiters' opinions were overheard on a recruiting forum.

- "By including their desired job title in the online objective statement, job seekers increase the chances that their resume will match an employer's search string."

- "I prefer to see 'Career Summary' in place of 'Objective'. If the objective doesn't match an employer's idea of the job, the resume will probably be discarded. By putting a one-paragraph 'commercial' as the very first thing the employer sees, you know that an overview of your qualifications is read."

- "As an in-house recruiter, any resume I receive without an objective tells me the applicant is either desperate and will take any job offered, or has not thought about his career enough to know what he wants. Both are huge red flags. I think an objective is essential."

- "We advise candidates to leave off the objective or may remove it before sending to a client. Use the objective space to include more information on accomplishments and experience."

- "When receiving resumes responding to a specific ad, I really don't have much appreciation for an objective statement. Wanting the job, the candidate will feed back the objective leaving me in the dark about what the candidate is truly looking for. In response to ads, I think a well-prepared cover letter runs circles around an objective statement. But I love objective statements on unsolicited resumes — they're typically more honest. This helps me determine what the job seeker's goals are and if I can even help him or her move to that next level at this time."

Advantages of an objective

Most studies show that employers prefer objectives for quick identification purposes. They like to see the name of their job openings and/or companies at the top of a resume. Because you cite those achievements that support your objective and forget random experiences, the finished product (when done well) shows that you and the desired job are a well-matched pair.

Disadvantages of an objective

Do you have the time to write a resume for each position (or career field) to which you apply? A narrow job objective may keep you from being considered by the same employer for other positions. And if the objective is too broadly focused, it becomes a meaningless statement.

The skills summary (asset statements)

A summary statement announces who you are and identifies your strengths. Take a look at the sections that follow for tips on when a summary statement is best.

When to use a summary

Use a summary statement when:

- You're a person with widely applicable skills. Recruiters especially like a skills summary atop a reverse chronological resume because it lets them creatively consider you for jobs that you may not know exist.

- You're in a career field with pathways to multiple occupations or industries (an administrative assistant, for example).

- You know that your resume is headed to an electronic database and you want to be considered for multiple jobs.

Advantages of a summary

A summary can be more appropriate to status — senior executives, in particular, can let their records speak for them. Recruiters believe that what you're prepared to do next should be pretty evident from what you've already done. Another argument is premised on psychology: Employers aren't known for being overly concerned with what you want *from* them until they're sure of what you can do *for* them.

Disadvantages of a summary

A summary doesn't explicitly say what you want and why the employer would want you. The technique of specifying a job objective in a cover letter attached to a skills-summary resume is common; the problems arise when the cover letter is inadvertently separated from the resume or the resume is passed out alone, as at a job fair. Furthermore, the fact that a skills summary resume leaves many doors open is a two-edged sword: Your accomplishments don't thrust you toward a specific target, so you may be abandoning a success strategy that's been proven again and again.

A summary can be stated in paragraph form or in four to six bulleted quick-hits, such as:

- Recruited and trained more than 300 people

- Installed robotics, standardizing product, reducing retraining cost by 16%

- Slashed initial training costs from $800,000 to $650,000 within one year

- Created dynamic training culture to support the introduction of a new product

---

What's first — education or experience?

The general rule in resume writing is to lead with your most qualifying factor.

With certain exceptions (such as law, where your choice of alma mater can dog you throughout life), lead off with experience when you've been in the workforce for at least three years. When you're loaded with experience but low on credentials, list your school days at the end — and perhaps even omit them entirely if you didn't graduate.

Young people just out of school usually start with education, but if you've worked throughout school or have relevant prior work history, start with experience.

Young readers, if your research shows that a prospective employer wants education and experience, provide a summary linking them together as interdependent. For example, explain how your education was part of your professional experience, or how your experience was an education itself. Following this consolidation, create a heading under which you can merge both sections — such as *Professional Preparation* or *Education, Training, and Employment*.

Education

List your highest degree first — type of degree, major, college name, and date awarded.

- ✔ New graduates give far more detail on course work than do seasoned aces who've held at least one job for one year or more.

- ✔ Omit high school or prep school if you have a college degree.

- ✔ If you have a vocational-technical school certificate or diploma that required less than a year to obtain, list your high school as well.

- ✔ Note continuing education, including seminars related to your work.

- ✔ If you fall short of the mark on the job's educational requirements, try to compensate by expanding the continuing education section. Give the list a name, such as *Professional Development Highlights*, and list every impressive course, seminar, workshop, and conference that you've attended.

Experience

Describe — with quantified achievements — your present and previous positions in reverse chronological order. Include dates of employment, company names and locations, and specific job titles. Show progression and promotions within an organization, especially if you've been with one employer for eons.

Consider using more than one Experience heading. Try headings, such as "Accounting and Finance-Related Experience," "General Business Experience," and "Healthcare and Administration Experience." This is yet another way of reinforcing your suitability for the job you seek.

Some resume formats use a more rigid approach than others, allowing little leeway as you fill in the blanks. Most formats, however, leave all kinds of room for stacking your blocks in a way that does you the most good.

Skills

Skills today are the heart and soul of job finding and, as such, encompass a variety of experiences. These are skills:

Collaborating, editing, fundraising, interviewing, managing, navigating (Internet), researching, systematizing, teaching

And these are skills:

Administering social programs, analyzing insurance facts, advising homeless people, allocating forestry resources, desktop publishing, coordinating association events, designing home furnishing ads, marine expedition problem-solving, writing police reports

And these are also skills:

Dependable, sense of humor, commitment, leadership, persistence, crisis-resilient, adaptable, quick, results-driven

And these are still more skills:

Brochures, UNIX, five years, 100% quota, telemarketing, senior management, spreadsheet, MBA, major accounting firms

Naming skills as a basic element of resumes may surprise you. I include them here because they've taken on new importance, and the skills concept has changed in the past two decades. Skills used to be thought of in the classic meaning of general and industry-specific abilities. Recruiting industry professionals expand the term to include personal characteristics, as well as past employers, special knowledge, achievements, and products.

Because the term is widely used in job searching today, a *skill* is any identifiable ability or fact that employers value and will pay for. That means that "five years" is a skill, just as "word processing" is a skill; employers pay for experience.

Top accomplishments

Top 12 accomplishments that most interest employers:

- ✔ increased revenues
- ✔ saved money
- ✔ increased efficiency
- ✔ cut overhead
- ✔ increased sales

- ✔ improved workplace safety
- ✔ purchasing accomplishments
- ✔ new products/new lines
- ✔ improved record-keeping process
- ✔ increased productivity
- ✔ successful advertising campaign
- ✔ effective budgeting

Where do skills belong on your resume? Everywhere. Season every statement with skills. Skills are indispensable. Whether you use an e-resume or a traditional paper resume, you must name your skills or be left behind.

What's the best way to name your skills? An excellent book with a comprehensive skills treatment aimed at adults is *CAREER SUCCESS: A Step-By-Step Workbook for Students, Job Seekers and Lifelong Learners, 3rd Edition,* by Urban Whitaker, O'Brien and Whitaker Publishers, P.O. Box 10973, Oakland, CA 94610; e-mail books@obrienandwhitaker.com.

Another skills-defining resource is a popular card-sorting exercise, *Motivated Skills Card Sort Kit,* available from Career Research & Testing; 2081-F Bering Drive, San Jose, CA 95131; phone 408-559-4945.

Skills is one part of the emerging concept of *competencies,* a discussion of which immediately follows.

Competencies

"Competencies" is a broader concept than "skills." Competencies and skills differ in that skills are applications of knowledge to solve a problem or perform an act. The competencies concept includes skills but also includes behaviors required in a career field position, such as persuasiveness or persistence in sales and marketing.

Richard H. Beatty, co-founder and board member of HR Technologies (www.hrscope.com), a leading competencies software firm in Purchase, N.Y., and author of *175 High-Impact Resumes,* 3rd Edition (Wiley), expands the concept's meaning: "Competencies are the knowledge, skills, characteristics, and behaviors essential to successful performance of a job."

But human resource professionals don't share universal agreement about the precise composition of *competency-based programs*. Some employers establish enterprise-wide *core competencies* that apply to all employees no matter what their position. The employer's signature core competencies (such as teamwork, goal setting, trustworthiness) are meant to aid in selecting new employees who are aligned with the company's mission and objectives. Essentially, the employer tries to figure out what makes its best performers tick (identify their competencies) and hire more people like them.

Some employers add to core competencies a number of *role competencies* that relate to the position held — an engineer's role competencies differ from an accountant's, for instance.

The following overview launches you on the road to understanding the nuts and bolts of the emerging *competency-based recruiting model*.

Competencies in corporate America

Most users of competency-based models are large companies or government agencies. The idea hasn't yet trickled down to the mass of employers. Each employer chooses the enterprise-wide core and role competencies that it prefers. Some employers articulate only a few enterprise-wide core competencies, and others have a dozen or more. An employer may have hundreds or even thousands of role competencies, assigning 20 or 30 to each position.

The competencies theory is an intellectual child of the 1990s, but its adoption popularity has surged only recently. Although the competencies concept is more commonly used in job interviewing, job seekers are beginning to integrate competencies into their resumes as growing numbers of employers adopt the approach to improving the quality of hiring.

Richard Beatty explains that competencies basically fall into two distinct classifications: *behavioral competencies* and *technical competencies*. Behavioral competencies — where most of the recent employer emphasis has been — are further divided into two distinct types, Beatty says. The two types are behaviors that are *job relevant* (important to job success) and behaviors that are *culture relevant* (important to fitting in well with the organization's culture of work environment).

I asked Beatty for an illustration. Here's what he says:

> ✔ **Technical competencies:** These are the specialized knowledge and skills needed to solve the key problems faced in a given position and get the results expected of the job.
>
> Specialized knowledge for a sales position includes product knowledge, market knowledge, customer knowledge, market trends, pricing, competitor products/ pricing/strategies, closing skills, knowledge of sales tactics, and techniques, for instance.

✔ **Behavioral competencies — job relevant:** These are the personal characteristics of excellent performers in the job.

Descriptions of job-relevant behavior in a sales position include self-confident, investigative, strategic, open/friendly, relationship builder, networker, good listener, strong communicator, attentive, responsive, and service-oriented.

✔ **Behavioral competencies — culture relevant:** These are where many of the corporate *core competencies* come into play. The core competencies reflect the behavior and attributes that the company's senior management believes are important to the organization's long-term survival and success.

Descriptions of culture-relevant behavior in a sales position include team-oriented, client-focused, change agent, strategic visioner, and continuous improvement-oriented.

Competencies in the animal kingdom

Animals have core competencies, too. Consider the story of the cat that thought it was a squirrel and applied for employment on the food production line at a huge acorn silo. The silo management thought that, based on its ability to leap from tree to tree, the cat would do an equally good job as the squirrels on its workforce.

Unfortunately, that assumption didn't prove true. Management hadn't factored into the hiring decision the knowledge and behavioral components of the cat's competency package.

At first, the cat dazzled management with its spectacular leaps, branch-to-branch, tree-to-tree. But the cat's productivity rating soon began to plummet. The cat that thought it was a squirrel brought home only a few acorns a week and was just exhausted at the end of each day. Puzzled, management investigated, watching the cat for a full week.

What management discovered was that you could put into a thimble the cat's knowledge of acorn gathering. The cat spent most of its day swiping at nimble-winged birds that kept flying away from the cat's enthusiastic pounces. Outmaneuvered, weary, and desperate, the cat did its best to gather the paltry few acorns it could find in the few minutes before quitting time.

Clearly, the cat lacked natural ability to gather acorns, and its behavior rankled bird lovers throughout management.

Too bad, management said, issuing the cat a pink slip. The cat just doesn't have the native "nut-gathering tree smarts" that squirrels use by instinct to do a bang-up job of squirreling away a winter's feast. And as for behavior, management explained that it wanted a high producer, not an avian predator.

Coworker squirrels, watching from the sidelines, wondered if the feline's competency failure in acorning while leaping may have inspired the familiar phrase, "What a cat don't know, a cat don't know."

Competency-based resumes

Competencies focus on how an employee contributes value (benefits) to the employer and on what's actually accomplished.

Most good resumes focus on knowledge, skills, and accomplishments. They only hint at competencies required to do the work. To capture behavioral competencies on a resume, you must show how your accomplishments confirm your competencies. Or to turn it around, you must show how your competencies made it possible for you to rack up home runs.

As an example, to connect your behaviors with your accomplishments, you can say:

Product development: Created new mid-market segment supporting an annual growth rate of 20% in a flat industry, demonstrating high energy and business acumen.

In the above example, the verb "demonstrating" connects the accomplishment (Created new mid-market segment supporting an annual growth rate of 20% in a flat industry) with the behaviors, or competencies (high energy and business acumen). Other verbs you can use to bridge the two types of information include:

- ✔ Confirming
- ✔ Displaying
- ✔ Exhibiting
- ✔ Illustrating
- ✔ Manifesting
- ✔ Proving
- ✔ Revealing

Very little outcome data has yet been collected on the construction of competency-based resumes. But here's a formula if you want to try your hand at incorporating competencies into your StandOut resume:

After noting your measurable accomplishments, add your personal behavioral competencies that made them possible.

Try to find out if the target company has adopted the competencies model. Start with professional organizations to which you belong. Look at the membership directory, see who you know who works where you're applying, and inquire about the company's competencies and any change in culture the company is trying to engineer.

If the professional society approach doesn't pay off, go direct. Look for the competencies tip-off on the company's Web site, where the company's core competencies may be embedded in its mission statement.

Alternatively, you can call the company's human resource department and ask, "Do you use a competencies model in recruiting?" If yes, ask if you can obtain a lexicon of the company's core competencies and the role competencies for the target position. Sometimes, the HR specialist will reveal the competencies and sometimes not. But you're missing a bet if you don't ask.

If the company uses the competencies model, apply the StandOut advice I mentioned previously: After noting your measurable accomplishments, add your personal behavioral competencies that made them possible.

Competencies statements don't make good keywords, and the company won't uncover your resume based on your behavioral competencies. So why do it? Accomplishment and skill keywords initially snag the interviewer's attention, but when he or she sees that you've also included competencies statements, the interviewer will note that there's no moss hanging from your hair and that you understand the emerging competency model. This sophistication will be a plus for interviewing purposes.

Be on guard against taking one particular wrong turn that spills the beans on any misunderstanding you may harbor about competencies. Some resume writers recognize competencies as a buzzword, but they don't know much about its workings. To compensate, they try to update keyword profiles or functional listings by pouring old wine into new bottles, which they then label "Core Competencies." That's a mistake. If you do this, HR professionals who "get it" will know that you don't.

Figure 10-1 is an abbreviated illustration of what to avoid.

Find more competency information through your professional organization, search engines (such as Google), personnel publications, and books with the word "competencies" in the title. The transferable skills list in Chapter 3 isn't a competency compilation, but it's a close relative and may provide inspiration and suggestions.

Chapter 1 discusses the way in which the concept is often used to screen out unqualified applicants in online recruiting.

Figure 10-1:
Not a
competent
listing of
compe-
tencies.

Core Competencies

* Public Relations   *Corporate Identity Analysis
* Dynamic Stock Merchandising   * P & L Forecasting
* Sales Marketing   * Crisis Communications

Activities

Activities can be anything from hobbies and sports to campus extracurricular participation. The trick is to analyze how each activity is relevant to the target job; discuss skills, knowledge, or other competencies developed; and list all achievements. Make sure that this section doesn't become meaningless filler.

In addition, avoid potentially controversial activities: Stating that you're a moose hunter won't endear you to animal-loving recruiters. If you've been able to research the reader and have found that you two have a common interest, however, that interest is worth listing on the resume, so that it can become an icebreaker topic during an interview.

Organizations

Give yourself even more credentials with professional and civic affiliations. Mention all important offices held. Relate these affiliations to your reader in terms of marketable skills, knowledge, and achievements. A high profile in the community is particularly important for sales jobs.

Just as you should be careful about which activities you identify, so too should you be sensitive to booby traps in organization memberships.

- ✔ Listing too many organizations may make the reader wonder when you'd have time to do the job.

- ✔ Noting that you belong to one minority group organization may work in your favor, but reporting your membership in five minority group organizations may raise red flags. The recruiter may worry that you're a trouble-making activist who's willing to exhibit poor work performance and unacceptable behavior in order to create a public issue if you're due to get fired.

- ✔ And, of course, you know better than to list your membership in religious or political organizations (unless you're applying for a job that requires such membership). They don't apply to your ability to do the job, and some readers may use them to keep you out of the running.

Honors and Awards

List most of the achievements for which you were recognized. If the achievement had zero to do with work or doesn't show you in a professional light, don't take up white space with it; for example, you probably wouldn't list a Chili Cook-Off Winner award (unless applying for a job as a chef).

Testimonials

After citing an achievement, you can follow up with a short, flattering quote from your boss or a client:

✔ (From an information systems technician): Bob Boss said he was "ecstatic" that I cut Internet access costs by 80 percent.

✔ (From a sales rep at a supercopy shop): Expanded the SoapSuds account by 15 percent. How? By contacting not the office manager but the chief financial officer and offering to remove signature authority of 250 terminated employees." "Jennifer Robertson's resourcefulness in getting inside SoapSuds after others had tried for months is truly impressive," said Barbara Boss, my direct supervisor.

Testimonials work, or advertisers wouldn't spend billions of dollars to use them. Be sure to check with your source before adding the quote to your resume, however. That way, there'll be no surprises.

Licenses and Samples of Your Work

If you're in the legal, certified accounting, engineering, or medical profession, you need to add to your resume the appropriate license, certifications, and other identifications required for the position. For a professional resume or CV, you may also need to list descriptions or titles of specific work that you've done or include samples of your work along with your resume. If asked to include samples of your work, be selective about what you send. No brainer: Make sure that your samples have no obvious flaws or errors.

References Gain New Importance

Do not include your references on your resume. Do create a second document filled with the names, correct telephone numbers, and addresses of references. Supply this sheet only when requested by an interested potential employer — don't burn out your references by allowing too many casual callers access to their names and contact information. In an earlier time, when supply and demand were roughly in balance, employers didn't always bother to check references. Small employers still may not, but midsize and large companies, afraid of making a hiring mistake, are taking aim on your past. Reference-auditing companies that specialize in uncovering reasons not to hire candidates contract with employers.

Rules vary slightly in different states, but employers can legally investigate not only references but an applicant's credit history, record of criminal convictions (not arrests), moving violations and accidents, performance at previous jobs, and workers' compensation claims.

What about salary history and requirements?

Never mention salary on your resume. If a job ad asks for your salary history or salary requirements, revealing dollar figures in a cover letter puts you at a disadvantage if you've been working for low pay — or if you've been paid above market.

Profile forms on job sites and online personal agents almost always ask for your salary information. If you decide to participate, state your expectations in a range ($xxx to $xxx), and include the value of all perks (benefits, bonuses), not just salary, in your salary history.

But first, do two things:

✔ Research the market rate for someone with your skills and experience. Start with the

Web site, Salary.com, which also provides the salary engine for most job sites.

✔ Find out why the smart money advises against being too quick to pipe up with hard figures on the money you've made and the money you want. What can you expect in return for revealing salary information, job unseen? You get a chance to name your price and hope you find takers, many of whom will want to talk your price down. Get advice by reading articles by Jack Chapman on JobStar.com. Absorb all you can — salary negotiation is as complex as buying a house.

Because so much information is available about you — probably more than you or I like to think about — make a project of handling your references. Key suggestions include the following:

✔ **Choose your references carefully.** List references who have direct knowledge of your job performance. If necessary, go beyond your immediate supervisor and include past or present coworkers, subordinates, customers, suppliers, members of trade associations, or anyone else who can praise your work. With the exception of your immediate boss, never — *never* — list a reference until you have gained that person's permission to do so. Make a dry run: Have a brave buddy call your references to make certain that no sly naysayers are hiding behind friendly faces.

✔ **Coach your references.** Providing them with your resume is standard operating procedure. Go further: Write a short script of likely questions with a summary of persuasion points under each question. In addition to general good words about your industriousness, creativity, and leadership, focus on the industry. If you're applying at a financial institution, suggest that your references dwell on trustworthiness, conservatism, and good judgment. If you're applying at a high-tech company that has proprietary software and inventions, ask your references to stress your ethics and loyalty.

- ✔ **Write your own reference letters.** A letter of reference isn't particularly effective, but it is better than nothing in cases where a company tanks out, your boss dies, or the reference is difficult to reach. When you want a reference letter, go after it StandOut style: Offer to draft or even to pre-pare for signature a letter of praise on your reference's letterhead. Routinely arrange for a reference letter when you leave a job.

- ✔ **Stamp out bad references.** If you were axed or pressed to resign, or you told your boss what you thought and quit, move immediately from spin control to damage control. Even if you were cool enough to obtain a letter of reference before you left, you absolutely must gulp down the bile and try to neutralize the reference.

  Appeal to a sense of fair play or guilt. Sometimes, just saying that you're sorry and you hope that the employer won't keep you from earning a living will be enough. Sometimes, though, it won't.

When you've done all you can to try to overcome a bad reference you can avoid supplying, such as your previous bosses, you have three options:

- ✔ Drown the poor reference in large numbers of favorable references.

- ✔ Find a lawyer who, for $200 or so, will write a letter to the person giving you a bad rap threatening legal action for libel or slander. This approach is surprisingly effective.

- ✔ Continue your job hunt, concentrating on small firms that may not check references or that may be more inclined to take a chance on someone.

No matter how super-powerful you've made your resume, weak or poor references can wipe out your job chances. That's why you write the sample question-and-answer scripts and the reference letters, and that's why you take the first step to patch things up with former adversaries. Your employment is a much higher priority by far to you than it is to reference-givers.

Start Fresh, Win Big

To capture the best job, you know that you can't simply add the latest job description and recirculate the same old resume with updated data. Like the small lad at the beginning of this chapter, you've got to convince employers that you will rake their leaves extremely well — and today, you're forced to compete with leaf-blowing machines!

Focus on your best content and present it forcefully. Because you have very few words to work with, choose precisely the correct words; Chapter 11 takes you to the word desk. Don't rush the construction of your resume: If you build it right, the interviews will come.

Application forms: Take them seriously

Although many job hunters tend to underestimate the importance of formal application forms, these tiresome profiles are legal documents. Lies can come back to bite you. Stick to the facts as you follow these rules and push some paper:

✔ If allowed, take the application home; photocopy it in case you spill coffee on your first effort.

✔ Verify all dates of employment and salaries to the letter.

✔ Enter the full name and last known address of former employers. If former employers are no longer available, don't substitute coworkers.

✔ If asked for salary history, give your base salary (or add commission and bonuses), omitting benefits.

✔ Give a complete employment history in months and years, including trivial three-week jobs that you wisely left off the resume. If you stint on telling the whole story, you leave a loophole of withholding information that later can be used against you if the employer decides that you're excess.

✔ Unless you have a condition directly affecting your ability to do the job for which you are applying, you need not elaborate on any disability.

✔ Divulge any criminal record unless your records are sealed; consult a lawyer about the possibility of "expungement" before job hunting.

✔ Be honest about having collected unemployment benefits (but remember that repeaters are frowned on); if you're caught lying about it later, practice your farewell speech.

✔ Autograph the application; you've been honest — why worry?

Chapter 11

Win with Words

. . . .

In This Chapter

▶ StandOut words: Action verbs that sell you

▶ Keywords: Nouns that sell you

▶ Resume grammar: Simple rules that sell you

. . . .

*W*ords: How powerful they are. It doesn't take many of them to change the world: The Lord's Prayer has 66 words, Lincoln's Gettysburg address numbers just 286 words, and the U.S. Declaration of Independence contains but 1,322 words.

Winston Churchill needed only two words to bind Russia to the *Iron Curtain*. A brief four words memorialized Martin Luther King's vision: *I have a dream*. And in a single sentence, John F. Kennedy set the challenge for a generation: *Ask not what your country can do for you, but what you can do for your country*.

Words are powerful — big words like *motherland* and *environmentalism* and small words like *peace* and *war* or *dawn, family, hope, love,* and *home*.

Words are pegs to hang your qualifications on. Words are the power that lifts you above the faceless crowd and sets you in Good Fortune's way. The right words can change your life.

Now, begin your hunt for the right words to build a StandOut resume. This chapter shows you how to use *StandOut words,* or action verbs, and *keywords,* or nouns, plus it provides resume grammar made simple.

StandOut words are action verbs describing your strengths: *improve, upgrade, schedule.* Keywords are usually nouns demonstrating essential skills: *technology transfers, PhD organic chemistry, multinational marketing.* A smattering of both can make your resume stand up and sing. An absence of either can make your resume sit down and shut up.

StandOut Words Can Bring Good News

Use power-play verbs to communicate your abilities and accomplishments. A punch-zip delivery keeps these achievement-oriented verbs campaigning for you. The important thing to do is to choose words of substance and power that zero in on your abilities and achievements.

Try not to use the same word twice on your resume — the thesaurus in a word-processing program can give you more possibilities.

Take a look at the StandOut words that follow and check off those words that work for you:

StandOut words for administration and management

advised	initiated	prioritized
approved	inspired	processed
authorized	installed	promoted
chaired	instituted	recommended
consolidated	instructed	redirected
counseled	integrated	referred
delegated	launched	reorganized
determined	lectured	represented
developed	listened	responded
diagnosed	managed	reviewed
directed	mediated	routed
disseminated	mentored	sponsored
enforced	moderated	streamlined
ensured	monitored	strengthened
examined	motivated	supervised
explained	negotiated	taught
governed	originated	trained
guided	oversaw	validated
headed	pioneered	
influenced	presided	

StandOut words for communications and creativity

acted	edited	proofread
addressed	enabled	publicized
arranged	facilitated	published
assessed	fashioned	realized
authored	formulated	reconciled
briefed	influenced	recruited
built	initiated	rectified
clarified	interpreted	remodeled
composed	interviewed	reported
conducted	introduced	revitalized
constructed	invented	scheduled
corresponded	launched	screened
costumed	lectured	shaped
created	modernized	stimulated
critiqued	performed	summarized
demonstrated	planned	taught
designed	presented	trained
developed	produced	translated
directed	projected	wrote

StandOut words for sales and persuasion

arbitrated	expedited	installed
catalogued	familiarized	integrated
centralized	identified	interpreted
consulted	implemented	investigated
dissuaded	improved	judged
documented	increased	launched
educated	influenced	lectured
established	inspired	led

liaised	produced	reviewed
maintained	promoted	routed
manipulated	proposed	saved
marketed	publicized	served
mediated	purchased	set goals
moderated	realized	sold
negotiated	recruited	solved
obtained	reduced	stimulated
ordered	reported	summarized
performed	researched	surveyed
planned	resolved	translated
processed	restored	

StandOut words for technical ability

analyzed	eliminated	lectured
broadened	excelled	maintained
charted	expanded	marketed
classified	expedited	mastered
communicated	fabricated	modified
compiled	facilitated	molded
computed	forecast	operated
conceived	formed	packaged
conducted	generated	pioneered
coordinated	improved	prepared
designed	increased	processed
detected	inspected	programmed
developed	installed	published
devised	instituted	reconstructed
drafted	integrated	reduced
edited	interfaced	researched
educated	launched	restored

revamped	surveyed	upgraded
streamlined	systematized	wrote
supplemented	trained	

StandOut words for office support

adhered	distributed	managed
administered	documented	operated
allocated	drafted	ordered
applied	enacted	organized
appropriated	enlarged	packaged
assisted	evaluated	planned
assured	examined	prepared
attained	executed	prescribed
awarded	followed up	processed
balanced	formalized	provided
budgeted	formulated	recorded
built	hired	repaired
charted	identified	reshaped
completed	implemented	resolved
contributed	improved	scheduled
coordinated	installed	screened
cut	instituted	secured
defined	justified	solved
determined	liaised	started
dispensed	maintained	

StandOut words for teaching

acquainted	apprised	certified
adapted	augmented	chaired
advised	briefed	charted
answered	built	clarified

coached	enabled	installed
collaborated	enacted	instituted
communicated	enlarged	instructed
conducted	expanded	integrated
coordinated	facilitated	lectured
delegated	fomented	listened
delivered	formulated	originated
demonstrated	generated	persuaded
designed	grouped	presented
developed	guided	responded
directed	harmonized	revolutionized
dispensed	implemented	set goals
distributed	influenced	stimulated
educated	informed	summarized
effected	initiated	trained
empowered	innovated	translated

StandOut words for research and analysis

administered	compared	drafted
amplified	compiled	edited
analyzed	composed	evaluated
applied	concentrated	examined
articulated	conducted	exhibited
assessed	constructed	experimented
audited	consulted	explored
augmented	critiqued	extracted
balanced	detected	focused
calculated	determined	forecast
charted	discovered	found
collected	documented	generated

grouped	measured	researched
identified	obtained	reviewed
integrated	organized	riveted
interpreted	pinpointed	screened
interviewed	planned	summarized
invented	prepared	surveyed
investigated	processed	systematized
located	proofread	unearthed

StandOut words for helping and caregiving

advanced	encouraged	reassured
advised	expedited	reclaimed
aided	facilitated	rectified
arbitrated	familiarized	redeemed
assisted	fostered	reeducated
attended	furthered	referred
augmented	guided	reformed
backed	helped	rehabilitated
balanced	instilled	repaired
boosted	liaised	represented
braced	mentored	served
clarified	ministered	settled
collaborated	negotiated	supplied
comforted	nourished	supported
consoled	nursed	stabilized
consulted	nurtured	streamlined
contributed	obliged	translated
counseled	optimized	treated
demonstrated	promoted	tutored
diagnosed	provided	unified

StandOut words for financial management

adjusted	economized	reported
administered	eliminated	researched
allocated	exceeded	reshaped
analyzed	financed	retailed
appraised	forecast	saved
audited	funded	shopped
balanced	gained	secured
bought	generated	sold
budgeted	increased	solicited
calculated	invested	sourced
computed	maintained	specified
conciliated	managed	supplemented
cut	marketed	systematized
decreased	merchandised	tested
developed	planned	tripled
disbursed	projected	underwrote
dispensed	purchased	upgraded
distributed	quadrupled	upsized
doubled	reconciled	vended
downsized	reduced	

StandOut words for many skills

accomplished	articulated	contributed
achieved	assured	coordinated
adapted	augmented	demonstrated
adhered	collected	dispensed
allocated	communicated	evaluated
appraised	composed	executed
arbitrated	conceptualized	facilitated
arranged	conserved	forecast

founded	navigated	repaired
governed	optimized	reshaped
guided	organized	retrieved
illustrated	originated	solved
improved	overhauled	stimulated
increased	performed	streamlined
initiated	prioritized	strengthened
integrated	promoted	trained
interpreted	proposed	upgraded
invented	reconciled	validated
launched	rectified	won
led	remodeled	

The last word on StandOut words: Little words never devalued a big idea.

Keywords Are Key to Finding You

Recruiters and employers use keywords to search and retrieve e-resumes in databases for available positions.

Keywords are chiefly nouns and short phrases. That's your take-home message. But once in a while, keywords can be adjectives and action verbs. Employers choose their own list of keywords — that's why no list is universal.

In computerized job searches, keywords describe not only your knowledge base and skills but also such things as well-known companies, big name colleges and universities, degrees, licensure, and professional affiliations.

Keywords identify your experience and education in these categories:

- ✔ Skills
- ✔ Technical and professional areas of expertise
- ✔ Achievements
- ✔ Professional licenses and certifications
- ✔ Other distinguishing features of your work history
- ✔ Prestigious schools or former employers

Employers identify keywords, often including industry jargon, that they think represent essential qualifications necessary for high performance in a given position. They specify those keywords when they search a resume database.

"Keywords are what employers search for when trying to fill a position: the essential hard skills and knowledge needed to do the job," is how systems and staffing consultant James M. Lemke classifies the words that describe your bundle of qualifications.

Rather than stopping with action verbs, connect your achievements. You managed *what?* You organized *what?* You developed *what?* Job computers look for the *whats,* and the whats are usually nouns.

Having said that, never say never. Employers scanning for management and administrative positions may search for verbs and adjectives that define soft skills — "assisted general manager," "outgoing personality," "self-motivated." But job computers normally prefer a hard skills diet.

If your resume has the sought-after keywords, the employer zooms you into focus; if not, you're overlooked for that particular job.

Examples of keywords

Obviously, keywords are arbitrary and specific to the employer and to each search-and-retrieve action that the employer wants done. The following lists provide a few examples of keywords for selected career fields and industries.

Keywords for administration/management

administrative processes	facilities management
bachelor's degree	front office operations
back office operations	office manager
benchmarking	operations manager
budget administration	policy and procedure
change management	production schedule
crisis communications	project planning
data analysis	records management
document management	regulatory reporting

Keywords for banking

branch manager

branch operations

commercial banking

construction loans

credit guidelines

debt financing

FILO (First In, Last Out)

financial management

investment management

investor relations

loan management

loan recovery

portfolio management

retail lending

ROE (Return On Equity)

trust services

turnaround management

Uniform Commercial Code Filing

workout

Keywords for customer service

account representative

call center

customer communications

customer focus groups

customer loyalty

customer needs assessment

customer retention

customer retention innovations

customer service manager

customer surveys

field service operation

key account manager

order fulfillment

order processing

product response clerk

records management

sales administration

sales support administrator

service quality

telemarketing operations

telemarketing representative

Keywords for information technology

automated voice response (AVR)

chief information officer

client/server architecture

cross-functional team

data center manager

director of end user computing

disaster recovery

end user support

global systems support

help desk

multimedia technology

network development analyst

project lifecycle

systems configuration

technology rightsizing

vendor partnerships

Keywords for manufacturing

asset management

assistant operations manager

automated manufacturing

capacity planning

cell manufacturing

cost reductions

distribution management

environmental health and safety

inventory control

just-in-time (JIT)

logistics manager

manufacturing engineer

materials coordinator

on-time delivery

shipping and receiving operation

spares and repairs management

union negotiations

warehousing operations

workflow optimization

Keywords for human resources

Bachelor of Science,
Business Administration (BSBA)

college recruitment

compensation surveys

cross-cultural communications

diversity training

grievance proceedings

job task analysis

labor contract negotiations

leadership development

organizational development (OD)

recruiter

regulatory affairs

sourcing

staffing

succession planning

team leadership

training specialist

wage and salary administration

Keywords are the magnets that draw nonhuman eyes to your talents.

Where to Find Keywords

How can you find keywords for your occupation or career field? Use a high-lighter to pluck keywords from these resources.

- ✔ **Printed and online help-wanted ads:** Highlight the job skills, competencies, experience, education and other nouns that employers ask for.

- ✔ **Job descriptions:** Ask employers for them, check at libraries for books or software with job descriptions, or search online. To find them online, just enter the term "job descriptions" on a search engine, such as Google (www.google.com).

- ✔ The *Occupational Outlook Handbook* and *Dictionary of Occupational Titles* (both published by the U.S. Department of Labor). Both books are at schools and libraries; the Handbook is online at www.bls.gov/oco.

- ✔ **Your core resume:** Look through to highlight nouns that identify job skills, competencies, experience, and education.

- ✔ **Trade magazine news stories:** Text about your career field or occupation should be ripe with keywords.

- ✔ **Annual reports of companies in your field:** The company descriptions of key personnel and departmental achievements should offer strong keyword clues.

- ✔ **Programs for industry conferences and events:** Speaker topics address current industry issues, a rich source of keywords.

- ✔ **Internet search engine:** Plug in a targeted company's name and search the site that comes up. Look closely at the careers portal and read current press releases.

  You can also use Internet search engines to scout out industry-specific directories, glossaries, and dictionaries.

- ✔ *1500 Key Words for $100,000+ Jobs,* by Wendy Enelow, Impact Publications (impactpublications.com).

Just as you should keep your resume up to date, ready to move in a flash if you must, you should also keep a running log of keywords that can help you reconnect to a new job on a moment's notice.

> ## Mining for keywords in job descriptions
>
> The excerpts below of two job descriptions posted on Business.com (business.com; search on job descriptions) illustrate how you can find keywords almost everywhere. In these examples, the keywords are underscored.
>
> Auto Dismantler:
>
> - Knowledge of proper operation of lifts, fork-lifts, torches, power wrenches, etc.
>
> - Knowledge of warehouse, core, and stack locations.
>
> - Skill to move vehicles without damaging vehicle, other vehicles or personnel.
>
> - Skill to remove body and mechanical parts without damage to part, self, or others.
>
> - Ability to read a Dismantler report and assess stock levels.
>
> - Ability to accurately assess condition of parts to be inventoried.
>
> Budget Assistant:
>
> - Reviews monthly expense statements, monitors monthly expenditures, and gathers supporting documentation for supervisor review and approval.
>
> - Performs basic arithmetic operations to calculate and/or verify expense totals and account balances.
>
> - Operates computer to enter data into spreadsheet and/or database. Types routine correspondence and reports.
>
> - Operates office equipment such as photocopier, fax machine, and calculator.

Get a Grip on Grammar

Resume language differs from normal speech in several ways described here. In general, keep the language tight and the tone professional, avoiding the following:

- **First-person pronouns (I, we):** Your name is at the top of each resume page, so the recruiter knows it's about *you.* Eliminate first-person pronouns. Also, don't use third-person pronouns (he, she) when referring to yourself — the narrative technique makes you seem pompous. Simply start with a verb.

- **Articles (the, a, an):** Articles crowd sentences and don't clarify meaning. Substitute *retrained staff* for *retrained the staff.*

- **Helping verbs (have, had, may, might):** Helping verbs weaken claims and credibility — implying that your time has passed and portraying you as a job-hunting weakling. Say *managed* instead of *have managed.*

✔ **"Being" verbs (am, is, are, was, were):** Being verbs suggest a state of existence rather than a state of motion. Try *monitored requisitions* instead of *requisitions were monitored.* The active voice gives a stronger, more confident delivery.

✔ **Shifts in tense:** Use the present tense for a job you're still in and the past tense for jobs you've left. But, among the jobs you've left, don't switch back and forth between tenses. Another big mistake: Dating a job as though you're still employed (2000–Present) and then describing it in the past tense.

✔ **Complex sentences:** Unless you keep your sentences lean and clean, readers won't take time to decipher them. Process this mind-stumper:

Reduced hospital costs by 67% by creating a patient-independence program, where they make their own beds, and as noted by hospital finance department, costs of nails and wood totaled $300 less per patient than work hours of maintenance staff.

Eliminate complex sentences by dividing ideas into sentences of their own and getting rid of extraneous details:

Reduced hospital costs by 67%. Originated patient independence program that decreased per-patient expense by $300 each.

✔ **Overwriting:** Use your own voice; don't say *expeditious* when you want to say *swift.*

✔ **Abbreviations:** Abbreviations are informal and not universal — even when they're career-specific. Use *Internet* instead of *Net.*

The exception is industry jargon — use it, especially in digital resumes. Knowledge and use of industry jargon adds to your credibility to be able to correctly and casually use terms common to the industry in which you're seeking employment.

Adopt a trick that writers of television commercials use to be sure that they give the most information in the fewest words: Set yourself an arbitrary limit of words to express a unit of information. For example, allow yourself 25 words to explain one of your former jobs. The 25-word limit guarantees that you'll write with robust language.

Remember, when your words speak for you, you need to be sure to use words that everyone can understand and that relate to the job at hand.

Chapter 12

Overcome Deadly Dilemmas

- -

In This Chapter

▶ Squashing the overqualified objections

▶ Standing tall as a reentering woman

▶ Dealing with disability issues

▶ Patching over employment gaps and demotions

▶ Adding focus to a busy resume

- -

*I*f you're tempted to skip over this chapter, which deals with reshaping perceptions, go ahead and fly by — if you're no older than 35 and have five years of experience that precisely matches the requirements for a job that you want. Otherwise, sit down, read up, and fight on!

This chapter spotlights major resume components that need spin control to ward off an early burial for your resume. These components are the quintessential and potential chance-killing perceptions that stem from your age; the abundance of your experience; and the experience that seemingly isn't there when you return to the job market. Other dilemmas are centered in unexplained spaces in your job history, stumbles in the workplace, or physical characteristics.

All the following common rejection issues call for *spin control,* or putting the best face on a perception.

Too Much Experience

Leading off the lineup of resume stumpers is a focus on the shady side of the four-letter word that's 10 letters long: *Experience.*

The E word's assignment to pejorative status is justified. Not only is inappropriate experience — too much or too little — often the real reason that you're turned down, but it's also too frequently a cover story for villainous rejections that are really based on any factor from bias to bad breath.

Too many qualifications or ageism?

A reader of my newspaper column, "Careers Now," who's rounding the 50s curve, writes that his qualifications for a training position are superior but too ample. He explains:

> *Preoccupation with age seems to be the pattern. I'm rarely called for an interview; when I call after sending a resume in response to an ad or a networking contact, I'm told I'm too experienced for the position — "You seem to be overqualified." How can I keep my resume from looking like lavender and old lace?*

Ageism often is the subtext in the *overqualified* objection. Deal with it by limiting your work history to the most recent positions you've held that target the job opening. To avoid seeming too old or too highly paid, limit your related experience to about 15 years for a managerial job and to about 10 years for a technical job. Concerns about how you moved up so fast will arise if you only go back 10 years for a managerial job, but 10 years is believable for a technical job.

What about all your other experience? Leave it in your memory bank. Or if you believe that the older work history adds to your value as a candidate, you can describe it under a heading of *Other Experience* and briefly present it without dates. Figure 12-1 gives an example of a resume that shows recent experience only.

The recent-experience-only spin doesn't work every time, but give it a try — it shows that you're not stuck in a time warp, and it's a better tactic than advertising your age as one that qualifies you for carbon dating.

If the employer is notorious for hiring only young draft horses, rethink your direction. Try to submit your resume to employers who can take advantage of your expertise, such as a new or expanding company operating in unfamiliar territory.

Fortunately, a new tool has come along in the past several years admirably suited to this purpose: Savvy job hunters now turn to the Internet's discussion groups to check out job leads, to name names of saint and sinner companies, and to ask about company cultures and anti-discriminatory practices. Based on your occupation, you can choose among the many millions of discussion groups available through forums and newsgroups. You may, for example, want to connect with other architects, financial planners, or technical writers. Use the keywords of your target employment field to find specific discussion forums at forumdirectory.net and forumscentral.com. Topica (www.topica.com) and NewsOne.Net (www.newsone.net) also help you easily locate active lists.

Recent Experience Only

Work Experience.

FEIN AND SONS – Operates continuously in Long Beach. **Sole Proprietor, Broker.**
Real estate brokerage, development, asset management, and consulting. In-house brokerage
company, specializing in eight- and nine-figure acquisitions, shopping centers, and
commercial space, obtaining entitlements and economic analysis. Personal volume: over
$100 million.

SONNHAARD INC. – Solana Beach. 2000 – 20XX. **Marketing Manager.**
Real estate development corporation. Primary project: Le Chateau Village, a French-theme
100-lot residential development in Del Mar. Sourced architect, designers, and contractors.
Limited liability company built 60 upscale custom homes by architect Jacques Donnaeu of
Toulouse. Supervised 10 sales representatives. Sales gross exceeded $40 million, selling 58
homes ahead of project schedule by six months.

WEST COAST ASSOCIATION – Los Angeles. 1992 – 2000. **Executive Vice President.**
International trade association with 190 firms holding annual fairs, from 25 states and all of
Canada, including two theme amusement parks, 15 affiliated breed organizations and 300
service members who provide goods and services to members. Annual convention attended
by over 2,000 executives. Acted as legislative advocate for California district and county
fairs, nine of which have horse racing and pari-mutuel wagering. Increased membership by
200%, administering seven-figure budget, with staff of five professionals.

Other Experience.

• BBH & Co., d.b.a. ENVIRONMENT AFFILIATED, **Executive Vice President.**
Administered six-figure budget and supervised 27 managers. Directed recruitment and
marketing activities.

• CSU Long Beach, **Development Director.** Managed 40-million-dollar project to expand
campus grounds 30%. Maintained lowest campus construction budget in state, including
contracting and materials.

• TRADE ALTERNATIVE, **Commercial Properties Manager.** Marketed, leased, and
acquired $900,000 in commercial property. Catered to such upscale clientele as high-end
law firms.

Figure 12-1: Focusing on recent experiences is an effort to avoid the problem of being seen as too old.

A bit harder to navigate, but with a complete 20-year archive, Google Groups (groups.google.com) allows you to wade through most newsgroups.

What if the overqualified objection is just that and not a veil for age discrimination? The employer legitimately may be concerned that when something better comes along, you'll set a sprint record for shortest time on the job.

If you really prefer to take life easier or to have more time to yourself, you can be forthcoming with that fact in your resume's objective. Writing this kind of statement is tricky. You risk coming across as worn-out goods, ready to kick back and listen to babbling brooks while you collect a paycheck. When you explain your desire to back off an overly stressful workload, balance your words with a counterstatement reflecting your energy and commitment, as in the example in Figure 12-2.

Figure 12-2:
A positive
resume
statement
for an older
worker.

Energetic and work-focused, but no longer enjoy frenzied managerial responsibility; seek a challenging nonmanagerial position.

Too much experience in one job

A reader writes:

> I've stayed in my current and only job too long. When my company cut thousands of workers, we received outplacement classes. I was told that job overstayers are perceived as lacking ambition, uninterested in learning new things, and too narrowly focused. What can I do about this?

Spin strategy A: Divide your job into modules

Show that you successfully moved up and up, meeting new challenges and accepting ever more responsibility. Divide your job into realistic segments, which you label as Level 1, Level 2, Level 3, and so on. Describe each level as a separate position, just as you would if the levels had been different positions within the same company or with different employers. If your job titles changed as you moved up, your writing task is a lot easier.

Spin strategy B: Deal honestly with job titles

If your job title never changed, should you just make up job titles? *No.* The only truthful way to inaugurate fictional job titles is to parenthetically introduce them as "equivalent to . . ." Suppose that you're an accountant and have been in the same job for 25 years. Your segments might be titled like this:

- ✔ Level 3 (equivalent to supervising accountant)
- ✔ Level 2 (equivalent to senior accountant)
- ✔ Level 1 (equivalent to accountant)

To mitigate the lack of being knighted with increasingly senior job titles, fill your resume with references to your continuous salary increases and bonuses and the range of job skills you mastered.

Spin strategy C: Tackle deadly perceptions head-on

Diminish any perception that you became fat and lazy while staying in the same job too long by specifically describing open-ended workdays: "Worked past 5 p.m. at least once a week throughout employment."

Derail the perception you don't want to learn new things by being specific in describing learning adventures: "Attended six semesters of word-processing technologies; currently enrolled in adult education program to master latest software."

Discount the perception that you're narrowly focused by explaining that although your employment address didn't change, professionally speaking, you're widely traveled in outside seminars, professional associations, and reading.

Spin strategy D: When nothing works, try something new

When you have followed these recommendations note for note but are still sitting out the dance, take a chance on something new.

Highlight the issue

In a departure from the normal practice of omitting from your resumes reasons for leaving a job, consider indicating why you're making a change after all this time.

Neutralize the issue burning in every employer's mind: "Why now? Why after all these years are you on the market? Excessed out? Burned out?" If the question isn't asked, that doesn't mean it isn't hanging out in the recruiter's mind. Even though you may be seen as a moss-backed antique, reveal yourself as interested in current developments by adding this kind of phrase in your objective:

Focusing on companies and organizations with contemporary viewpoints

In an even more pioneering move to solve the same problem, create a whole new section at the tail of your resume, headed *Bright Future,* with a statement such as the one in Figure 12-3.

Figure 12-3:
Being seen
as dynamic
and experi-
enced with
this add-on.

BRIGHT FUTURE
Layoffs springing from a new management structure give me the welcomed opportunity to accept new challenges and freshen my work life.

Consider contract work

An employer's perception of highly experienced people may be that they're too rigid and hold expectations that the new environment will replicate the old — a perception that assassinates their job prospects.

Sometimes, going the second mile to prove you're dynamic and experienced, as well as generous and forward-looking, still doesn't generate job offers. This is particularly true for professionals over 40 in technical fields.

An example from an Oklahoma City reader of my newspaper column:

> *"I have a PhD in physics and more than 20 years of computer programming experience, including Fortran, C/C++, ADA, HTML, and Java. At my own substantial expense, I'm currently completing a year's course work in Cobol, Visual Basic, Web-page administration, and advanced LAN theory."*

The Oklahoma reader laments that he hasn't had a nibble on a job interview. Yes, he's tried the internship remedy.

> *"I enrolled for an internship, but after I donated 40 hours to the company, building five computers for free for them, the company pulled out of the internship program, negating a verbal agreement to give me hands-on experience. Because I have a doctorate, almost routinely I'm asked, 'Why would you want to be a programmer?' The implication is that I'm overqualified. The reality is that ageism is alive and well, and employers are unwilling to pay for senior talent."*

In such cases, I advise seasoned personnel to consider contract work. For contract work, start your resume with a keyword profile and include as many skills as you legitimately can.

In addition to following the resume tips for seasoned aces offered in Chapter 4, get other ideas of how technical personnel can surmount "overqualified" objections and age discrimination by cruising this Web site: Science, Math, and Engineering Links (`www.phds.org`).

Also, you can tap into the nation's largest database of information describing age discrimination against technical personnel and some ideas on how to fight it by subscribing to the e-mailing list of Dr. Norman Matloff, a computer science professor at the University of California at Davis. For a free subscription, e-mail Dr. Matloff at `matloff¢.ucdavis.edu` and ask to be put on his age discrimination list.

Too Long Gone: For Women Only

The reentering woman still has it tough. Usually, Mom's the one who puts her career on hold to meet family responsibilities. When she tries to reenter the job market, by choice or economic necessity, she feels as though she's been living on another planet, as this letter shows:

> *Employers don't want to hire women if they've been mothers and out of the market for more than a year or two. Hey, ya know, for the last 10 years, I've worked my tail off! Don't they understand that? Doesn't intelligence, willingness to work hard, creativity, attention to detail, drive, efficiency, grace under pressure, initiative, leadership, persistence, resourcefulness, responsibility, teamwork, and a sense of humor mean anything these days?*

Every characteristic that this reader mentions is still a hot ticket in the job market, but the burden is on Mom to interpret these virtues as marketable skills.

- ✔ Grace under pressure, for example, translates to *crisis manager,* a valuable person when the electricity fails in a computer-driven office.

- ✔ Resourcefulness translates to *office manager,* who is able to ward off crank calls from credit collection agencies.

- ✔ A sense of humor translates to *data communications manager,* who joshes a sleepy technical whiz into reporting for work at two in the morning for emergency repair of a busted satellite hovering over Europe.

You can't, of course, claim those job titles on your resume, but you can make equivalency statements: Like a crisis manager, I've had front-lines' experience handling such problems as electrical failures, including computer crashes.

If you're a returning woman, develop a StandOut resume, like the one shown in Figure 12=4, that connects what she can do with what an employer wants done using the tips in the following sections.

Look back in discovery

Review your worksheets (see Chapter 13) to spot transferable skills that you gained in volunteer, civic, hobby, and domestic work. Scout for adult and continuing education, both on campus and in nontraditional settings.

Reexamine the informative television programs that you've watched, the news magazines that you've monitored. Go to the library and read business magazines and trade journals to make a lexicon of up-to-date words, such as *Please compare my skills* (not *I'm sure you will agree*).

Avoid tired words like *go-getter* and *upwardly mobile*. Yesteryear's buzzwords, such as *management by objective* and *girl Friday* won't do a thing to perk up your image, and will, in fact, make you look as old as Rosalind Russell — the original girl Friday.

In recounting civic and volunteer work, avoid the weak verbs: *worked with* or *did this or that*. Instead say, *collaborated with*. What other strong verbs can you think of to sound more businesslike?

Incorporate professional terms

The use of professional words can help de-emphasize informal training or work experience. But you must be careful when doing this to show good judgment about the work world.

Professionalizing your domestic experience is a tightrope walk: Ignoring it leaves you looking like a missing person, yet you can't be pretentious or naive. Don't say *housewife;* say *family caretaker* or *domestic specialist*. Refer to *home management* to minimize gaps in time spent as a homemaker. ***Important:*** Fill the home management period with transferable skills relevant to the targeted position.

Delve into what you did during your home management period. You did not hold a paid job, but you did do important unpaid work. Dissect your achievements to find your deeds — they can be impressive. Examples range from time management (developing the ability to do more with less time) to budgeting experience (developing a sophisticated understanding of priority allocation of financial resources). Other examples include using the telephone in drumming up support for a favorite charity (developing confidence and a businesslike telephone technique) and leadership positions in the PTA (developing a sense of authority and the ability to guide others).

Despite more than three decades of media attention to skills developed by homemakers, employers continue to be dismissive of parenting and other abilities acquired inside the home. Many employers believe that identifying yourself as a domestic specialist is no more workplace-useful than claiming to be a "seasoned husband" or "experienced friend."

Make your homemaker skills difficult to disrespect by showing their relevance to a given career field. Be careful to avoid sounding as though you attended a workshop where you memorized big words.

Whatever you do, you can't ignore the issue — like where have you been for the past few years? When you lack skills developed outside the home in community work, you have to do the best you can to pull out home-based skills.

Selected home-based skills

Don't overlook these skills that you may have acquired inside the home. I've included a few examples of occupations in which they can be used. This illustration assumes that you lack formal credentials for professional-level work. If you do have the credentials, upgrade the examples to the appropriate job level.

✔ **Juggling schedules:** Paraprofessional assistant to business executives, physicians. Small service business operator, dispatching staff of technicians.

✔ **Peer counseling:** Human resources department employee benefits assistant. Substance abuse program manager.

✔ **Arranging social events:** Party shop manager. Nonprofit organization fund-raiser. Art gallery employee.

✔ **Conflict resolution:** Administrative assistant. Customer service representative. School secretary.

✔ **Problem-solving:** Any job.

✔ **Decorating:** Interior decorator. Interior fabric shop salesperson.

✔ **Nursing:** Medical or dental office assistant.

✔ **Solid purchasing judgment:** Purchasing agent. Merchandiser.

✔ **Planning trips, relocations:** Travel agent. Corporate employee relocation coordinator.

✔ **Communicating:** Any job.

✔ **Shaping budgets:** Office manager. Department head. Accounting clerk.

✔ **Maximizing interior spaces:** Commercial-office real estate agent. Business furniture store operator.

Reentry

JOY R. NGUYEN

12 Watt Road, Palmira, Florida 34567   (321) 654-9876

SUMMARY OF EXPERIENCE

More than five years' experience in event-planning, fundraising, administration and publicity. More than nine years' experience in administration for retail and manufacturing firms. B.A. in Business. Florida Teaching Certificate.

NONPROFIT/VOLUNTEER SERVICE

2002-Present   Palmira Optimists' Association, Palmira, Florida Membership Committee Chair

Planning, organizing programs, exhibits and events to recruit association members. Coordinated annual new member events.

1994-2002   Okeefenokee County Y.M.C.A., Okeefenokee, Florida Member, Board of Directors and Executive Committee

Spearheaded first Y.M.C.A. organization in county. Designed programs, procedures, and policies, monitoring trustees in the construction of $3 million facility. Led $2.5 million fundraising campaign.

• **Fundraising Chair**, 1997-2001 Raised funds for entire construction project, establishing hundreds of donors and supervising project. Sourced contractors and directed fundraising activities, using strong interpersonal and networking skills.

HOME MANAGEMENT EXPERIENCE

• **Scheduling:** Assisted business executive and two children in the scheduling of travel and 160,000 miles of transportation. Arranged ticketing, negotiated finances of $12,000 in travel expenses.
• **Conflict Resolution:** Arbitrated personal, business issues. Effective interpersonal skills.
• **Relocation:** Launched inter state relocation of entire family, coordinating moving services, trucks, and packing schedules.
• **Budget & Purchasing:** Managed family finances, including budgeting, medical, dental, insurance packages, two home purchases, three auto purchases, expenses, and taxes. Developed finance and math skills.

ADDITIONAL PROFESSIONAL EXPERIENCE

1994-1996   Sunrise Books, Cabana, Florida
                 Assistant Manager, Sales Representative

Managed daily operations of coffee house and bookstore, directing staff of 35. Supervised entire floor of merchandise and stock. Purchased all sideline goods.

• Spearheaded store's first sales campaign, resulting in tripled sales.
• Designed system for inventory analysis, streamlining purchasing. and display control.
• Redirected staff duties for more effective work hours.
• Promoted from sales to supervisor in 38 days; three months later to asst. mgr.

EDUCATION

• **Bachelor of Science in Business,** 1994, University of Miami, Miami, G.P.A.: 3.75
• **Florida Teaching Certificate,** Business and English, 2001, Florida State, Palmira

Figure 12-4: A sample resume showcasing the skills of a domestic specialist reentering the work world.

Use years or use dates — not both

Some advisers suggest that in referring to your home management years, you use a *years-only approach* and list years, not dates, as in Figure 12-5, to avoid the gap in paid work experience.

Figure 12-5:
Examples
of the
years-only
approach to
list house-
hold man-
agement
skills.

> • *Family Care 10 years*
> Child care, home operations, budgeting and support for a family of four. Participation in parent/school relations, human services, and religious organization.
>
> • *Leadership Positions*
> Vice President, Curriculum Committee, PTA; Chair 8 years, Fund-Raising, American Humane Society; Subcommittee Chair, Budget Committee, First Baptist Church

This approach is unlikely to make a favorable impression on a person who hires often. Employment professionals prefer concrete facts and dates. But the years-only resume can work at small businesses where the hiring manager also wears several other hats and doesn't pay much attention to hiring guidelines.

Don't make the mistake of using both forms on the same resume, assigning dates to your paid jobs but only years to your homemaker work.

Know the score

Gender bias lives, and, of course, you should omit all information that the employer isn't entitled to, including your age, marital status, physical condition, number and ages of children, and husband's name. Even though the law is on your side, in today's interview-rationed job market, your resume must qualify you more than the next applicant. If you've been out of the job market for some years, you have to work harder and smarter to show that you're a hot hire. To help in your quest, seek out seminars and services offered to reentering women.

Job Seekers with Disabilities

More than 40 million Americans are protected by the *Americans with Disabilities Act* (ADA), which makes it illegal for an employer to refuse to hire (or to discriminate against) a person simply because that person has one or more disabilities.

ADA protection covers a wide spectrum of disabilities, including acquired immunodeficiency syndrome (AIDS) and human immunodeficiency virus (HIV), alcoholism, cancer, cerebral palsy, diabetes, emotional illness, epilepsy, hearing and speech disorders, heart disorders, learning disabilities (such as dyslexia), mental retardation, muscular dystrophy, and visual impairments. The act does not cover conditions that impose short-term limitations, such as pregnancy or broken bones.

Generally, the ADA forbids employers who have more than 15 employees and who are hiring from doing the following:

- Discriminating on the basis of any physical or mental disability

- Asking job applicants questions about their past or current medical conditions

- Requiring applicants to take pre-employment medical exams

The ADA requires that an employer make reasonable accommodations for qualified individuals who have disabilities, unless doing so would cause the employer "undue hardship." The undue hardship provision is still open to interpretation by the courts.

If you have a disability that you believe is covered by the ADA, familiarize yourself with the law's specifics. The U.S. Department of Justice's ADA home page can be found at www.ada.gov. For even more information, call your member of Congress, visit your library, or obtain free comprehensive ADA guides and supporting materials from the splendid Web site maintained by the Job Accommodation Network (janweb.icdi.wvu.edu).

Deciding when and whether to disclose a disability

The ADA watches your back to prevent discrimination based on your disability, but recruiters may still weasel around the law to avoid what they perceive as a liability. Use street savvy: When you can't win and you can't break even, change the game.

In your game, spin control begins with choosing whether to disclose your disability on your resume. Use these tips:

✔ If your disability is visible, the best time to disclose it is after the interview has been set and you telephone to confirm the arrangements. Pass the message in an offhanded manner: "Because I use a wheelchair for mobility, I was wondering if you can suggest which entrance to your building would be the most convenient?"

✔ Alternatively, you may want to reserve disclosure for the interview.

✔ If your disability is not visible, such as mental illness or epilepsy, you need not disclose it unless you'll need special accommodations. Even then, you can hold the disclosure until the negotiating stage once you've received a potential job offer.

No matter what you decide to do, be confident, unapologetic, unimpaired, and attitude-positive.

Explaining gaps in work history

Disclosure in the job-search process is a complex quandary. What can you do about gaps in your work history caused by disability?

In years past, you may have been able to obscure the issue. No longer. New computer databases make it easy for suspicious employers to research your medical history. And with health insurance costs so high, they may do exactly that. If your illness-related job history has so many gaps that it looks like a hockey player's teeth, I've never heard a better suggestion than writing "Illness and Recovery" next to the dates. It's honest, and the "recovery" part says, "I'm back and ready to work!"

If you have too many episodes of "missing teeth," your work history will look less shaky in a functional format, discussed in Chapter 9. Online resume discussion groups, which you can find through the Job Accommodation Network (`janweb.icdi.wvu.edu`), can serve as further sources of guidance on this difficult issue.

Asking for special equipment

If you need adaptive equipment, such as a special kind of telephone, I wouldn't mention it — even if the equipment is inexpensive or you're willing to buy it yourself. Instead, stick with the "time-release capsule" method of sharing information: Dribble out those revelations that may stifle interest in hiring you only when necessary. Never lose sight of your objective: to get an interview.

When Demotion Strikes

Kevin Allen (real person, phony name) was the district manager of five stores in a chain when he was demoted to manager of a single store. The higher-ups were sending him a message — they hoped he'd quit so that they could avoid awarding a severance package of benefits. Kevin ignored the message, retained a lawyer, kept his job, and started a job hunt after hours.

He finessed his resume by listing all the positions he had held in the chain, leaving out dates of when each started and stopped.

> **Demoting Store Chain, Big City**
>
> District Manager, 5 stores
>
> Store Manager, Windy City
>
> Store Assistant Manager, Sunny City
>
> Store Clerk, Sunny City

Throwing all of Kevin's titles into one big pot seemed a clever idea, but it didn't work for him. After a year of searching, Kevin got interviews, yes; but at every single face-to-face meeting, he was nailed with the same question: "Why were you demoted?" The interviewers' attitudes seemed accusatory, as if they'd been misled. Kevin failed to answer the question satisfactorily — he did not receive a single offer during a year's search. How did all the potential employers find out the truth?

Among obvious explanations: (A) Kevin worked in a "village" industry where people know each other and gossip. (B) Employers ordered credit checks on him; credit checks show employment details. (C) Employers authorized private investigations, an uncommon but not unheard-of practice in private business.

No one knows what really happened, but in hindsight, Kevin may have done better had he accepted the message that the chain wanted him out, negotiated a favorable severance package that included good references, and quit immediately while his true title was that of district manager.

After two humiliating years of demotion status, Kevin took action by "crossing the River Jordan," a Biblical phrase that universities have adapted. It refers to those who seek a new beginning by returning to college for a law or business degree. Kevin enrolled in law school. (A happy ending: Six years later, Kevin is a happily employed city attorney.)

In cases like Kevin's, a strategy that's forthright but doesn't flash your demotion in neon lights may work better than trying to cover up the demotion. Combine only two titles together, followed quickly by your accomplishments and strengths, as shown in Figure 12-6.

1999 - 2002 Demoting Company Name
Assistant Manager, Manager

As assistant manager, support the manager and carefully monitor detailed transactions with vendors, insuring maintenance of products and inventory; use skills in invoicing, billing, ordering, and purchasing. As manager, supervise all aspects of purchasing, display, and merchandise sales. Trained team of more than 30 employees in two-week period. Trained three assistant managers in essential functions of customers, employees, and finance. Increased sales revenues 25 percent in first six months.

Figure 12-6: Sample of combining a demotion with a higher position.

No matter how well you handle your resume entry, the reference of the demoting employer may ultimately end your chances of landing a new job that you want. In trying to mend fences, you may appeal to the demoting employer's fairness or go for guilt. Point out how hard you worked and how loyal you've been. Find reasons why your performance record was flawed. Ask for the commitment of a favorable reference and a downplaying of the demotion. If fairness or guilt appeals are denied, see an employment lawyer about sending the demoting employer, on law-firm letterhead, a warning against libel or slander.

The basic way to handle demotions throughout the job-hunting process is akin to how you handle being fired: by accentuating the positive contributions and results for which you are responsible. *But being demoted is trickier to handle than being fired.* Surprisingly, being fired no longer suggests personal failure — being demoted does.

Gaps in Your Record

Periods of unemployment leave black holes in your work history. Should you (A) fill them with positive expressions such as *family obligations,* (B) fill them with less positive but true words such as *unemployed,* or (C) show the gap without comment?

Choosing B, *unemployed,* is dreary. Forget that! Choosing C, *leave-it-blank-and-say-nothing,* often works — you just hope that it isn't noticed. My choice, however, is A: Tell the truth about what you were doing but spin it in a dignified, positive way. A few examples: *independent study . . . foreign travel . . . career renewal through study and assessment.*

An infoblizzard of tips has been published on how to repair resume holes. Unless you were building an underground tunnel to smuggle drugs, the principles are simple:

- ✔ Present the time gap as a positive event.

- ✔ Detail why it made you a better worker — not a better *person,* but a better worker with more favorable characteristics, polished skills, and mature understanding, all of which you're dying to contribute to your new employer.

How can these principles be applied? Take the case of a student who dropped out of college to play in a band and do odd jobs for four years before coming back to finish his biology degree and look for a job. The student knows that employers may perceive him as uncommitted. In the resume, he should treat the band years like any other job: Describe the skills that were polished as a band leader. Identify instances of problem solving, teamwork, leadership, and budgeting.

You do the real problem solving in the cover letter that accompanies such a resume, as Abilene Christian University Director of Career Services Jack Stewart outlines in Figure 12-7.

Figure 12-7:
Excerpt explaining a job gap in a cover letter.

After completing two years of undergraduate study, it was necessary for me to work to continue my education. Using my talents as a musician, I organized a band and after four years was able to continue my education. I matured and learned much about the real world and confirmed that an education is extremely important in fulfilling my career goals.

The chief mistake people make is assuming that a positive explanation won't sell. Instead, they fudge dates from legitimate jobs to cover the black holes. You may get away with it in the beginning. But ultimately, you'll be asked to sign a formal application, a legal document. When a company wishes to chop staff without paying severance benefits, the first thing that happens is an intense investigation of the company's database of application forms. People who lied on their applications can be sent out into the mean streets with nothing but their current paychecks on their backs.

Lying isn't worth the risk — it's a mistake.

The consultant/entrepreneur gap

Professional and managerial job seekers are routinely advised to explain black holes by saying that they were consultants or that they owned small businesses. Not everyone can be a consultant, and there's substantial risk in the small-business explanation.

If it should happen to be true that you were a consultant, name your clients and give a glimmer of the contributions you made to each. If you really had a small business, remember: Employers worry that you'll be too independent to do things their way or that you'll stay just long enough to learn their business and go into competition against them. Strategic antidotes: Search for a business owner who is within eyeshot of retirement and wouldn't mind your continuing the business and paying him or her a monthly pension. Resume antidotes: Describe yourself as "manager," not "CEO" or "president," and if you have time, rename your business something other than your own name: "River's End Associates, Inc.," not "Theresa K. Bronz, Inc."

Another method of papering-over glaring gaps is to include all your work under "Work History" and cite unpaid and volunteer work as well as paid jobs.

Suppose that you've been unemployed for the past year. That's a new black hole. Some advisers suggest the old dodge of allowing the recruiter to misperceive the open-ended date of employment for your last job: "2000–" as though you meant "2000–Present." The open-ender solution often works — until you run into a reader who thinks that it's way too calculating.

Black holes are less obvious in a functional format, as discussed in Chapter 9. *If you can't find a positive explanation for a black hole, say nothing.*

If you possess a not-so-pristine past, stick with small employers who probably won't check every date on your resume.

Here a Job, There a Job, Everywhere a Job, Job

I once interviewed a man who had held 185 jobs over the course of his 20-year career, encompassing everything from dishwasher to circus clown and from truck driver to nursing aide. He wrote to me, not requesting resume advice, but to complain that a potential employer had the nerve to call him a *job hopper!*

Omit inappropriate data

The best way to handle some land mines on your resume is to ignore them. Generally, revealing negative information on a resume is a mistake. Save troublemaking information for the all-important job interview, where you have a fighting chance to explain your side of things.

Stay away from these topics when constructing a resume:

✔ Firings, demotions, forced resignations, and early termination of contracts

✔ Personal differences with coworkers or supervisors

✔ Bankruptcy, tax evasion, or credit problems

✔ Criminal convictions or lawsuits

✔ Homelessness

✔ Illnesses from which you have now recovered

✔ Disabilities that do not prevent you from performing the essential functions of the job, with or without some form of accommodation

Should you ever give reasons for leaving a job? In most instances, resume silence in the face of interview-killing facts is still the strategy of choice. But the time has come to rethink at least one special issue: losing a job.

Now that jobs are shed like so many autumn leaves, losing a job is no longer viewed as a case of personal failure. It may be to your advantage to state on your resume why you left your last position, assuming that it was not due to poor work performance on your part. If you were downsized out, the recruiter may appreciate your straightforward statement, "Job eliminated in downsizing."

But remember, if you elect to say why you lost one job, for consistency, you have to say why you left all your jobs — such as for greater opportunity, advancement, and the like.

Talk about an antiquated term — in the 21st century, the notion of job hopping is as far out of a reality circle as the concepts of job security, company loyalty, and a guaranteed company pension. The Great American Dumping Machine will continue to sack people who then may have to take virtually any job they can to survive.

Adding insult to injury, some employers cling to a double standard — hiring and firing employees like commodities, then looking with disfavor on applicants who have had a glut of jobs by circumstance, not by choice.

You're not alone

Large numbers of people have to write resumes that explain holding too many jobs in too short a time. The harsh realities of business may force you to detour from a single career path to alternative tracks where you can acquire new skills and experiences, even if they're not skills and experiences of choice. If so, you need serious creative writing to keep your resume focused on the work history that is relevant for the next job sought.

Use these tips when you find that you have too many jobs in your history:

- ✔ Start by referring to your *diversified* or *skills-building* background.

- ✔ Use a functional or hybrid resume format (see Chapter 9) and present *only your experience relevant to the job you seek.*

- ✔ Express your work history in years, not months and years.

Focus your resume

Too many jobs in your background threaten your focus. *Unfocused* is an ugly word in job-search circles. Being judged as "unfocused" is saying that you lack commitment, that you're perpetually at a fork in the road. It's a reason not to hire you.

When your resume looks as though it will collapse under the weight of a mishmash of jobs unconnected to your present target, eliminate your previous trivial pursuits. Group the consequential jobs under a heading that says *Relevant Work Experience Summary.*

What if this approach solves one problem — the busy resume — but creates another, such as a huge, gaping black hole where you removed inconsequential jobs? Create a second work history section that covers those holes, labeling it *Other Experience.* Figure 12-8 shows an example.

Dealing with an unfocused career pattern on paper is easier when it's done under the banner of a temporary service company. The spin in this case lists the temporary services company as the employer. You choose one job title that covers most of your assignments. Under that umbrella title, identify specific assignments. Give the dates in years next to the temporary services firm, skipping dates for each assignment. Figure 12-9 shows an example.

What if you work for several temporary services at the same time? The simple answer is that you use the same technique of dating your work history for the temporary service firms, not for the individual assignments. This dating technique is a statement of fact; you legally are an employee of the temporary services firm, not of the company that pays for your temporary services.

When excess jobs or focus isn't a problem, you may choose an alternative presentation for a series of short-term jobs, as illustrated in Chapter 4. The alternative doesn't mention the staffing firm(s) but only the names of the companies where you worked.

Impacted Resume with Focus

Professional Experience

UNITECH, Hamburg, Germany
Computer Laboratory Assistant, 2002-Present
> Manage and troubleshoot hardware and software systems. Recover data, create programming architecture, and install parts and software. Assist a team of 18 engineers.

TECHNIK TECH, Hamburg, Germany
Assistant to System Analysts, 1998-2001
> Participated in construction, repair, and installation of systems at local businesses. Diagnosed faulty systems and reported to senior analysts, decreasing their workload by 25%.

TRADE NET, Berlin, Germany
Applications and Network Specialist, 1996-1998
> Set up and monitored a Windows-based BBS, including installation, structure, security, and graphics. Authored installation scripts for Trade Net, licensing U.S. software use in Europe.

Other Experience

AMERICAN TOY STORE, Berlin, Germany, Sales Representative, 2001-2002
Arranged and inventoried merchandise, directed sales and customer relations. Developed strong interpersonal skills and gained knowledge of retail industry.

CAMP INTERNATIONAL, Oslo, Germany, Activities Director, 1996-1998
Organized daily activities for more than 300 children from English-speaking countries, including sports, recreation, and day classes. Supervised 10 counselors and kitchen staff of five, developing responsible and effective management skills.

Figure 12-8: Solving the black-hole problem in a jobs-impacted resume by creating a focus plus a second work history section.

Focusing with Temp Jobs

Professional Experience

Relia-Temps 2002-present

Executive Secretary

- North Western Banking Group
Perform all clerical and administrative responsibilities for 10-partner investment and loan firm, assisting each partner in drafting contracts, reviewing proposals, and desiging various financial programs. Supervise 7 staff members. Introduced 50% more efficient filing system, reducing client reviews from 4 to 3 hours.

Administrative Assistant

- Mosaic Advertising
Supervised 3 receptionists and 4 clerical specialists, reporting directly to president. Administered daily operations of all accounting and communication transactions. Using extensive computer savvy, upgraded company computer networks withWindows 98.

- Blakeslee Environmental, Inc.
Assisted 8 attorneys at interstate environmental protection agency, scheduling meetings and conferences, maintaining files, and updating database records. Redesigned office procedures and methods of communication, superior organizational skills.

Figure 12-9: Listing your temporary job assignments without looking unfocused.

When Substance Abuse Is the Problem

Substance abuse is a disability under the Americans with Disabilities Act. If you're recovered from the addiction, you're entitled to all the Act's protections. If you are still abusing a substance, such as alcohol or illegal narcotics, you're not covered by the Act. Don't disclose previous substance abuse on your resume.

Cover gaps in your work history with the *Illness and Recovery* statement (see the "Job Seekers with Disabilities" section earlier in this chapter) or simply do not address the issue at all. Be careful what information you put on a job application — remember that it's a legal form and that lies can come back to haunt you (see the "Gaps in Your Record" section earlier in this chapter).

If you were ever arrested for smoking pot or being intoxicated — even once in your life — the fact may surface to damage your employment chances. Asking about arrest records is illegal, but a few private database companies don't let that stop them — they compile electronic databases of such arrest information and sell them to any employer who will buy.

The upshot: Avoid mentioning booze or drugs, be careful about application forms, and be honest at interviews — *if* you have recovered or *if* the experience was a brief fling or two.

If you're still held prisoner by a chronic, destructive, or debilitating overuse of a chemical substance that interferes with your life or employment, no resume tweaks will benefit you. Get help for your addiction.

A Bad Credit Rap

Job seekers who won't be handling money are surprised that employers may routinely check credit records.

Credit histories — called *consumer reports* — hold much more than payment history. A consumer report on you contains data from names of previous employers and residential stability to divorces and estimated prior earnings.

Employers are wary of hiring people awash in debt because they fear that stress will impact job performance, or that you have inadequate management skills or even that you may have sticky fingers with the company's funds.

Consumer reports have serious implications for students who graduate with sky-high education loans and credit card balances. They or their families may have missed payments to keep up college study. Divorced individuals often need spin control to address credit problems.

An amendment to the Fair Credit Reporting Act took effect in 1997; among new consumer protections against unfair credit treatment is the requirement that employers must get your permission in a stand-alone document to check your credit — no blending the request into fine print in the employment application.

And after an employer receives the report on you — but before any adverse action is taken, such as rejecting your application for a job — the employer must give you a free copy of the report with related legal documents. Receiving a copy of the documents gives you a chance to correct mistakes and spin control your issues.

For details of your rights, get a free copy of the Federal Trade Commission's publication, *Fair Credit Reporting,* by writing to the Public Reference Branch, FTC, Washington, DC 20580. You can also get the publication online at `www.ftc.gov/bcp/conline/pubs/credit/fcra.htm`.

Credit checking isn't a resume concern as such, but after you understand how a negative consumer report — true or erroneous — can torpedo your employment chances, you'll work all the harder on getting great references. (I discuss background-check concerns in Chapter 1.)

Resources to Solve Many Dilemmas

The array of resume dilemmas known to humankind is too long, too challenging, and too complex to comprehensively chronicle in this dollop of space.

The topic of strategies for ex-offenders, for instance, needs its own book to adequately address this issue. Fortunately, a few good books for people who've been in trouble with the law have emerged in the past couple of years.

Of course, the ex-offender issue isn't the only hard problem that keeps individuals unemployed. Until now, there hasn't been a single vendor offering resources aimed at helping people with a backdrop of trouble.

Impact Publications Publisher Dr. Ron Krannich has compiled a unique catalog of books, videos, and software designed to assist individuals with not-so-hot backgrounds. The catalog includes resources dealing with employment issues concerning substance abuse, addictive behaviors, ex-offenders, and juveniles, to name a few.

One book, for instance, is titled, *No One Will Hire Me!* For more information, download the free catalog, "Change Your Job! SuperSource . . . for People With Difficult But Promising Backgrounds," from the publisher's Web site (`impactpublications.com`), click on "catalogs," and then click on the catalog title. You can also request the catalog by mail from Impact Publications, 9104-N Manassas Dr., Manassas Park, VA 20111, or call 800-361-1055.

Spin Control Is in the Details

A white ruffled blouse stained only slightly with one dab of spaghetti sauce is 99 percent clean. But every person who saw me wear it at a public event remembers the red spot, not the white part of the blouse. Similarly, you can have a 99 percent StandOut resume, but any one of the deadly perceptions identified in this chapter can ice it without your knowing why. Practice spin control — present possible negative perceptions in a flattering light.

A positive explanation goes a long way in overcoming a resume land mine. It won't work all the time, but it will work some of the time, and all you need — for now — is one good offer to hit the job jackpot.

Chapter 13

Move from Worksheets to Finished Resume

. . . .

In This Chapter

▶ Focusing on what you want and do not want

▶ Sizing up your education and training

▶ Examining your skills and competencies

▶ Writing worksheets, summaries, and asset statements

▶ Producing great-looking resumes

. . . .

1 f there were a Grand Prix pit crew to fine-tune your resume in this modern age, it would consist of you, you, and you.

That is, everything in your StandOut resume starts with what you want and can do, and how effectively you write it down. This chapter helps you do exactly that by guiding you through the compilation of three self-discovery documents. You will work in three steps:

1. **Detailed worksheets on which you write all employment-related aspects of your life to date.**

2. **Summary worksheets on which you write key information drawn from your detailed worksheets.**

3. **Asset statements (power-packed self-marketing statements drawn from your summary worksheets), which can be used to open your resume or cover letter with a flourish.**

Harried career? Use worksheets to rethink your direction

Do you find yourself working too many hours a week and neglecting other parts of your life — friends, family, hobbies, community, and spiritual activities?

Women are especially prone to burnout from the work-go-round grind of rising early, struggling through the day, falling asleep wondering how you'll get it all done, and then getting up again the next morning and starting all over.

Do you really want a career change?

If you're overwhelmed and overworked, the worksheets in this chapter can help you with more than resume preparation. You may be ripe for a career change — or a flexible work schedule, telecommuting, or starting your own business.

Use the worksheets as a diary for discovery.

Use these worksheets to fuel an introspective look at who you are and where you've been. Think of them as a kind of work/life diary to identify the experiences you most enjoyed and did well at, as well as those you never want to repeat.

The personal inventory you create in these worksheets can take you a long way toward identifying solutions to a work/life dilemma that's eating away at your happiness. You may realize that you really don't want a career that's all-consuming — you want one with more balance. The personal inventory you create for resumes also serves as a straightforward tool to guide you toward a more fulfilling future.

Step One: The Detailed Worksheets

The worksheets in this chapter are your first line of defense against repeating sour experiences in your previous jobs, and they also help you to reincarnate cherished experiences in your future jobs. If you haven't held a job before, this chapter can help guide you to the kind of position that you'll most appreciate.

Think of the worksheets in this chapter as a kind of Swiss Army Knife, giving you the tools to get in touch with your innermost thoughts and desires about the following:

- ✔ The real reasons you left previous jobs
- ✔ Beneficial transferable lessons you learned in previous jobs
- ✔ The components that you really must have in a job to be happy
- ✔ The skills and responsibilities that you most enjoy using
- ✔ The skills and responsibilities that you never want to use again

Make copies of the New Job Worksheet, which begins on the next page, for each job you want to review.

New Job Worksheet

(Photocopy and complete one worksheet for each relevant job.)

Reasons for Leaving Job

Employer:_____ From:_____(Year) To:_____(Year)

What did you most like about your job here, and why did you apply for it in

the first place?_____

_____

_____

_____

What did you most dislike about your job here?_____

_____

_____

_____

Why did you choose to leave (pay, title, no promotion, unfulfilling)?_____

_____

_____

Areas of Highest Performance

Of the skills you used here, which gave you the most satisfaction

(give example)? Why?_____

_____

_____

_____

Of the duties, which made you feel your best? Why?_____

_____

_____

Which skills and responsibilities would you like to use in your next job?_____

_____

_____

_____

What You Never Want to Do Again

Of the skills you used here, which were the least fulfilling?

_____

_____

_____

Which tasks did you dread most? Why?_____

_____

_____

_____

Your Most Attractive Attributes

In your leisure activities, which competencies and skills have you used that

can transfer to your next job?_____

_____

_____

_____

Note: Don't bother writing a summary of this exercise; its message will be indelible in your mind.

Knowing What You Have to Offer

You can't present the best of yourself until you have a handle on the goods. Harold W. Ross, founding editor of the urbane and wildly successful *New Yorker* magazine, got that gem of wisdom dead straight when he drolly assessed who he was in the scheme of things.

Ross, a high school dropout and a Colorado miner's son who blew out of the Silver West a century ago to become a famous figure in American journalism and letters, once advised a staff member of the magazine:

> "I am not God," he reportedly said. "The realization of this came slowly and hard some years ago, but I have swallowed it by now. I am merely an angel in the Lord's vineyard."

On these pages, you get a chance to show why you, too, are an angel. I assume that you already have labored in the vineyards of career determination and have a fair idea of the kind of job or career field that you want to lay siege to. If not, back up and pursue the issue of career choice in *Changing Careers For Dummies,* by Carol L. McClelland, PhD (Wiley).

Working the Worksheets

Each worksheet that follows looks at your life in a wide-angle, rear-view mirror and then narrows the focus by suggesting that you target the most useful and vital accomplishments and competencies.

Many people lose the resume derby because they merely report where they have worked and enumerate the duties they were assigned. That information alone won't roll over the competition. You need to provide effective answers to the following questions:

- ✔ What did you accomplish?
- ✔ What value and competencies did you bring to a specific position?
- ✔ What did it matter that you showed up at the office most days?
- ✔ How have you put your education to work?
- ✔ What good has your education done anyone?

The *identification* and *measurement* of *results, outcomes,* and *achievements* are what make recruiters book you for interviews.

Begin your personal inventory now. Fill out these worksheets:

- ✔ Education
- ✔ Competencies (paid and unpaid work skills, knowledge and abilities)
- ✔ Hobbies and activities translated to skills
- ✔ Employability skills (personal characteristics)

Education and Training Worksheet

Name of institution/program _____

Address/Telephone _____

Year(s) attended or graduated _____ Degree/diploma/certificate _____

Overall GPA _____ Major GPA _____ Class rank (if known) _____

Work-relevant study

(Photocopy and complete one worksheet for each relevant course.)

Course _____

Knowledge acquired _____

_____

_____

Skills acquired _____

_____

Accomplishments (with concrete examples) _____

_____

Relevant projects/papers; honors _____

_____

Keywords/StandOut words _____

Quotable remarks by others (names, contact data) _____

_____

_____

Paid Work Worksheet

(Photocopy and complete one worksheet for each job.)

Name of employer_____

Postal address, e-mail address, telephone _____

_____

_____

_____

Type of business/career field _____

Job title _____Dates _____

Direct supervisor's name, contact information (if good reference; otherwise, note coworkers or sources of good references)_____

_____

_____

Major accomplishments (Promotion? Awards? Business achievements? — "increased sales by 30 percent" or "saved company 12 percent on office purchases?" What credit can you claim for creating, implementing, revamping, designing, saving? Jog your memory by recalling problems faced and action taken.) _____

_____

_____

_____

Problems faced _____

_____

_____

Action taken _____

_____

_____

_____

_____

Skills acquired _____

_____

_____

_____

Knowledge/abilities acquired_____

_____

_____

_____

Job responsibilities _____

_____

_____

_____

Keywords/StandOut words_____

_____

_____

_____

_____

Quotable remarks by others (names, contact data) _____

_____

_____

_____

_____

Unpaid Work Worksheet

(Photocopy and complete one worksheet for each relevant unpaid job.)

Name of employer_____

Type of organization_____

Volunteer job title_____Dates _____

Direct supervisor's name, contact information _____

_____

Major accomplishments (What credit can you claim for creating, implementing, revamping, designing, saving? Jog your memory by recalling problems faced and action taken.) _____

_____

_____

_____

Problems faced _____

Action taken _____

Skills acquired _____

Knowledge/abilities acquired_____

Keywords/StandOut words _____

Quotable remarks by others (names, contact data) _____

_____

_____

_____

Hobbies/Activities-to-Skills Worksheet

(Photocopy and complete one worksheet for each relevant work-related activity.)

Name of hobby, organization, club (location)_____

Dates _____

Title/position (officer/member) _____Elected (yes/no) _____

Accomplishments _____

_____

_____

_____

_____

Work-related skills acquired _____

_____

_____

Knowledge/abilities acquired_____

_____

_____

_____

Keywords/StandOut words_____

_____

_____

Quotable remarks by others (names, contact data) _____

_____

_____

_____

Employability Skills Worksheet

(Photocopy and complete one worksheet for each relevant position.)

Name of company/supervisor _____

Aspects of your work ethic that the employer appreciated_____

_____

_____

Example _____

Facets of your personality that the employer valued _____

_____

_____

Example _____

Name of coworker/client/industry contact _____

Aspects of your work ethic that the person appreciated _____

_____

_____

Example _____

Facets of your personality that the person valued _____

_____

_____

Example _____

Keywords/StandOut words _____

_____

Step Two: The Summary Worksheets

The worksheets you've just filled out are rich in raw material for the worksheet summaries in your next step toward a glorious StandOut resume. On your worksheet summaries, highlight the data that most clearly show how well you qualify for the job (or jobs) you desire.

Photocopy the blank summary worksheet and fill out one copy for each job that catches your eye. In the left column, jot down what the employer wants. You obtain this information from job ads, job descriptions, and occupational literature. If you're working with a recruiter, the data should be easy to get.

In the opposite right column, drawing from your worksheets, make note of how well you fill the bill. How good is the fit between each requirement and your qualification? Some career coaches call the matching process *T-boning*.

When the job calls for specific skills, an employer doesn't necessarily care how or where you obtained the requisite skills in the summary worksheet, so the headings in the left column merely say Skills Required.

By contrast, the headings in the right column of the summary worksheet correspond to their worksheets in this chapter. They are noted specifically as yet another reminder to include your skills obtained from any source, paid or unpaid.

The more successful you are at tailoring your resume to fit a specific job, the more likely you are to be in the final running.

Step Three: Drafting Asset Statements

To open a resume or cover letter, you may want to use an *asset statement*.

An asset statement is essentially a skills summary — although other ingredients of competencies can be inserted, specifically your knowledge, abilities, and personal characteristics. An asset statement is known by many names in the recruiting industry. Some of these other names are:

- Highlights statement
- Keyword summary (or profile)
- Marketing summary
- Objective summary

> ✔ Power summary
>
> ✔ Professional history capsule
>
> ✔ Profile section
>
> ✔ Qualifications summary
>
> ✔ Synopsis

The asset statement typically contains the three to five best skills (sales points) that support your job aspiration. The exception to this definition is the keyword profile, which uses a listing (rather than sentences) of virtually all the relevant skills you possess.

The data in your asset statement need not be proven with examples in this brief section — for now, it stands alone as assertions. In effect, you are saying, "Here's who I am. Here's what I can do for you." This is a tease, encouraging the reader to hang in there for proof of what the opening claims.

The information you've written in the previous worksheets paves the way for your powerful asset statements. Figure 13-1 gives you examples of power-packed asset statements.

Why You Need Asset Statements

An asset statement opens your resume with a bang but provides several other benefits as well:

✔ **Summary page:** Asset statements can be expanded to an entire summary page, which you place atop a reverse chronological resume (in effect turning your reverse chronological resume into a hybrid resume format, as discussed in Chapter 9).

✔ **Old successes:** An asset statement can revive a fading job achievement. Suppose you have an achievement that took place four or five years ago and is now needed to qualify you for a job. By amplifying the old achievement in a summary statement (and perhaps choosing a functional format for your resume), you don't bury it in a bazaar of your past jobs. When crystallized in a focused power summary, the golden oldie achievement still works for you.

✔ **Basis for achievement statements:** Asset statements provide the raw material for achievement sections (paragraphs) and brief (one- or two-line) high-voltage statements that you use later in your resume.

Summary Worksheet

The Employer Wants You Have

Education and Training Required	Education and Training Skills Including Achievements
1)	
2)	
3)	
4)	
5)	
6)	
7)	
8)	
9)	
10)	
Skills/Knowledge/Abilities Required (Competencies)	**Paid** Skills/Knowledge/Abilities
1)	
2)	
3)	
4)	
5)	
6)	
7)	
8)	
9)	
10)	

(1 of 2)

Summary Worksheet

The Employer Wants **You Have**

Skills/Knowledge/Abilities Required (Competencies)	**Unpaid** Skills/Knowledge/Abilities
1)	
2)	
3)	
4)	
5)	
Skills/Knowledge/Abilities Required (Competencies)	Hobby/Activity Skills Including Achievements
1)	
2)	
3)	
4)	
5)	
Employability Skills Required (Personal Characteristics)	Employability Skills Including Achievements
1)	
2)	
3)	
4)	
5)	

(2 of 2)

Human resources manager

Well-rounded experience in all human resource functions. Focus: Benefits and Labor Relations. Managed an HR staff of 200,000-population, unionized city. Reputation for progressive programs attractive to both city and employees.

Marketing account executive

Award-winning marketer with impressive performance record in Internet merchandising. Proficient in international conventions and customs. Attentive to details while focusing on the big picture. Excellent at organizing, tracking, and managing projects. Relate well to both customers and coworkers.

Construction manager

General construction-manager experience covers all areas: start-up and financing, site selection, building design, and construction. Hire and train. Properties never litigated. Work ahead of schedules. Rehired several times by same developers.

Figure 13-1:
Asset statements that turbo-charge a resume.

Communications graduate

Entry opportunity in print or broadcast news. Completing rigorous communications degree, with minor in English. Interned as editorial associate in newspaper columnist's office, achieved top performance review; editor of college newspaper; instructor of adult students at writing lab.

Data in achievement statements must be proven by *examples,* the best of which are *quantified.* Measure, measure, measure!

What's the difference between an asset statement and the achievement statements that are used later in your resume? The difference is that in an *achievement statement*, you should incorporate documentation, or "storytelling," to authenticate what you're saying. By contrast, *asset statements* are credible without examples or results.

E-Z asset statements

Remember, you don't have to prove what you say right there in the opening statement or summary — but you do have to prove it later in your resume in achievement statements. Here's a collection of write-in forms to start you off. Just fill in the blanks.

✔ After __ (number of years, provided the number is not too high) years in _____ (your occupation), seek opportunity to use extensive experience and _____ (your favorite skills) as a (your target position).

✔ Knowledge of (your expertise) and familiarity with _____ (type of product, industry, or clientele). Seek position as _____ (job title) using intensive experience as a _____ (occupation).

✔ Developed new _____ which resulted in increased _____; maintained an aggressive _____ program that increased employer's revenues by __%. Seeking a position as a _____ (your objective) in an organization needing expertise in _____ (your top skills).

✔ A position as a _____ (a job slightly higher in rank than your top employment), specializing in _____ (a skill unique to you).

✔ A _____ (type of) position that needs _____ (list skills and accomplishments). Demonstrated by _____ (list of paid and volunteer responsibilities and successes). Will _____ (an improvement that your prospective employer appreciates).

✔ Offering _____ (your field) skills in _____ (related industry), with ability to solve _____ (one or more problems common in the field), including _____ (your top skills).

✔ Encyclopedic knowledge of _____ (your top skills in technical aspects of position), familiarity with _____ (qualifying duties of position), and effective management of _____ (your lesser job-related skills).

Aim for Powerful but True Statements

Wait until the next day to review your finished asset statement. Did you get carried away with fantasy writing? Ask yourself, "Can I live up to this advance billing?" If not, tone it down to reality — that is, your *best reality*. Unfortunately — you smooth writer, you — when you land a job based on hype that you can't back up, you'll be renewing your job search.

After working your way through Step 1 (worksheets), Step 2 (summary worksheets), and Step 3 (asset statements), you're ready to put your keyboard in action, either electronically or on paper. The following tips apply chiefly to paper, but some suggestions apply to formatted online resumes as well.

Write Until It's Right

Can you write a decent resume in nanoseconds? Several resume books on the market sport titles insisting that you can do just about that. Bogus! A well-developed resume requires adequate curing time to form, mellow, and develop — you must think, write, think some more, rewrite, proofread, get feedback, and rewrite.

All too many job hunters scatter hundreds of thrown-together resumes. Then they wait. Nothing happens. Why do you think nobody bothers to call with an interview offer? Perhaps thrown-together too often gets thrown out?

If you don't want to be left behind because of a thrown-together resume, write a StandOut resume. It works.

After tailoring your StandOut resume, must you also customize a cover letter? Here's the *wrong answer:* No, just roll out the old I-saw-your-ad-and-I-am-enclosing-my-resume cliché. Here's the *right answer:* Yes, a tailored cover letter is the perfect sales tool for a tailored resume.

But that's a topic for another book. Check out *Cover Letters For Dummies,* 2nd Edition (Wiley), for everything you need to know about cover letters and more.

Paper Resumes That Resonate

Although the market is moving away from paper resumes toward digital resumes, tree-and-ink products are here for the foreseeable future. Here's how to look outstanding on paper and make the first cut in the employment screening process.

Word processing

You need a computer equipped with word-processing software to produce your resume. Typewritten copies are still acceptable, but most people don't type well enough to produce crisp, clean, sparkling copies. If word processing is not yet one of your skills, scout out a word-processing class — you'll need this ability in nearly any job you take. In the meantime, find a friend who will key in your resume. If you have the skill but not the tools, can you use a friend's computer? Or use a computer at a school's computer lab or career center, or try your local public library? If none of this is possible, take your handwritten resume to a professional office support firm and hire someone to do the production work.

Unemployed people can use computers for free at Public One-Stop offices nationwide; to find a One-Stop office near you, go online to `www.doleta.gov/usworkforce/onestop`.

Printing

Producing your resume on a laser or inkjet printer is today's standard. The old-fashioned dot matrix printers lack the firepower to print resumes that compete in today's job market. If you photocopy a core resume — rather than custom-tailor each resume to the job at hand — make sure that the copies look first-rate. No blurring, stray marks, streaks, or faint letters.

Paper

How good must your paper be? For professional, technical, managerial, and executive jobs, the stock for a paper resume should be quality paper with rag content, perhaps 25 percent, and a watermark (a faint image ingrained in the paper). Office supply stores, small printing firms, and specialty-paper mail-order catalogs offer a wide range of choices. Restrict the color of your paper to white or off-white, eggshell, or the palest of gray. Print on one side of the sheet only.

The ink on a StandOut resume is evenly distributed across each page, which is best achieved with a smooth paper stock. The image evoked by a high-quality paper is diminished when it looks as though the ink just didn't flow consistently — the print looks alternately dark or faded, may be streaky or smeared. Linen (*textured*) paper is impressive, but the ink from a laser printer or photocopier may not move smoothly across a sheet, making your resume hard to read. Try before you buy. If there's the slightest doubt about readability, switch to laid (*smooth*) paper.

The quality of paper is immaterial when your resume is to be scanned into job computers or spun across the Internet. Hiring managers never see the quality of paper or printing you have selected.

Open spaces

Which style of reading do you prefer: a paper so packed with text that your eyes need a spa treatment before tackling it or a paper so generous with white space that you *want* to read it? Too many people, hearing that they must not exceed one page, try to cram too much information in too little space.

A ratio of about one-quarter white space to text is about right. Line spacing between items is vital. Do not justify the right side of the page — that is, do not try to have the type align down the right side of the page — leave it ragged. Right justification creates awkward white spaces. An overcrowded page almost guarantees that it will not be read by younger recruiters and hiring managers who grew up in an age of television and *USA Today*-style newspapers. And older readers? Their eyes won't take the wear and tear of too many words crashing in too small a space. White space is the master graphic attention-getter.

Typefaces and fonts

A *typeface* is a family of characters — letters, numbers, and symbols. A *font* is a specific size of typeface. Helvetica is a typeface; Helvetica 10-point bold, Helvetica 12-point bold, and Helvetica 14-point bold are three different fonts.

No more than two typefaces should appear on one resume; if you don't have an eye for what looks good, stick to one typeface. Either Times Roman or Helvetica used alone is a fine choice for your resume. But if you want to mix the two typefaces, I recommend that you choose Helvetica for the headings and Times Roman for the text and lesser headings.

Paying attention to the spacing of your resume contributes much to its readability. Printing your name in small capital letters can be pleasing. Using larger type for headings (12 or 14 pt.) or boldface can give necessary prominence. Use italics sparingly — you don't want to overdo emphasis, and italicized words lose readability in blocks of text.

Design structure

Your name and contact information can be flush-left, centered, or flush-right. Look at examples in Chapter 17.

Some recruiters suggest that you type your name flush-right because they thumb through the right-hand corner of resume stacks.

Aim for a tasteful amount of capitalization and bold lettering for emphasis.

Important information jumps in the recruiter's face when set off by bullets, asterisks, and dashes.

Typos and spelling errors are unacceptable. They are seen as carelessness or a lack of professionalism. It is far better that I have a spelling mistake in this book than you have one in your resume. In the tens of thousands of resumes mistakenly sent to me for review as a syndicated columnist (a service I do not offer), spelling has, at times, been creative. One man claimed to be *precedent* of his company. Do you think he was a good one? Use your computer's spell-check feature, read your finished resume carefully, and ask a friend to read it also.

Do not staple together a two- or three-page resume or put it in a folder or plastic insert. The resume may be photocopied and distributed, or it may be scanned into a database. To minimize the risk of a page becoming an orphan, put a simple header atop each page after the first: your name and page number. In a multiple-page resume, you may want to indicate how many pages there are, as in page 1 of 2, in case the pages get separated. You can also put the page number at the bottom.

Your StandOut Resume Is Moving Right Along

Take the time to make sure your resume is as strong as it can be to attract the employer who has the right job for you. The resume samples in Chapter 17 can give you a good idea of the variety of clean-cut, appealing resume designs you can adopt.

The resume design: Does it make a difference?

Recruiters essentially agree that resume design counts, as these excerpts from an online recruiting forum reveal:

Recruiter #1: "Is there a 'best' resume design? I'm told by a self-proclaimed expert that a format with about one third of the page left blank on the left-hand side (for example, a heading of 'Education' all the way to the left margin, then information is indented about one third of the way into the page) is best. This space allows recruiter/interviewers to have a place to make notes."

Recruiter #2: "Recruiters and interviewers should not be writing on anyone's resume."

Recruiter #3: "Attention to detail should not be overlooked. But to say that there should be a margin here or there, or everything should be on one page, is an outdated point of view. Resume design can be indicative of someone's personality, telling much more from the beginning."

Recruiter #4: "The resume design makes a great deal of difference. Most managers don't have time to search through a resume looking for information. If it's not easy to spot, the resume will go into the 'do not call' pile. The better the design of the resume, the more likely we are to interview."

Part IV
StandOut Resumes Online

The 5th Wave   By Rich Tennant

"I like your resume, Mr. Chan — 4 cups of culinary school, 3/4 tablespoon internship, and a pinch of restaurant management. The only problem I have is finding the pound of dough it'll take to hire you."

In this part . . .

You find the latest news about e-resumes: what's in, what's out. You get insider tips on how to decide which technology to entrust with your StandOut resume, including the exact words to use.

Chapter 14

The Changing E-Resume: Technology in Transition

• •

In This Chapter

▶ Defining e-resumes

▶ Gaining e-resume benefits

▶ Understanding keyword flimflams

▶ Asking how to submit e-resumes

▶ Using an easy work-flow model

• •

*1*f you're new to the mysterious world of the e-resume, a quick scoot by a few terms gets you clicking on the right keys. (If you're an old e-resume hand, go straight to "The Invisible Keyword Flimflam" section later in this chapter.)

The term *e-resume* can mean any of the following:

✔ A file sent as an e-mail attachment; usually, the distribution format is MS Word or WordPerfect. Less frequently it is Adobe Acrobat's PDF (portable document format).

✔ A resume that is incorporated into the body of an e-mail message.

✔ A resume posted on a commercial Web job site, such as CareerBuilder or Monster.

✔ A resume submitted to a company Web site's career portal.

✔ A resume/portfolio on a Web page created by a job seeker.

✔ A resume/portfolio on a CD-ROM.

If you're wondering why the word "scannable" didn't make the cut, it's because a scannable resume starts out as a paper (printed) document and becomes an e-resume only after it is scanned into an electronic database.

The Rise of the E-Resume

An e-resume may be called a *digital* or *online* resume because it appears in digital format (meaning that it's electronic, not printed on paper) and is sent through a computer connected to a computer network.

The Net (Internet) is the world's biggest computer network. The Web (World Wide Web) is a graphical overlay on the Internet that makes possible sound, film, video, and various special effects as well as text.

With the Net and the Web as background, boundless change is inevitable in the way we do business, and the resume industry is no exception. The transformation within the resume industry is irreversible. The newest trends are described in Chapter 1, but these two developments underpin all resume change:

- An amazing acceleration of computer software over the past 15 years drives the reinvention of the way you *prepare and submit resumes* and in the way others *read and manage them.*

- The Internet, in connecting the globe's computers, continues to restructure forever the way resumes are sent from one place to another.

These two developments sparked the explosion of the e-resume. Millions and millions of e-resumes float like inexhaustible soap bubbles throughout cyberspace each day. Their collective volume threatens to overwhelm the recruiting industry.

The Invisible Keyword Flimflam

Feeling as if they're stuck in a rerun of the movie *Groundhog Day,* recruiters searching resumes online are seeing the same dozen people perched atop search results again and again.

Suppose an applicant named Charlie Brown turns up high on search results for an HR representative and high again on search results for a sales representative. Applicant Tillie Glutz is a top-rated contender for medical assistant and top-rated for respiratory therapist as well. How can this be? Do superworkers walk among us?

Not exactly. The reason the same people keep turning up at the top of search results for many job openings is not that they're supremely talented in multiple directions. The reason is online shenanigans.

Some technically sophisticated job seekers have discovered the "Invisible Keyword Flimflam." These crafty individuals are packing e-resumes with every keyword they can find, whether or not the words actually describe their qualifications. They highlight keywords they don't want to show up, then change the font color from black to white to match the background color. In a normal onscreen review, the eye doesn't see the misleading keywords.

Why go to all this trouble? They hope to improve their employment chances by scoring a high ranking in search results when search engines, sifting through a database of qualified applicants, find those keywords and raise them to the top of the electronic heap.

Unraveling the ruse is simple but time consuming, irking the recruiter who's doing the digging. To discover hidden keywords, the recruiter highlights the applicant's entire resume, then pastes it into an MS Word document. Next, the recruiter highlights the text and changes the font color to black. That's when the recruiter sees the deceit: Standing between the paragraphs are all the keywords that were not visible or printable until they were highlighted and the font color changed from white to black.

How do the understandably irritated recruiters respond when they come across the hidden keyword gambit? Just what you think: They trash it. The offending applicants who truly may be desperate are perceived as such — and desperate doesn't sell. Moreover, all versions of resumes from applicants who pepper their documents with inappropriate keywords are kicked out of that company's database. The company-wide wipeout means the offending applicant not only loses one particular job, but all jobs there.

If use of the invisible word trick grows, clogging e-recruiting systems that rely on keyword searches and turning their databases into swamps of unqualified job seekers, the systems will be severely damaged, perhaps even disabled.

Employers' countermeasures to combat hidden keywords and other less dramatic causes of database overload are being debated as you read these words.

But the e-resume, in all its variations, is effectively the Elvis of the recruiting industry — the king who will live forever. Recruiters say they're underwater, soaked with maddening swells of e-resumes and gasping for air. The overload has created problems that could well affect your job search.

Get the Loot, Not the Boot

To avoid the cyberwall-to-cyberwall competition in e-resumes described in the previous section, do you automatically throw up your hands, forget about e-resumes, and claim you'd rather dig ditches for a living? No, because if you do decide to "just forget about doing an e-resume," a shovel may well become your only work tool.

Except for small businesses that don't use computers and companies that prefer you come into the employment office and fill out an application for hourly work, e-resumes have become essential.

Instead of swearing off e-resumes, review the aspects and advantages of an e-resume, especially if you are on the world's "A list" of job seekers — a younger person with a bit of experience and hot skills in demand:

✓ **Career management tool:** Using a variety of privacy-protecting methods, a number of employed people position themselves to trade up jobs by parking their resumes on carefully chosen job sites that use (computer) personal job agents. (See Chapter 2.) When a better job turns up that matches their requirements, they're notified by e-mail. This category of employed person is termed *passive job seeker* and is the most prized of recruits; a widely held theory says that the person who has been hired by someone must be a desirable candidate.

✓ **Resume of choice:** Recruiters and hiring managers increasingly prefer to receive e-resumes because they are easier to deal with than stacks of paper.

✓ **Fewer resume readers:** The downsizing of a vengeful employment god over the past 25 years has taken its toll on human resource departments like everywhere else. The old conventional dilemma: The leaner staffs are drowning in paper resumes. The new conventional dilemma: The leaner staffs are submerged in e-resumes. Even so, browsing e-resumes is easier than scaling paper-resume mountains.

✓ **Ever-changing workforce:** Flexible employees — temporary, part-time, contract, and self-employed — need efficient connections for quick job changes. E-resumes may shorten search and response time.

✓ **Information technology workforce:** Anyone in IT fields must use an e-resume or else be considered IT's Biggest Pinhead.

✓ **Tightening recruitment budgets:** Employers say that online recruiting costs less than most other kinds of recruiting and that's why they're using more of it.

Newspapers aren't standing still for job site competition for advertising: Newspapers are combining online with print ads for a slight additional cost. Online recruiting typically calls for e-resumes.

✓ **Requests for online response:** Job ads increasingly instruct applicants to send e-resumes. Some advertisers refuse to reveal postal mail addresses.

✓ **Modernization of recruitment agencies:** Virtually all third-party recruiting agencies (read *headhunters*) use digital databases to manage their resume volume.

Stop and Ask Directions

When you're not sure what technology is being used where you send your resume (which, today, is most of the time), telephone or e-mail the employer's human resource department or company receptionist and ask the following question:

> *In submitting my resume, I want to be sure I'm using the correct technology at your organization. Can I submit my resume to your company electronically?*

If the answer is yes, then ask

> *Can I send my resume as an attachment?*

If the answer is yes, then ask

> *If I send my resume as an attachment (MS Word, WordPerfect), will managers see my resume in the original format, or do you convert the attachment to text?*

If the company converts the original resume to a pure text resume, avoid a bad wrap. Send your resume as a plain text (ASCII) file (Chapter 15 has info on ASCII resumes). Why? Some systems that convert an attachment to text do so at the expense of readability. They mess up the line-wrapping formatting so badly that the result looks as though your typing is tacky. Figure 14-1 shows an example of a plain text resume that began life as an attachment.

Resume Production, 1-2-3!

Are you puzzled about where to begin, what to write first, and what to do next? Follow these steps that Jim Lemke (this book's technical reviewer) and I recommend to fire up your resumes after you've created the core document, from which all targeted resumes flow.

1. **Create your resume in a word-processing program, such as MS Word or WordPerfect.**

   Stylize the resume to reflect your persona by choosing a typeface you like. Visually emphasize focal points with boldface, bullets, and underlined characters, as well as words. Save as "yourname.doc" (like "JimLemke.doc"). This document is your fully formatted resume for general usage. Print paper copies as needed.

Limit yourself to using characters found on a standard keyboard so that they translate correctly. For example, use asterisks to mark bulleted items, and forget about using the fancy arrows you can choose in the MS Word program.

2. **Convert your formatted resume (MS Word or WordPerfect) into plain text by following these steps:**

    1. Using the Edit menu, click "Select all."

    2. Click the "Start" button, then "Programs," then "Accessories." Select "Notepad" and paste your resume from the fully formatted original in Step 1.

    3. Select the "Wordwrap" feature from the "Edit" menu.

       Some minor tweaking may be necessary to line up dates and job titles if they were indented or you used bullets in your formatted resume.

    4. Save the resulting document as "yourname.txt" (for example, "JimLemke.txt").

   This is your plain text (ASCII) e-resume, which is compatible with all systems for use in e-mailing and posting to job sites.

3. **Use either your .doc file (created in Step 1) or .txt file (created in Step 2) to import your e-resume to other applications, such as an Adobe Acrobat PDF file.**

   You also can save your MS Word document as HTML from the MS Word "Save As" toolbar.

That's it. You're ready to roll.

And Away You Go . . .

The e-resume has gained ground during the last few years in the transition from paper to electronic self-marketing. Although paper won't go away in our lifetime, it's now on the downward slope of the popularity curve.

Paper will always be valued with some traditional employers and at job interviews when cranking up a computer is distracting. For most job seekers, a dual-resume track — with a heavy dose of e-resumes — is the one to follow in the opening years of the twenty-first century.

```
TARGET COMPANY
Category:  Consulting Services
Description of my ideal company:
To obtain a position in the Information Technology field which
provides a challenging atmosphere conducive to professional
achievement and the ability to advance while contributing to
organizational goals. To work for a company that lives a credo
and holds commitment to personal integrity and pursuit of
excellence as core values.
TARGET LOCATIONS
Relocate:  Yes
US-CO-Boulder/Fort Collins  US-CO-Denver  US-DC-
Washington/Metro
US-VA-Fairfax  US-VA-Vienna  US-VA-Northern
US-CO-Denver South  US-VA-Alexandria  US-VA-McLean/Arlington
WORK STATUS
US  I am authorized to work in this country for any employer.
EXPERIENCE
7/2000 - Present  Broadbase Software, Inc.  Menlo Park, CA
Application Consultant
?       Install and configure Broadbase Foundation and Brio
Enterprise Server to create a decision support environment.
?       Customize out of the box Broadbase Applications and Brio
Reports to customers decision support needs.
?       Reverse engineer transactional databases with ERwin to
build a logical dimensional model for physical deployment onto
Broadbase db.
?       Create custom applications in Broadbase Foundation
Application Workbench to perform ETL into physical dimensional
model within Broadbase db.
?       Administer Broadbase db.
?       Provide support after engagement is over for problems
that may arise.
?       Work mainly on transactional systems in SQL Server,
Sybase and Oracle. To develop dimensional models for
analytical reporting from Brio or MS OLAP server.
9/1999 - 7/2000  Genesis ElderCare  Kennet Square, PA
Senior Application Analyst (Applications DBA)
Designed an assessment database to track patient medical
outcomes and company defined scoring system
```

Figure 14-1: What can happen when you don't use ASCII.

Chapter 15

Fading Technology: Scannable and Plain Text Resumes

Scannable resumes were all the rage in the 1990s. These days, scannable resumes are on their way out. Plain text resumes (also called ASCII resumes) are sauntering toward history, too — just more slowly.

New technology is the reason scannable and plain text resumes are joining DOS operating software in computer museums. Recruiters now prefer slick intake systems that allow resumes to travel smoothly online and move straight into an electronic resume management database with no muss, no fuss.

Older systems that pass resumes through scanners often require manual doctoring to correct goofy readings. As for plain text resumes, well, recruiters and line managers say they're ugly and hard to read.

Even so, don't trash the scannable and plain text versions of your resume just yet. If an employer or job site directs you to send a resume that can be scanned or to send an online plain text resume, do it. This chapter gives you what you need to know.

Help Computers Find Your Scannable Resumes

A *scannable resume* is a paper resume scanned into a computer as an image. It can be postal mailed, hand delivered, faxed on a fax machine, or faxed from your computer to the employer, printed on paper and then scanned into a computer.

Scanning of resumes into electronic databases is done by human resource departments, which often outsource the task to service-bureau-like firms, and also by third-party recruiters.

A computer's scanning technology is programmed to extract (pull out) a summary of basic information from each resume image. This includes name, address, telephone number, skills, work history, years of experience, and education.

The extracted information summary is also stored in the electronic database along with the resume image. The summary is categorized by qualifications or kept as a searchable *plain text document* (described later in this chapter).

Resumes and their extracted summaries sleep peacefully until an HR specialist or recruiter searches (usually by keywords) the summaries to retrieve candidates of applicants that match the requirements of the job opening. The technology ranks candidates, from the most qualified to the least qualified. The relevant resumes get a wake-up call and pop to the recruiting screen.

Your mission: Take the correct steps to make your scannable resume *searchable* and *retrievable*. Make sure that scanning technologies can distinguish the letters and that your keywords (see Chapter 11) are spelled correctly so computers can find them.

When your resume goes AWOL in a database, your name just never comes up for the right jobs, or maybe any jobs. Fortunately, you can take steps to prevent scanning errors from putting you on the sidelines.

By following the technical tips in Table 15-1, you can ensure that your resume survives 99.9 percent of all types of scanning software in resume databases. Figure 15-1 shows a resume prime for scanning, and Figure 15-2 demonstrates many of the items from the "No, Don't Do This" columns of Tables 15-1 and 15-2.

Table 15-1	Tips to Charm Computer Eyes
Yes, Do This	*No, Don't Do This*
Do use white 8.5-inch x 11-inch paper.	Don't use colored paper. Paper that's too dark (or type that's too light) is a risky read for computers. Don't use paper that has a background pattern of any type: marble, speckles, lacy, or abstract designs. The software tries to read the designs and gets very mixed up. Avoid odd-sized paper. Especially don't use 11-inch x 17-inch paper and fold it over like a presentation folder (the fold-over has to be cut apart and painstakingly fed through the scanner's automatic document feeder on the front side and then again on the back side). A corollary is don't use colored typeface.
Do print on one side of the paper.	Don't print on two sides of the paper.
Do provide a laser-printed original that has good definition between the type and the paper. Your resume needs all the help it can get if it's faxed from one location to another: Each successive generation of copying degrades the quality of the reproduction.	Don't send a typewritten original (it makes you look like an old fud), a photocopy (unless you're certain that its reproduction quality is tops), or dot matrix printouts. Inkjet printers can be okay, but with the wrong paper, slightly smeared ink can cause the letters to bump into each other.
Do use standard typefaces, such as Helvetica, Futura, Optima, Univers, Times, Courier, New Century Schoolbook, and Palatino.	Don't use a condensed typeface. White space separates letters; no space smushes them together. Letters must be distinctively clear with crisp, unbroken edges. 'Avoid arty, decorative typefaces.
Do make sure that none of the letters touch together; in some typefaces, the letter "r" touches the following letter and looks like an "n." Computers relate to correctly spelled words, and so a "misspelled" word will not be read.	Don't try to crowd too much on one page by using 8-point or 9-point fonts. (Technically, some 9-point fonts are computer readable, but older human eyes may hate squinting to read your prose packed tightly with petite type.)

(continued)

Table 15-1 *(continued)*

Yes, Do This	No, Don't Do This
Do feel free to use larger fonts for section headings and your name: 14 to 16 points are good. Larger headings look better on the electronic image of your resume when humans read it (which they don't always do). Personally, I like the body of resumes in a 12-point font size, the section headings in 14-point, and the name in 16-point.	Don't worry about using 12-point fonts for your section headings and name if that's what you prefer. Scanning software will convert everything into the same size font no matter what's on the image, and you may need the space taken up by larger fonts to add a skill point.
Do use boldface and/or all capital letters for section headings.	Don't use any of these bad-scan elements: • italics or script • underlining • reverse printing (white letters on a black field) • shadows or shading • hollow bullets (they read like the letter "o") • number (#) signs for bullets (the computer may try to read the line as a phone number) • boxes (computer try to read them like letters) • two-column formats or designs that look like newspapers • symbols (such as a logo) • vertical lines (computers read them like the letter "l") • vertical dates (use horizontal dates: 2002–2007)
Do keep your scannable resume simple in design and straightforward — what recruiters call "plain vanilla."	Don't overdo the use of special characters when alternatives are available. Rather than write "telephone/fax number," write "telephone-fax number."
Do use white space to define sections.	Don't overdo the use of horizontal lines, and leave plenty of white space (about ¼ inch) around each section.

Yes, Do This	*No, Don't Do This*
Do place your name on the top line. If your resume runs more than one page, put your name as the first text on the other pages. Use a standard address layout below your name. List each telephone number on its own line; list your e-mail address on its own line; list your Web site on its own line. If you combine contact information, such as your telephone and e-mail address on the same line, put six spaces of white space between them.	Don't use unusual placements of your name and contact information.
Do send your resume without staples. Paper clips are okay.	Don't use staples (can cause processing of two pages as one).
Do send your resume flat in a 9-inch x 12-inch envelope; remember to add extra postage.	Don't fold or crease your resume. Laser print and copier toner may flake off when your resume is folded, or the software may just look at the fold and shrug in defeat.

After you examine the mechanics of scanner-savvy resumes, consider the content. Table 15-2 contains tips and tricks for human scanners.

Table 15-2	**Tips to Charm Human Eyes**
Yes, Do This	*No, Don't Do This*
Do include a one-page cover letter to all employers and recruiters, or when special instructions are needed. Be sure to use keywords (see Chapter 11) in your cover letter.	Don't bother to send a cover letter if you're sending your resume to a resume database where its insertion into the database is understood. An exception: When you're posting in a company database where the match between your resume and the job may not be obvious — an engineer applying for a sales engineering position, for instance.

(continued)

Table 15-2 *(continued)*

Yes, Do This	*No, Don't Do This*
Do realize that multiple-page resumes are not discouraged. Computers can easily handle multiple-page resumes, allowing you to give more information than you might for a formatted (paper) resume. As soon as the computer begins to search and retrieve for skills and other points of background, it laps up information to determine whether your qualifications match available positions. Generalized guidelines: • New graduates, one page (two with heavy facts) • Most job seekers, one to two pages • Senior executives, two to three pages • CV users, three to six pages	Don't cram-jam so much data onto a single page that it looks like the fine print on an insurance policy. Be concise, but use the pages you need to effectively sell your abilities.
Do consider putting a keyword profile or approximately 20 to 30 words at the beginning of your resume. It's an attention grabber and a jiffy picture of the essence of your qualifications. Although a keyword profile isn't technically necessary — computers can extract your skills anywhere on your resume — leading off with a keyword preface assures that human eyes see your strengths on the first screen, enticing them to scroll down and see in what context your skills are offered. If you fail to grab their interest on the first screen, they find it too easy to click to the next resume. And, creating a keyword profile forces you to specifically think of the keywords you need to use.	Don't be redundant by layering summary upon summary. If you use a keyword summary, don't follow up immediately with a qualifications summary.
Do be generous with your keywords to define your skills, experience, education, professional affiliations, and other marketable points of background. Generally, keywords are such nouns as "writer," "Excel," and "Spanish."	Don't assume that your action verbs will place you among the candidates chosen for an interview.

Yes, Do This	No, Don't Do This
Do incorporate the resume-writing guidance given in other chapters of this book (with the exception of heavy reliance on action verbs). For example, focus your resume. If you use a job objective with a keyword profile, remember to make sure that the profile supports your objective.	Don't throw out all you've ever learned about writing formatted paper resumes; the problem-solving concepts also apply to scannable resumes.
Do handle with care shortfalls in experience.

Suppose that the job ad calls for five years' experience in manufacturing technology, and you have only three years, but you have an engineering degree. Computers don't handle the counting of years of experience very well. If you've had two jobs in manufacturing technology but one lasted two years and the other three years, the computer won't add it up. So just say it: "Have five years' experience equivalent: three years' direct experience plus two years' college training in subject." In this technique, use "years' experience in" (apostrophe replaces the preposition "of") instead of "years of experience."

The five years' experience requirement may be somewhat arbitrary. What employers want are skills; if you can come close to the requirement and you've got the skills, you've got an excellent chance of being chosen. | Don't (in an educational shortcoming) put down two dates (the date you started and the date you left college) beside the name of your college. Double dates flag your disqualification as a college graduate. If you're a graduate, the graduation year is enough.

Don't write more years than a job ad asks for. If the job requires five years and you write that you have eight years, some software programs will whiz right by your resume. So write "more than five years' experience." By mimicking the job's requirements, older applicants also get a fair chance to be seen. Suppose you've got 30 years' experience. You still write "more than five years' experience." |
| Do keep your resume updated with new keyworded skills and achievements; computers automatically date and call up the last resume received with your name and telephone number. | Don't send multiple resumes with differing objectives to the same database, using the same name and telephone number — you'll look unfocused. |

(continued)

Table 15-2 *(continued)*

Yes, Do This	*No, Don't Do This*
Do call to follow up and be assured that your resume was received, is in the database, and has been routed to the appropriate line managers. If you can determine which line managers received your resume, try calling them before or after the start of the normal business day.	Don't end your follow-up with a call to a specified number for an employer's automated applicant tracking system. An impersonal inquiry to an automated response system android won't do much to advance your cause.
Do use industry jargon and familiar, standard words that computers are likely to search for. Say "candidate sourcing," not "candidate locating," for example. Some scanning software can come up with synonyms, but other software can't. If you use initials (MIT) in a keyword preface, spell it out later in the text (Massachusetts Institute of Technology).	Don't use unfamiliar words that computers may not be programmed to search for. Industry jargon is an exception to this caution — employers almost always use jargon in searching for the best candidates. They expect you to understand the lingo if you're in the industry.

Fast Key to ASCII: The Plain Text Option

ASCII is pronounced "AS-kee." It's an acronym that stands for *American Standard Code for Information Interchange* and is used to describe *plain text* files that have no graphics, no rule lines, no bullets, no italics, and so on.

No-frills files may be referred to simply as ASCII, or plain text, or ASCII plain text; all three terms mean the same thing — files that can be universally understood by computers everywhere in the world. An ASCII message is straight text and allows for almost no formatting.

ASCII is so dreary in design that even its mother (if it had one) couldn't love it. Even so, almost everyone has been using this one-size-fits-all file to avoid communications miscues between such popular word-processing programs as MS Word and WordPerfect that run on various computer platforms, such as PCs, Macintosh, UNIX workstation, or mainframe terminal.

Although ASCII resumes are heading into the sunset, until the recruiting world is totally living large with handsomely formatted e-resumes, you may be stuck with the plain-Jane look. So here's the drill.

Bad Scannable Resume

WALDO DOOFUS

4400 MacBeth Circle
Central City, CA 94322

Messages: (414)332-2999
Home: (414)332-8765

EXECUTIVE MANAGEMENT ... BUSINESS DEVELOPMENT
MBA

> *Double column, lines, and underscores are risky for computer's eyes.*

> *Even if made scanner readable, where did all this experience occur? What years?*

PROFESSIONAL EXPERTISE

Product Marketing

Sales Management

Business Development

Customer Service

Operations Management

Manufacturing Processes

Material Flow

Inventory Management

Accounting & Finance

Financial Justification

Risk Management

Human Resources

Public Relations

> *Skills will be extracted, but what do they mean?*

> *Total lack of dates plus huge list of functional talents ages candidate.*

EDUCATION:

M.B.A. Degree,
University of La Morris
La Morris, CA

B.S., Accounting/
Business, Catfish &
Crystal College,
Portland, OR

PROFILE

A professional manager with many years of successful business experience gained in private industry, non-profit and government sectors. Accustomed to profit and loss responsibilities. Effective leader with imagination and vision. Marketer of industrial equipment in multi-level channels. Former President/CEO and Regional Sales Manager.

FUNCTIONAL SUMMARY OF EXPERIENCE

General Administration

Thoroughly experienced in managing the efforts of others. Direct leadership involvement in accounting, banking, credit, insurance and risk management. Experience with hiring, training, redirection and safety programs. Examples of general administration accomplishments:

- As President/CEO of a start-up material handling equipment company, exercised full profit and loss responsibility for all operations.
- Planned and implemented company strategy, including selection of product lines, fabrication to accommodate special applications, outsourcing manufacture of component parts.

Marketing & Sales Management

Diversified experience marketing industrial equipment products through established and new independent distributors.
Experienced in all types of product marketing, including cooperative advertising programs, selecting and training new distributors, encouraging and replacing established distributors, interacting with customers; assisting in the bidding process; preparing sales reports and forecasts. Examples of marketing accomplishments:

- As Regional Sales Manager with a major industrial hardware manufacturer, managed annual sales of $1.5 million in five western states while faced with shrinking product offering, many production problems, sales office reallocations and major personnel changes.
- Developed and implemented marketing strategies to maintain profitability as many competitors were failing.

Figure 15-1: Hold on, there! This resume's not ready yet!

Good Scannable Resume

Mark Rawl Michovich

683713 Marilea Circle
Murrieta, CA 92562
(123) 456-7890
e-mail: mmichovich@jjnet.com

Note linear treatment with ample keywords.

OBJECTIVE

Microcomputer network administration/analysis/training

PROFILE

10 years' A+ Certified Computer Service Technician/ Includes laser printer maintenance and repair, network administration, PC hardware and software configuration

- Software: MS DOS, All Windows inc. Windows XP Professional, HTML
- "Excellence in Customer Service" award
- Member and past officer, S. Cal Computer Tech's Association
- Systems integration, analysis and trouble shooting experience
- PC, Macintosh, and multi-user system experience

Professional societies are keywords that employers often search for.

EXPERIENCE

What would have to change to make this a resume to send via e-mail? Answer: Turn solid bullets into asterisks, make type all one size, and substitute uppercase for boldface.

Electrismart Inc.   Moreno Valley, CA   2002 to Present
Consultant/Webmaster

Consultant for local Internet Service Provider (ISP).

- Assist with e-mail setup and configuration.
- Provide instruction for use with Macintosh and IBM/Compatible computers.
- Help new clients with web page design.

FreshImports Inc.   Norco, CA   1998-2001
Marketing and Sales Representative

- Marketing and product management of electronic microcomputer components for electronic manufacturing company.
- Managed all help-desk technical support, troubleshooting (hardware/software), integration and interface to PC compatibles (desktop and notebook), Macintosh and server environments.
- Created support manuals and user guides for proprietary and distributed products. "Improved overall customer service and technical support by 65%" (Employer's quote).

Candidate lacks bachelor's degree, often a requirement. Observe how education is handled for computer scans.

EDUCATION B.S.B.A * - California Baptist College, Pasadena, CA
              * Pursuing, expect to complete in 2008.

Figure 15-2: This baby's ready to roll!

To create a plain text resume, start with your formatted, printable resume. Open your formatted resume, make a copy of the computer file, name it yourname.txt (or anything else with the ".txt" extension) and tell the computer to save it as a *text-only* document.

Alternatively, type your electronic version from scratch in your favorite word-processing program, saving it as a *text-only* document and naming it yourname.txt.

Because your resume now has ASCII for brains, it won't recognize the formatting commands that your word-processing program uses. So be on guard against the common errors in the following sections.

Typeface/fonts

Don't expect a particular typeface or size in your ASCII resume. The typeface and fonts appear in the typeface and size that the recipient's computer is set for. This means that boldface, italics, or different font sizes will not appear in the online plain text version.

Word wrap

Don't use the word wrap feature when writing your resume because it will look as weird as a serial letter "E" running vertically down a page. Odd-looking word wrapping is one of the cardinal sins of online resumes. Set your margins at 0 and 65, or set the right margin at 6.5 inches. Then end each line after 65 characters with hard carriage returns (just press the Enter key) to insert line breaks.

Proportional typefaces

Don't use proportional typefaces that have different widths for different characters (such as Times Roman). Instead, use a fixed-width typeface (such as Courier). Then, you will know that you have a true 65-character line. For example, if you compose and send your resume in Courier 12 and it's received in the Arial typeface, it should still work well with most e-mail programs, surviving transport with a close resemblance to the original line length.

Special characters

Don't use any characters that aren't on your keyboard, such as "smart quotes" (those tasteful, curly quotation marks that you see in this book, not the straight, wooden, inch-mark variety) or mathematical symbols. They don't convert correctly, and your resume will need fumigating to rid itself of squiggles and capital U's.

You know that you're off in the wrong direction if you have to change the preferences setting in your word processor or otherwise go to a lot of trouble to get a certain character to print. Remember that you can use dashes and asterisks (they're on the keyboard), but you can't use bullets (they're *not* on the keyboard).

Although you can't use bullets, bold, or underlined text in a plain text document, you can use plus signs (+) at the beginning of lines to draw attention to part of your document. You can also use a series of dashes to separate sections and capital letters to substitute for boldface. When you don't know what else to use to sharpen your ASCII effort, you can always turn to Old Reliable — white space.

Tabs

Don't use tabs because they get wiped out in the conversion to ASCII. Use your spacebar instead.

Alignment

Don't expect your resume to be full-justified. Your ASCII resume is automatically left-justified. If you need to indent a line or center a heading, use the spacebar.

Attachments

Paste your resume with a cover note (a very brief cover letter) into the body of your e-mail. You can, if you want, also attach a nicely formatted resume.

Page numbers

Don't use page numbers. You can't be certain where the page breaks will fall, and your name and page number could end up halfway south on a page.

Spell check

Don't forget to spell check *before* you save your resume as an ASCII file.

The subject line

The subject line can bring you front and center to a recruiter's attention.

- When responding to an advertised job, use the job title. If none is listed, use the reference number.

- When you send an unsolicited resume, write a short "sales" headline. For example: Bilingual teacher, soc studies/6 yrs' exp. Or, Programmer, experienced, top skills: Java, C++.

   Never just say Bilingual teacher or Programmer. Sell yourself! Keep rewriting until you've crammed as many sales points as possible into your "marquee."

Should you show a "cc" for "copy sent" on your resume? If you're e-mailing a hiring manager (such as the accounting manager), copy the human resources department manager; that saves the hiring manager from having to forward your resume to human resources and is more likely to result in your landing in the company's resume database to be considered for any number of jobs.

Do a Final Check

After you think that your resume is ready to roll, write a short cover note (using the same technical guidelines as for your resume). Leading off with the cover note, cut and paste the text of both your note and resume into the body of an e-mail message. Send the message to yourself and to a friend, and then compare responses. This last check should reveal flaws in your technique, giving you a chance to mend before you send.

Look over the following plain text resume for Della Hutchings (Figure 15-3), and you can see why it should never leave home without a bag over its face.

Plain Text Resume

```
Della Hutchings
890 Spruce Ave.
Las Vegas, NV 22222
945-804-5829
   E-mail: dellah@aol.com
Admin Assist,4 yrs exp, 6 software pgms, time mgt skills

SUMMARY
================================================================
Word. WordPerfect. Lotus. Excel. PageMaker. QuickBooks
Bilingual: Spanish. Time management. Budgeting. Organizational
skills.

EMPLOYMENT
================================================================
University of Upper Carolina               2003-Present
Church Knoll, NC


ASSISTANT TO DIRECTOR OF ACADEMIC TECHNOLOGY
Use and support a wide variety of computer applications
Work with both Macintosh and IBM computers
Communicate with clients in South America
Apply troubleshooting and problem solving skills
Maintain complex scheduling for employer, staff, self
Responsible for dept. budget administration; 100% balanced

Mothers for Wildlife Inc.                  2002-2003
ADMINISTRATIVE ASSISTANT

Edited/wrote newsletter
Organized rallies and letter-writing campaigns
Maintained mailing lists
Saved organization $1,200 changing equipment

EDUCATION
================================================================
University of Upper Carolina at Chapel Hill, NC
BA with honors in International Studies, May 2000

Won Gil award for best honors thesis on Latin America
GPA in Major: 3.8/4.0

AFFILIATIONS
================================================================
Carolina Hispanic Students Association
Amnesty International
Concept of Colors (Multicultural modeling group)

HOBBIES
================================================================
Like details: Writing and Web design

AWARDS
================================================================
On present job: Administrative Assistant of the Month four times
-- 3/03, 8/03, 3/04, 9/05
Recognized for productivity, organization, attention to detail
and interpersonal skills.
```

Figure 15-3: Yikes! What a mess!

E-Forms: Fill in the Blankety-Blanks

The e-form is just a shorter version of the plain text resume, usually found on company Web sites. The company encourages you to apply by setting your plain text into designated fields of the forms on the site.

The e-form is almost like an application form, except that it lacks the legal document status an application form acquires when you sign it, certifying that all facts are true.

Follow the on-screen instructions given by each employer to cut and paste the requested information into the site's template. You're basically just filling in the blanks with your contact information that's supplemented by data lifted from your plain text resume.

Remember that e-forms can't spell check, so cutting and pasting your resume into the e-form body, instead of typing it in manually is your best bet. Because you spell checked your resume before converting it to ASCII (of course, you did!), at least you know that everything is likely to be spelled correctly.

Virtually all company Web sites now encourage you to apply online through their applicant portals. You're asked either to cut and paste your resume or to fill out an online form. Most companies ask you to answer demographic questions about race, gender, and so forth as a way of collecting data for the *Equal Employment Opportunity Commission* (EEOC). You aren't required to include this information to be considered for employment. Nevertheless, women and minorities are well advised to oblige the demographics request. What if you're a white male? Your call.

When you're finished, send your e-form. That's all there is to it. No big deal.

E-forms work well for job seekers in high-demand occupations, such as nursing, but they don't work so well for job seekers who need to document motivation, good attitude, and other personal characteristics and achievements that computers don't search for. When you rely on an e-form to get an employer's attention, you're playing 100 percent on the employer's turf.

A Game Plan for Scannable and Plain Text Resumes

To cover all bases, create multiple versions of your resume. You may never need to provide a scannable or plain text resume, but then again, you might. Plan ahead. Follow this straightforward process:

1. **Write a core resume formatted to flatter your background and styled in an eye-appealing manner with boldface, indentation, underlining, italics, and any graphic features that look good. Use all the action verbs you want.**

   Hold on to this good-looking, formatted resume and take copies with you to job interviews.

   Advantage: SUPER PRESENTABLE.

2. **Working from your formatted resume, strip away the graphic baggage of underlines, italics, designs, and so forth.**

   Advantage: SCANNABLE.

3. **Add muscle to your scannable resume with keywords even if you have to delete some action verbs (check out Chapter 11 for keywords).**

   Advantage: SEARCHABLE.

4. **Working from your scannable resume, convert your resume to plain text (ASCII).**

   Advantage: SENDABLE.

5. **Add a Keyword Summary at the top of your *plain text resume* if it doesn't already have one.**

   Advantage: SALEABLE.

6. **Working from your plain text resume, copy and paste requested data into employers' e-forms posted on their Web sites.**

   Advantage: SPELLCHECKABLE.

Save all versions of your resume on your hard drive, ready to print, revise, update, or e-mail in an instant.

Chapter 16

In Search of an Uncommon E-Resume

"*L*et me try something new!" your inner creative person screams. "I'm comfortable in my skin, and I want to be comfortable in my resume. The colorless, button-down, one-dimensional resume isn't me."

Well, dudes and dudettes, if that's the tune running through your head, you don't want to miss this chapter, which explains the variety of high-tech resume options available.

Before the tour begins, you should know that recruiting professionals discourage atypical resumes, adamantly arguing that they don't work. Recruiting professionals tell me that a mere *5 percent* (or fewer) of e-resumes venture out of the mainstream, and those that do are often ignored.

By *mainstream,* I mean straightforward documents that are fully formatted and technologically born again to ride the online rails as attachments to e-mail (see Chapter 1), usually MS Word attachments. Those, of course, are in addition to mainstream resumes that journey across the Internet, riding not on the rails but inside the cybercar as ASCII plain text documents (see Chapter 15).

But despite the overwhelming body of employment industry insiders — like 95 percent — who advise against being *too* different, you may find just the right uncommon e-resume to entice a recruiter or employer who is in the market for an independent thinker.

Having explained the odds, let the tour begin.

Seven Resumes You Don't See Every Day

Although recruiting professionals generally dismiss off-the-road resumes, you may think one of the following seven creations could carry your message with style.

- ✔ PDF file
- ✔ Web and e-portfolio
- ✔ E-newsletter
- ✔ Beamer
- ✔ Smart card
- ✔ Talker
- ✔ Flash

I explore each type in the following sections.

PDF resume

"PDF" really stands for *portable document format,* but a document using this format comes to readers looking *pretty darned fine* — exactly the way you sent it.

A PDF resume is a *read only* document. That is, it can't get bent out of shape when a reader, say an in-house corporate recruiter, is looking at a resume on a computer monitor, then somehow manages to graffiti it up by dropping a book on the keyboard or inadvertently tapping a key or two and changing the content. A non-PDF resume (a Word attachment, for example) could be altered to a wacky, tacky version and sent downstream to hiring managers who would wonder, "Why am I getting this messy resume?" But a PDF resume won't change — it has the equivalent of a protective coating around it.

PDFs are an invention and trademark of Adobe. You've probably seen online catalogs with all the lines, text, and pictures in the right places and no bulging in the middle — the catalogs were created as PDFs. Now, the technology is increasingly turning up in online resumes.

One reason that it's getting around is that PDFs can be viewed by any computer platform — Windows, Macintosh, even Linux. You can download the latest version of the Adobe Acrobat Reader software for free at adobe.com.

To create your own PDF files (for a resume), you will need to have the Adobe Acrobat program (which unlike the Adobe Acrobat Reader is not free) installed on your computer. You can purchase the latest version from Adobe (adobe.com) for less than $250. Or you can look at online competitive shopping sites such as Cnet.com (cnet.com) for cheaper prices.

To convert your resume into a PDF, first review it to be certain it's precisely the way you want it — very little editing can be done after your resume is effectively "set in stone." Then open MS Word (or the word processor you used to create your resume), open your resume document, and select "Print." Select the PDF print driver as your "printer." This process converts your resume into PDF format viewable by Acrobat Reader.

Readers viewing your attached PDF resume also need the free Adobe Acrobat Reader. You should include a hyperlink in your resume which allows a quick download of the Reader in case the employer or recruiter doesn't already have it.

PDF resumes have experienced a recent surge in popularity. They are particularly attractive to recruiting professionals who spend hours and hours in front of a computer reading coma-inducing ASCII text resumes.

Web resume and e-portfolio

Web resumes — also called HTML resumes — are electronic documents posted on a personal Web site, permitting easy transmission to links of information that flesh out your basic resume facts — samples of your work, for instance. With the right "tags" (like street signs), your resume will appear on numerous search engines and be easily accessible to recruiters and employers. Companies that pride themselves on being "cutting edge" or that do a lot of e-commerce business are prime prospects for Web resume job seekers.

Web resumes, with their links to sound and graphics, are a glamorous alternative to the one-dimensional resume. Although a Web resume can't pop to life in the pages of a book, I have included a heavily-linked version in Figure 16-1 created by Glenn Gutmacher, who teaches advanced online recruiting techniques to companies and staffing agencies. (The resume is real but the dates are fictional.) Gutmacher's resume is lined with links. This version is cut to two pages, and the links are represented by underlined text. You can see the entire resume and click through the links on Gutmacher's Web site, recruiting-online.com.

Web Resume

GLENN S. GUTMACHER
33 Keith Drive, Norton, MA 02766-1868 USA
tel: 508-930-9391 email: findwork@recruiting-online.com
sample project management assignments | Glenn's media credits/speeches
download this resume as: Microsoft Word (.doc) | rich text format (.rtf) | ASCII plain text
(.txt) | Adobe Acrobat (.pdf)

EXPERIENCE:
Recruiting-Online.com, Inc., Norton, MA. President, 9/02 - present.

- Research, develop, market and present _Advanced Online Recruiting Techniques_ seminar in varied formats to associations and recruiters from hundreds of companies of all sizes and industries.
- Official Internet recruiting certification instructor for NEHRA.com (2000), Jobfind.com / Boston Herald (2001) and BostonWorks.com / Boston Globe (2002).
- Created and presented employer and internal group trainings on BostonWorks.com products (4/02 - present).
- Consultant to BostonWorks.com (11/01 - present): E-newsletters strategist and writer; developed and presented training of BostonWorks.com product line to Boston Globe sales staff and select customers; developed job-seeker seminars track and secured roster of presenters and personal career counselors for all BostonWorks job fairs.
- Webmaster: developed and designed numerous web sites (list at www.seedesignworks.com/web)

ReadyAbout Interactive, Boston, MA. Project Manager & Director of Internet Recruiting, 11/00 - 4/02.

- Project manager for various high-end interactive projects (web, CD-ROM, etc.) for external and internal clients from Fortune 500 firms on down, utilizing staff and contracted resources in application development and graphic design. (See annotated descriptions of sample project management assignments.)
- Spearheaded recruiting and applicant tracking efforts, and corporate e-marketing initiatives for the company, including full editorial responsibilities (see www.readyabout.com/newsletter).

VillageGenie.com, Inc. (now ExecuPlanet.com), Boston, MA. Vice President, Content, 3/00 - 10/00.

- Developed content strategy for rich content/functionality modules that are supplied as private label plug-ins to client Web sites. Company acquired by leading outplacement firm, Lee Hecht Harrison.
- Worked closely with Web development vendors towards beta release of product.
- Wrote or co-wrote all copy for corporate Web site and client/investor marketing materials.

Figure 16-1: Sometimes, employment comes through a well-linked resume.

Community Newspaper Co., Needham, MA. Interactive Product Manager and Commercial Content Editor, 10/98 - 3/00.

- Oversaw launch of and maintained CommunityClassifieds.com and its component sites: Town Online *Working* (CNC's career resources Web site for Eastern Massachusetts); ParentandBaby.com (parenting resources); Town Online Real Estate (for *Boston Homes*, *South Shore Homes*, etc.); Town Online Newcomers (Newcomers Guide); and Town Online *Introductions* (online personals).
- Developed and systematized new sources of online content to complement what comes from print publication weekly (e.g., career experts for live chats, special columnists, etc.).
- Wrote and supervised compilation of content from various departments for corporate intranet.

Home Box Office, Inc., New York, NY. Secretary, Area Marketing, 8/96 - 4/98.

- Researched and maintained periodic marketing campaign reports.
- Liaison between HBO corporate departments and regional sales staffs to help handle field issues.

EDUCATION, DISTINCTIONS AND SKILLS:

- Yale University, New Haven, CT. B.A., cum laude, Psychology/Organizational Behavior, 5/96.
- Archibald MacLeish/Garry Trudeau Prize, Yale University. For graphic and literary style in a college newsletter, 5/96.
- MS Office; graphics and publishing software; web site development tools; medium Spanish fluency.

BOARDS AND MEMBERSHIPS:

- Northeast Human Resource Association (NEHRA), Member, 2000 - present and Internet recruiting certification instructor, 2002 - present.
- Maple Common Neighborhood Association, Trustee/Officer, 4/02 - present.
- National Association of College Broadcasters, Providence, RI. Chairman of the Board, 1/95 - 1/96.

OTHER KEYWORDS:

seminar developer, seminar courseware writer, user documentation writer, training course documentation writer, seminar instructor, course instructor, training instructor, seminar trainer, online content editor, online content manager, online content writer, internet content editor, internet content manager, internet content writer, internet recruiting trainer, internet recruiting consultant, marketing collateral writer, print collateral writer, javascript, html, Microsoft Office 2000: word, excel, powerpoint, outlook, project, access; visio, sourcesafe; photoshop, pagemaker, quarkxpress, filemaker pro, infogist, copernic, adobe acrobat, eudora, ulead, quickbooks pro

You can find out everything you ever wanted to know about Web resumes from Rebecca Smith, an online educator living in the Silicon Valley. She didn't invent the breed, but she has certainly been a leading advocate of its use. Smith's site, `eresumes.com`, is robust with tips on how to prepare a Web resume and boasts an extensive gallery of Web resumes categorized by profession.

Web resumes are very useful for people who need to show their work, such as individuals in engineering, architecture, art, or modeling, and when you're working as a free agent marketing your workplace wares on various job sites that cater to contract gigs.

Martin Kimeldorf, an educator and author in Tumwater, Washington, is the godfather of the paper-portfolio-for-all concept (see Chapter 9). In earlier years, only artists and other creative professionals who needed to show their work carried big leather cases filled with work samples to job interviews. In Kimeldorf's reinvention, the portfolio goes to interviews and employee evaluation meetings. Professionals share their portfolios online. Institutions of higher education everywhere have grown enthusiastic about the portfolio concept as a job-hunting tool to give employers a big picture of who their students are.

Your e-portfolio should include, at minimum, says Dr. Randall S. Hansen of Quintessential Careers (`quintcareers.com`), a copy of your resume; skills and abilities; samples of your own work; testimonials and letters of recommendations; awards and honors; conferences and workshops; transcripts, degrees, licenses, and certifications; military records, awards, and badges; and three to five references.

You may want to check out some Web sites that feature portfolio information. Two good ones are the Kimeldorf Portfolio Library (`amby.com/kimeldorf/portfolio`) and Professional Employment Portfolios from the Career Center at Ball State University (`bsu.edu/careers`).

What is the difference between Web HTML resumes and e-portfolios? E-portfolios are so similar to linked-loaded Web resumes that many people say there's little difference. Kimeldorf separates the two by describing the Web resume as a work of words and the e-portfolio as a work of pictures.

"One of my criteria is that the portfolio be primarily visual rather than text-based in conveying its message," Kimeldorf says.

Web resumes and e-portfolios have not caught on broadly across the employment spectrum because they're generally viewed as too time-intensive for recruiters. Even tech-savvy job seekers are advised to use Web resumes as a supplement to one-dimensional versions.

Beamers

Dateline: Resume of the Future Department . . . A *beamer* — or beamable resume — is a quick version of your resume read on a *personal digital assistant* (PDA) or wireless handheld device or digital phone. Your handheld electronic device broadcasts your contact information, qualifications, and experience in a format suitable for a small screen.

Cutting-edge recruiting professionals say that millions of these resumes will silently travel through the airwaves of future conferences, business meetings, and power lunches. Most of the technology already exists, but some standardization issues are yet to be resolved. The potential for the design and delivery of the beamer resume may be enormous. "Beam me up" takes on whole new shades of meaning.

E-newsletters

Knowledge of all things intergalactic isn't a prerequisite to qualify you to send out an e-newsletter as a networking tool for job leads, but knowing what you're talking about is essential.

Fred Pike and Tom Tucker have experimented with e-newsletters (e-mailed to recipients) with encouraging results. Their discovery: The trick is to give something in return for the assistance you hope to get. That something is *information*.

Fred Pike's online newsletter

Pike's four-page communication — *Fred Pike's News from the Job Search Front* — is presented in a layout swimming in white space for easy reading. Small graphics brighten the newsletter throughout, complimenting the editorial content, which offers original philosophical and business-oriented essays.

In an early issue, Pike discussed the topic of "Differentiation" as a marketing tool, explaining how it could help your business succeed. Following the essay, Pike concludes with a brief job pitch, which he amusingly calls "My Shameless Plug," and the graphic is, yes, an electric plug.

After selling a successful business several years ago, Pike now wants back in the game. He explains in "My Shameless Plug" the type of managerial position he's looking for, and he then closes with a polite and warm request for job leads: "If you know any companies where I could be a good fit, or any people I should contact as part of my ongoing networking, please let me know!"

A reader's overall impression is not one of being pressured, but of an opportunity to lend a networking hand to a charming and very knowledgeable job searcher. At press time, Pike was considering two offers.

Tom Tucker's online newsletter

Tips from Tom Tucker opens with a crowd pleaser — a photo of Tucker's classic 1967 Corvette. Tucker's gift to the reader is a collection of important tips for maintaining old cars and airplanes, Tucker's hobby for 25 years.

Sample tip: "Change the engine oil if the car has been in storage for any length of time. Why? (a) Allowing the bearings to set in dirty oil will cause problems later and (b) To insure there is no moisture in the oil so that your engine won't rust internally."

Tucker's newsletter has an engaging feel to it, and quickly after launching, an old college pal who runs a trucking company saw the newsletter and asked Tucker to take a contract stint as his trucking company's safety director until Tucker lands a permanent executive position.

Smart card

A *smart card* is a piece of plastic embracing a microchip capable of storing data, as well as a microprocessor to pass it on to a computer network. The essential smart card is a thirtysomething in the world of technology. Since the 1970s, the smart card been used for a multitude of purposes — from campus meal plans to security key systems to banking debit cards.

Technically, resumes can be adapted to smart cards and swiped through smart card readers to be downloaded into a system. The hitch is that smart card readers are relatively scarce and standardization issues stand in the way. Another concern: Losing your smart card resume is a privacy loss as great as losing your wallet. The smart card as a resume platform is definitely a wait-and-see.

Talkers

The Brits, don't you know, started the talking streak to transform the resume into a multimedia version with voice and video. Known more formally as the talking CV (*curriculum vitae,* explained in Chapter 9), there isn't much difference between the talking CV software model and the video online job interview that I describe in *Job Interviews For Dummies* (Wiley).

After the talking resume (or interview) is completed, you, the owner of the chatty document, give out a private ID and password to recruiters whom you want to view and listen. You can see illustrations of talking CVs at www. talkingcv.com.

This format could take off when broadband online service (Internet technical capacity) becomes widely available.

Flash

Reflecting the ultimate in animated movement and rock-concert audio, this resume product is made possible by Flash software. You never know what theme you'll find on a Flash resume, from space-age motifs to Spiderman to video games.

The Flash resume package may include additional elements, such as a photo (a big no-no in the recruitment world because of possible discrimination) and cover letter. The Flash model isn't for bankers or accountants, but it could net you a job as a Web or club designer.

Creative specialists at video game companies, theme park workplaces, advertising agencies, graphics studios, or virtually any enterprise requiring inventive thinking could find a flash of excitement to be just what the bored recruiter ordered.

Type "Flash resumes" into your favorite search engine for examples and companies that provide the service.

Just When You Thought Resumes Were Boring

The slightly off-kilter but potential star resume presentations described in this chapter prove once again that everything under the sun has not yet been invented.

Part V
Samples of StandOut Resumes

The 5th Wave   By Rich Tennant

"I'm updating my resume to make me appear more youthful. I'm including a street name, what do you like— 'PR-Diddy', 'JJ Kool-Data', or 'Ice-Cubicle'?"

In this part . . .

You find resume samples that have been carefully crafted so you can be inspired by different ways to handle your own StandOut effort. Your resume is your marketing spokesperson. So give it your best.

Chapter 17

A Sampling of StandOut Resumes

In This Chapter

▶ Model resumes for various skill and experience levels

▶ Model resumes for nine different career fields

Prepare to meet the graduates of StandOut boot camp, from entry- to management-level job seekers. Real people wrote the originals of these resumes, but I tore them up and rewrote them to meet StandOut standards. All names and contact information are fictional, but the raw selling power behind every one is real.

Although StandOut formats (illustrated by the templates in Chapter 9) are loaded with sell-power, they're by no means rigid — not every section heading works for every resume. Choose your section headings carefully to flaunt your strengths.

In the interest of not chopping trees, I chopped material — that is, some resumes in this chapter would have been two pages had I not eliminated text. Occasionally, as another conservation measure, I used ampersands (&) to replace the word "and." Should you use ampersands on your own resume? Yes, but very gingerly. Ampersands are okay for

▸ Company names

▸ Copyrights

▸ Logos

▸ Phrases common in the targeted industry, such as "P & L Statements" (Profit & Loss)

Otherwise, spell out the word "and."

This chapter gives you a selection of StandOut model resumes.

Assistant Retail Manager
ACCOMPLISHMENT

Contact data too close together to scan.

Jack Straw

2424 Heavensent Lane, Wichita, Kansas 67056   (316) 446-5513   E-mail: jstraw@aol.com

OBJECTIVE
Position as **assistant retail manager** using my eight years of experience in retail, technical sales, and software experience.

SUMMARY
- Hard-won and successful experience in many aspects of retailing: sales, marketing, operations, training, and service.

- Can open and manage retail software and other technical products. Qualified as assistant manager of retail store; qualified as department manager of superstore. Managed new retail location ranking in top ten of 64 stores within first year.

- Internet/World Wide Web merchandising start-up study.

Web merchandising is buzzword; "start-up study" means Straw studied topic, is ready to implement new selling technology for new employer.

HIGHLIGHTS OF SKILLS

- Opening, operating **new locations**
- **Growing sales:** make **customer first**
- **Budgeting, extending credit**
- **Recruiting** and interviewing
- **Training** and retraining staff
- **Telemarketing**
- Product display
- Promotion, advertising strategies
- **Software licensing, electronics, purchasing**

- All major **point-of-sale equipment**
- **Computer skills:** PCs and Macs; General Store, Excel, Lotus 1-2-3, QuickBooks, Aldus PageMaker, CAD, CorelDraw, Desktop Publisher, Superpaint, Windows Office including Word.
- **Internet skills:** World Wide Web, e-mail, FTP

Can be made computer friendly by eliminating vertical design lines.

PROFESSIONAL EXPERIENCE

Video Tape Tub, La Costa, KS -- Customer Representative   2003-Present
Customer service, product display, inventory maintenance, video rentals and returns. "Best help I've had in five years" (Owner Cal Showers).

Custom Names, Delmar, KS -- Consumer Service Representative   2002
Extensive retail sales and technical support for software, computer equipment, satellite TV, electronics and home theater equipment. Maintained average monthly sales of $30,000, ranking fourth in sales. Heavy telemarketing component.

(1 of 2)

Jack Straw

The Cutting Edge, Rancho, KS -- Assistant Manager   2000-2002
Serviced upscale clientele in high-end software, electronics and video game retail store. Handled sales, purchasing, staff training, work schedules, product inventory and display, technical support for electronics and software, bank deposits and staff management.

Software Bug, Carlsbad, KS -- Night Manager   1997-2000
Evening management of software retail store. Innovative sales strategies brought store from 47th in sales ranking to 8th in a 64-store chain. Other work: employee recruiting and dismissal, training, retraining, scheduling, staff management, technical support. Awarded Employee of Month four separate months.

Temp-a-Medic, La Jolla, CA -- Healthcare Staffer   1996-1997
Matched healthcare temps with hospitals in Los Angeles and San Diego. Developed organizational skills, calm resilience when chaos threatened and acceptance of high-pressure, detail-reliant environment. Sold new accounts at seven hospitals.

EDUCATION

62 academic hours toward bachelor's degree; have kept nose to grindstone taking 3-6 hours per semester for past five years. Anticipate testing out of 18 hours; expect degree June, 2008.

VOLUNTEER AND PERSONAL EXPERIENCE

-- Coach, Roller Hockey Little League of North County. Coached winning North (San Diego) County team of more than 30 youths, ages 7-12. Grateful for opportunity to develop strong interpersonal, cross-generational, cross-cultural and community networks. Proven talent with teamwork, organization, people of various economic classes.

-- Interests include computers, electronics, ice hockey, computer drafting and freehand illustration.

> Straw's goal is completion of college degree. To indicate intent to enroll for more than 3 to 6 hours per semester while working in retailing, noted for long hours, would be risky.

(2 of 2)

Chemist
PROFESSIONAL

DIXON MARBEND
123 Moon Road, Flanders, New Jersey, 07836 (201) 584-0150

Chemist ← *Objective replaced with job title, summary follows – personalizes the format.*

Six years' research experience with increasing responsibility and successful record of instrumentation and scientific achievement. Specialty: Silicon. Designed computer systems (mainframe to micro) for laboratory instrument automation, including patented design. Published presenter.

EDUCATION

- Ph.D., Chemical Design & Engineering, University of Rochester, Rochester, New York. Dissertation: Manipulation of Luminescent Porous Silicon Structures
- Master of Science, Chemistry, University of Rochester, Rochester, New York
- Bachelor of Science, Physics, Honors, University of New Jersey-Elizabeth, Elizabeth, New Jersey

EXPERIENCE AND ACCOMPLISHMENTS

Quantifies achievements and responsibilities.

2000-Present **Research Assistant, University of Rochester, Rochester, N.Y.**
- Patented procedure for "Engineering of Luminescent Images on Silicon" and coauthored seven publications (see addendum).
- Conducted research investigations of luminescent silicon, and spearheaded procedure for abricating structures with photoelectricity; managed staff of 5 assistants.
- Delivered 14 presentations of results and research in progress to professors in department.
- Tutored 37 undergraduates in research and chemistry theory, increasing teaching skills.
- Purchased $79,000 in chemicals and equipment for starting research lab .

1999-2000 **Research Assistant, University of New York, New York City**
- Built non-vibrating 1.5 ton aluminium platform for NMR management. ← *Shows results of achievements.*
- Assisted professor with construction of super-conducting NMR spectrometer.
- Designed and manufactured integrated circuits in lab.

Minimizes less relevant jobs.

1999 **Research Assistant, University of New Jersey-Elizabeth, Elizabeth, N. J.**
- Investigated methods for feature distortion in scanning tunneling microscopy.

1998-1999 **Laboratory Assistant, University of New York, New York City**
- Prepared and maintained delicate equipment and chemicals for chemistry labs, ensuring maximum performance and efficiency.
- Worked with 57 teacher assistants and students, developing training skills.

Skills section added to format, enhancing abilities and using more keywords.

TECHNICAL SKILLS

Steady state photoluminescence	Machining aluminum and Plexiglas
Raman, FTIR and UV-Vis spectroscopy	Macintosh: Word, KaleidaGraph,
Inert atmosphere (Schlenk and dry box)	Canvas, Aldus PageMaker, MacDraw,
Standard electrochemistry/photochemistry	Hypercard, Chem 3D, Excel, Internet
AFM, STM, and SEM	

(1 of 2)

Dixon Marbend   **(201)584-0150**

PUBLICATIONS

"Engineering of Luminescent Images on Silicon." Marbend, U.S. Patent No.1,234,567; Jan 1, 2005

"Silicon Technology." Saynor and Marbend in 2004 *Martin-Marietta Yearbook of Science Technology*; Martin-Marietta: New York, N.Y. 2003, 123-4

"Optical Cavities in Silicon Film." Saynor, Curbin, and Marbend in *Electrochemic Journal*, 2003, 21

"Emission from Etched Silicon." Marbend and Piner in *Material Research Symposium*, 2003, 12, 3456-7

"Color Image Generation on Silicon." Marbend and Saynor in *Chemical Science*, 2002, 123, 4567-8

"Porous Silicon Micro-Dension." Marbend and Saynor in *Physics Applied*, 2002,45, 678-9

"Stoichiometric Cadmium Electrodeposition." Krass and Marbend, *MaterialChem*, 2001, 1, 23

HONORS, MEMBERSHIPS & PRESENTATIONS

Chemical Symposium Research Fellow, Undergraduate Honors Fellows, Winter Research Fellow

Chemical Symposium, Chemical Alliance, Electrochemistry Association

Marbend, Saynor and Curbin. *Emission from Etched Silicon*. Presented at 123rd Chemical Symposium, Detroit, Michigan, January 2005

Marbend. *Porous Silicon Micro-Dension*. Presented at 234th Chemical Alliance, New York City, New York, January 2003

New scanning software reads italics; old ones do not. Marbend telephoned recruiter to determine scanning software. When old programs are used, Marbend substitutes a second version of his resume, replacing italics with quotes around same typeface used in rest of resume.

(2 of 2)

Health Club Manager
REVERSE CHRONOLOGICAL

Hilda Larson
347 Appleview Drive, Chicago, IL 60611
(312) 555-9876

*** CONFIDENTIAL ***
Work (brief messages only) (312) 555-9876

Larson leads with graduate degree because health clubs are subject to legal liability for client injuries, aggravated by employees without formal credentials.

Larson's boss doesn't know she's job-hunting; note "Confidential" and work telephone number with mention to keep calls to arrangement-making only.

Objective and Qualifications:

Health and Fitness Industry Management: Master's and undergraduate degree in Health and Fitness. Eight years' individual and group health education and exercise leadership. Extensive background in equestrian skills, dance, gymnastics, martial arts, swimming, and strength work. Use wellness and preventive-medicine techniques.

Professional Experience:

5/01-Present University of Chicago Center for Disease Research & Health, Chicago, IL
- **Health Promotion Specialist, Researcher, Exercise Physiologist**
Provide monthly nutrition testing and counseling to 120 individuals, 300 in group. Conduct health and fitness classes -- 350 per month. Organization and promotion skills recognized with selection for Health Promotion Coordinator to Chicago Executive Program.

10/99-5/01   Wheaton College Health and Fitness, Wheaton, IL
- **Instructor and Program Consultant**
Produced bimonthly newsletter, wellness counseling, and campus-wide publicity, leading to 25% membership increase in health and fitness club in 3 months.

11/99-5/01   Fitness Plus Enterprises, Inc., Winnetka, IL
- **Personal Fitness Trainer, Group Exercise Instructor**
Taught group exercise classes and designed personal fitness programs for 550 individual clients. Popular trainer among special groups (disabled and elderly).

5/99-7/99   Aerobics Activity Center, Winnetka, IL
- **Assistant to the Associate Director**
Designed activity program, teaching, lecturing, and performing market research.

9/98-5/99   University of Chicago, Chicago, IL
- **Graduate Teaching Fellow**
Designed and taught. Advised 24 independent study projects for undergraduate students. Wrote two proposals to Health/Fitness Department Chair, initiating development of new graduate instruction program; result $5,000 grant from school.

(1 of 2)

Hilda Larson   (312) 555-9876

Education:

Master of Health Science, Health Education Concentration, University of Chicago, 2000
Bachelor of Science, Honors, Kinesiology, Adult Fitness Concentration, University of Chicago, 1996
Guest Scholar, Physical Education Professional Division, University of Chicago, Winter and Spring 1999

> It's okay to list the education section on the 2nd page because Larson refers to it in the qualifications section.

Certifications:

2003   Exer-Safety Associates Step/Bench Certification
2001   American College of Sports Medicine Health and Fitness Instructor
2000   American Council on Exercise Certified Personal Trainer

Presentations:

- University of Chicago Executive Program, Summer 2003 and 2004
- Sport Cardiologists and Nutritionist National Conference, Spring 2000
- Buen Salud Annual Gathering, Mexico City, Mexico, Spring 2000
- University of Chicago Individual Fitness Design, Fall 1999

Conferences:

- World Fitness IDEA International Conference, Las Vegas, NV, 2004
- IDEA Personal Trainer's Conference, San Jose, CA, 2003
- Regional Northeast Wellness Conference, Boston, MA, 1999

Awards and Honors:

- Academic Honors, University of Chicago, 1993 and 1994
- Harriet Wilson Award for Kindness and Receptivity to Others, 1991
- Cross Cultural Awareness Award for Achievement in Cross Cultural Skills, 1991
- Varsity Letters in Dance and Gymnastics, University of Chicago, 1991
- Honored as "Outstanding in public relations and efficiency," 1997
- National Amateur Champion at the National Horse Show, Madison Square Garden, 1991

> Despite national standing in equestrian skills, urban health clubs aren't known for horse stables, thus award is placed last. Yet such a prominent skill can't be omitted -- further, recruiter may be a rider and identify with Larson.

(2 of 2)

Nonprofit Manager
REVERSE CHRONOLOGICAL

MARSHA ANN WHITELAND

231 Montrose Heights
Manchester, NH 03104

(603) 456-9876
E-Mail: mwhite@mci.mail.com

> Nonprofits struggle for funds; a manager who is an attorney is a value-added candidate — a resume opener.

....

NONPROFIT MANAGER-ATTORNEY: Significant experience with urban issues and nonprofit organizations. Successful manager of complex multimillion-dollar programs requiring constant attention to bottom line. Skilled advocate effective in stressful environment requiring personal diplomacy mediation among conflicting groups.

....

PROFESSIONAL EXPERIENCE

STANFORD RESOLUTION, INC., Montpelier, Vermont

Senior Counsel, Professional Liability Section, June 2004 to present

> Quantifies all achievements.

> Upward mobility shown by dividing jobs by heading.

Manage professional liability (34 members including section chiefs, attorneys, paralegals, and clerical staff), and substantive legal work involving approximately 175 failed savings and loans. Close investigations, bring suit, and settle litigation. "With Marsha in charge, we are a legal powerhouse!" -- Jack Ricemaster, Co-Senior Counsel.

Counsel, Professional Liability Section, November 1998 to May 2004

> Quantifies all achievements.

Managed investigation and litigation of civil claims against 25+ failed savings and loans, as well as liaisoned with attorneys, accountants, brokers, appraisers, insurers, and fidelity bond companies; supervised investigators and counsel, assuring cost-effectiveness. Budgeted more than $15 million for S&L project. Coordinated with federal agencies: Department of Justice, Office of Thrift Supervision, and Federal Deposit Insurance Corporation.

OSWALD, LEICHT, AND SCHULTZ, Washington, D.C.
Associate, September 1996 to September 1998

Focused civil litigation on real estate issues, HUD regulations, and franchise laws.

> Minimizes less pertinent jobs.

LEAGUE OF FEMALE CITIZENS' FUND, Washington, D.C.
Project Director, October 1992 to September 1996

> Includes apt volunteer services in work history.

Directed 100+ volunteers in national Community Development Block Grant Monitoring Project; executed volunteer training program; organized national conference allowing volunteer participant conferences with officials of Department of Justice and Housing and Urban Development resulting in grant extensions.

> Shows results with achievements.

EDUCATION

STANFORD LAW SCHOOL, Juris Doctorate, Bar Admission, Washington, D.C.

NEW HAMPSHIRE UNIVERSITY, Bachelor of Arts, Urban Studies, Magna Cum Laude

Speech-Language Pathologist
PROFESSIONAL and TARGETED

Brian N. Hawes
123 Northumbridge Avenue Nashville, Tennessee 37203
(615) 456-7891   E-mail bhaw@aol.com

Replaces objective with job title. → **Speech-Language Pathologist**

EDUCATION

1996 to 1998, and 2000   **University of Tennessee, Chattanooga, TN**
Ph.D., 1993; dissertation pending.
Minor: Audio/Visual Media, G.P.A.: 4.00   *Includes top achievements.*
Awarded assistantship for clinical research.

1994 to 1995   **Wolgrel University, Bartlett, TN**
Master of Science in Speech-Language Pathology, Minor: Psychology, G.P.A.: 4.00
Wrote and produced radio and television commercials and promotional videos.

1985 to 1989 and 1995   **Tuskeegee University, Tuskeegee, TN**
Bachelor of Arts in Language, Minor: History, G.P.A.: 3.86
Graduated summa cum laude, after three study-abroad terms, serving as multimedia laboratory
assistant, student government representative, and club president.

Skips summary— saved for cover letter.

Shows extra-curricular achievements.

PROFESSIONAL EXPERIENCE AND ACCOMPLISHMENTS

1997 to Present   **Radius Vox Laboratories, Millington, TN**   Director
Describes prestigious employer. Firm delivers computer and video imaging and audio signal analysis (voice spectrography). Marketing
targets hundreds of physicians and healthcare providers treating laryngeal, craniofacial dental, and
neurologic disorders.

1996 to 1997   **University of Tennessee, Chattanooga, TN**   Lecturer, Researcher
Restructured research laboratory, adding new facilities for voice analysis, videoendoscopy, and
biofeedback. Employed sound spectrography, stroboscopy, photography, and electrophysiologic
measurement techniques. Lectured to 233 linguists on articulation and voice disorders analysis.
Supervised Orofacial Clinic (staff of 37), developed familiarity with fiberoptic endoscopy,
videofluoroscopy, and nasometry.   *Quantifies achievements.*

1995 to 1997   **The Sound & Sight Center, Bartlett, TN**   Speech-Language Pathologist
Provided assessment and therapy to over 3,000 patients (neurologic, orofacial, vocal and pediatric).
Designed medical forms and computer-based therapy, decreasing procedure time by 30%. Coordinated
patient referral plans with local medical centers.   *Shows industry knowledge.*

OTHER SKILLS AND CERTIFICATIONS
Computer: Windows (latest version), numerous applications, Microsoft certified, AI (Prolog), SAS, and SPSS.
Specialized Certifications: American Speech Association, International Association of Forensic Phonetics,
Association of Phonetic Sciences, Zertifikat Deutsch, Goethe Institute Summer Abroad Fellowship, and Lake
Search and Rescue Team. Licensed Tennessee Speech-Language Pathologist, FCC Radiotelephone Operator's
Permit.

Financial Executive
LINEAR

Contact information placed on right so it can be read easily when recruiter thumbs through a stack of resumes.

Diana Carter
12 Wollenstromcraft Way
Princeton, NJ 07921
(908) 345-6789
dcart@aol.com

Objective: FINANCIAL MARKETS MANAGEMENT POSITION

Experience:

Great Eastern Bank, Princeton, NJ   July 2000-July 2005
Second Vice President -- Global Markets Project Manager
• Developed, outlined, and scheduled 98 conferences covering spectrum of financial risk management issues
• Launched 53-page quarterly newsletter on new products and fluctuations. Researched and edited copy from technical specialists and regulatory agencies
• Expanded circulation of client newsletter more than 500% in three years
• Managed $1.2 million budget and monitored department expenses
• Provided marketing support for Senior Vice President
• Traveled to Hong Kong, Singapore, and London delivering educational seminars on derivative products and uses
• Administered 17 bank personnel policies for seven staff members
• Directed office closure due to downsizing

Divides job by title, emphasizing upward mobility.

Reason for leaving okay here — widespread banking mergers.

Assistant Treasurer -- Global Risk Managment Project Coordinator
• Assisted establishment of Risk Management Education & Marketing department
• Created presentation materials for over 30 conferences and education programs in 2001
• Promoted to Project Manager/Second Vice President

PC Leaser Inc., Newark, NJ   November 1997-June 2000
Assistant Vice President
• Negotiated and prepared loan documentation for 23 financing lease transactions
• Scheduled and finalized fundings with 15 financial institutions

Trims down less relevant jobs to focus resume on target job.

Computer Borrowers Corporation, New York City, NY   May 1996-November 1997
Lease Finance Administrator
• Managed company's secured credit lines, market activity, and interest rates
• Arranged financing for transactions up to $2 million and interim financing for all leases
• Served as financial liaison with 5 departments within the company

Education:

Graduate School of Management, University of New York, New York City
• Currently pursuing an MBA (part-time), credits earned: 38 of 60
Cambridge College, Cambridge, MA
• Bachelor of Arts in Sociology, May 1993

GPA not high, thus not mentioned.

Nuclear Engineer
REVERSE CHRONOLOGICAL

Anthony T. Barbosa

Graceland Avenue
St. Louis, MO 677777
319.789.3393 Home
319.366.2525 Cell
atbarbosa@earthlink.net

CONFIDENTIAL RESUME

Also a keyword resume; no keyword summary but keywords throughout — good technical jargon

EXPERIENCE

Text is well separated from horizontal lines; asterisks (rather than solid bullets) make it easy transfer to plain text.

| 2005-Present | Giant Power & Light Co. | St. Louis, MO |

Reactor Operator Candidate, Hot License Class 97-01

* Chosen by management to attend Reactor Operator-Hot License class 97-01

* Passed the National BWR GFES Exam with a score of 93%

| 2001-2005 | Giant Power & Light Co. | St. Louis, MO |

Auxiliary Operator Nuclear - A

Entire resume stresses accomplishment, impressive striving to demonstrate skills.

* Member of operations unit which upgraded the San Bern Nuclear Plant from a forced shutdown condition on the NRC watch list to both NRC SALP-1 and INPO-1 ratings, company dual unit record breaking performance, and established world records for BWR single and dual unit continuous operations.

* Operated reactor, turbine, and auxiliary support systems to support the safe, reliable, economical, and environmentally sound production of power.

* Selected by operations management as one of three operators for extended assignments as Radwaste Control Operator, to pursue system, operational and programmatic upgrades. Received awards for results produced in this area.

Note how candidate divides tenure at a single employer into segments reflecting advancement.

* Developed several computer programs to assist the operations unit with managing operator exposure and error free performance.

| 2001-2002 | Giant Power & Light Co. | St. Louis, MO |

Radiological Engineer

* Developed a remote valve decontamination device that saved the utility in excess of $450,000 of critical path time during its first use.

* Performed a hydrogen water chemistry impact study to determine the impact of increased injection hydrogen rates on site exposure.

* Designed the containment and developed procedures used for the recovery of a damaged Americium-Beryllium neutron calibration source.

Anthony T. Barbosa
Page 2

| 1998-2000 | Nuclear Associates | Various sites |

Health Physics Supervisor/Lead Technician

* Clemente Nuclear Generating Station, Towanda, GA (BWR)

* Paired with GE on full system decon (fuel installed) testing for EPRI

* Heddon's Fort, Cincinnati, OH (PWR)

| 1997-1998 | Careful Waste Management, Inc. | Tampa, FL |

Field Chemist

* Supervised packaging and shipping of hazardous materials

* OSHA 40-HR Hazmat trained

* On-call emergency supervisor/safety officer for field ops

| 1989-1997 | U.S. Navy | Bangor, WA |

Engineering Watch Supervisor/Lead Engineering Lab Tech

* Managed 13-man engineering watch section in port/underway for Trident sub

* Supervised chemistry and radiological control department

* Article 108 rad con monitor

* Navy prototype staff instructor

EDUCATION

New York Regents is a well-regarded distance education institution; candidate studied while aboard submarine.

| 2005 | Virginia Polytechnic University | Blackburn, VA |

Bachelor of Science in Nuclear Engineering

* GPA 3.8/4.0

| 1999 | New York Regents College | Albany, NY |

Associate Degree in Liberal Arts

INTERESTS

* Competitive offshore sailing, computers, bicycling, backpacking, Frisbee dog competition.

Personal interests convey image of competitiveness, technology priority, yet rounded out with healthful activities.

Business Specialist
REVERSE CHRONOLOGICAL/PLAIN TEXT

This one-page resume is shown for technique; in real life, elaborate on skills, name software, explain skills claims. Back up your brags. Remember, digital resumes can be longer than paper resumes.

ALBERTO LAFUENTE
7806 Palm Drive
Plano, TX 70890
(832) 704-2694
e-mail: alf@newbiz.com
www.newbiz.com

Skills summary at top, skills summary at end: Resume is stuffed with skills, just what computers feed on.

NEW BUSINESS SPECIALIST
>>>

Client relationship management. Client planning. Product
Development. Marketing materials. Capitalization. Venture funding.
Start-up specialist.

EXPERIENCE

Sawyer Enterprises, Inc. Kansas City, MO
Director of Marketing
2003-2005

No mention that company folded.

Founding principal in this health-product corporation. Produced
300% revenue increase in second year of operation from six-figure
base. Travel up to 75%, including distributor contact and
training, site demos, trade shows.
* Sourced medical and technical services.
* Wrote company marketing plans.
* Served on executive team.
* Brought in company's largest contract, $875,000.
* Bid with procurement contracts from government; 45% success.

Contintentwide Bank   Kansas City, MO
New Business Account Executive
2001-2003
Responsible for soliciting large corporate accounts and loans;
enlarged base by $2.8 million. Hired and trained associates.

EDUCATION

The Ohio State University   Columbus, Ohio
Bachelor of Arts, History
2001
Continuing Education:
Marketing, Sales, Finance, Accounting
2002-Present

HARD SKILLS
PC programs: word processing, spreadsheets (accounting and
analysis). Heavy Internet research skills. Technology savvy.

SOFT SKILLS
Communications: technical information to technical and
nontechnical managers. Bilingual (English and Spanish).

Information Technology
REVERSE CHRONOLOGICAL/PLAIN TEXT

Plain text resume can go over the Net and slide right into a scannable database.

GEORGIA K. ESTRADA
107 Begonia Terrace
Lexington, MA 02165
Cell Phone: (617) 999-0808
Email: gkestrada@bu.edu

Giving mobile phone number is a good idea; adds immediacy to contact.

JOB OBJECTIVE
++
MICROSOFT WINDOWS OR NETWORK PROTOCOL DEVELOPMENT

SKILLS
++
C, C++, CGI, CScript, DOS, HTML, HTTP, Java, Javascript, MFC, SQL,
SSI+, TCP/IP, UNIX, Lotus, Visual Basic, Visual C++, WebDBC,
Windows, Windows XP Professional, Windows .NET Enterprise Server,
Microsoft Small Business Server

EMPLOYMENT
++
Clarion Systems, Inc.   2005-Present
PROGRAMMER
Develop, maintain, and monitor product-building tools and
processes using Visual C++ and MFC on Win NT 4.0. Began as intern;
promoted to regular status job.

Wonderwheels, Inc.   09/2004-01/2005
JUNIOR SOFTWARE ENGINEER
Internship: Team member responsible for design and development of
MS Project 2002. Implement code to improve application's
performance. Enhance GUI features, assist in test and troubleshoot
application.

RHI Labs, Inc.   05/2004-08/2005
APPLICATION PROGRAMMER
Co-op job: Designed and developed two project tracking programs
using MS SQL, Javascript, and HTML. Member of team to maintain,
enhance, and create NTSQL server applications. Tested programs,
gathered user requirements, and created help documentation and
released applications.

Boston University Computer Sci. Dept.   2002-2006
PROGRAMMING ASSISTANT/TEACHING ASSISTANT
Assisted undergraduate students in C & C++ programming. Provided
technical support and acted as lab assistant. Projects: Java
Poker Game, War Gamescore, Inventory Database Manager, Assembler
and Linker.

EDUCATION
++
Boston University
Boston, MA
BACHELOR OF ARTS COMPUTER SCIENCE - May 2005.
GPA: 3.75; Attended on 4-year partial scholarship; internships

Chapter 18

A Sampling of Special Needs Resumes

*H*aving to fight to advance your career isn't unusual — neither are the job-war wounds on your resume. Many people who seek employment today have a few special issues that should be stamped "handle with care."

New graduates and reentry homemakers need jobs but lack extensive paid experience. Career changers, including ex-military personnel, face the challenge of transferring skills and learning entire new job languages. Seasoned aces may have "too much" experience, and must defend themselves against being labeled "overqualified." People who have gaps in their records, who were demoted down the power chain, or who were exposed to too many temporary jobs must manage their resumes to sell skills rather than experience.

The following model resume samples generally match the templates in Chapter 9. In some instances, the sample section headings may not match the templates exactly. The templates contain the whole range of heading options, so you can pick and choose the best way to market your unique needs and interests.

Gap in History
TARGETED

> Computer can't read graphic or shading; name will not retrieve. For human eyes only.

Paula G. Cramer
271 Redus Ave.
Mustang, OK 73064, (405) 123-4567

OBJECTIVE: KELLEY-KENNEDY PRINTING COMPANY PRODUCTION MANAGER
to use 12 plus years of print production management experience and graphic art knowledge

QUALIFICATIONS SUMMARY
- Handle all print project phases from design through prepress to final
- Budget management — competent, careful
- Education (college degree plus seminars) in management backs up experience-based skills

SKILLS SUMMARY

Desktop Publishing	Staff Management
Color Separation Technology	Vendor Contract Negotiations
WP Suite, Lotus 123, MS Office XP, QuarkXPress,	Purchasing
PageMaker, Internet, All Word-Processing Software	Blueline Approvals

> Good treatment of two gaps — the first one was nearly three years, the other was six months. You have to read carefully to find the gaps because they are buried in the copy.

ACCOMPLISHMENTS AND EXPERIENCE

Lewisburg Marketing, Inc., Ada, OK
PRODUCTION MANAGER AND PRINT BUYER (Direct Mail):
Managed direct mail print production from design development through mail date for 40+ concurrent projects, meeting deadlines for 2.5 million per week, 12/96-3/00
- Directed prepress, design review, proofing, blueline approval, layout, print and finishing schedules. Insured compliance with U.S. Postal requirements.
- Purchased for all job components and effectively managed $13 million annual budget; price and contract copywriters, designers, and printer negotiations.

The Maupin Company, Edmond, OK
PRODUCTION COORDINATOR AND PLANNER
Planned and executed print production needs for clients, coordinated efforts of Account Executive, Designers, and Production Staff, 4/95-6/96
- Managed estimating, purchasing, job production layout, and projects submission to graphic design, camera and stripping, providing proofreading, scheduling, and blueline approvals, working closely with press room manager to meet delivery deadlines.

PRIOR EXPERIENCE

Investment Litho Company, Edmond, OK
GENERAL ASSISTANT
Worked part-time throughout college. Learned printing business from master printers, 6/88-6/92

EDUCATION Bucknell University, Ada, OK - B.S. in Business and Marketing, 1991
Massbank Management Institute, Edmond, OK - 12 seminars, management

College Intern
HYBRID

This resume puts all contact data on the same line although general scanning rules call for separate lines; newer systems will read one line, but put a minimum of six spaces between address, telephone, and e-mail.

Hard-sell language omits Chinese proficiency and is designed to counteract employer's potential assumption that Davidson (in USA on student visa) will return to Asian nation. Otherwise, bilingualism should appear in objective. Using professors' names and testimonials encourages further interest.

Alexander Davidson

36 W. Garnet #4   Pacific Beach, CA 92012   (619) 435-5555   E-mail: alexd@ddd.edu

Objective   **Internship or career-related summer position in Electrical Engineering;**
"Highly motivated — an all-American go-getter" (says professor Bob Smith) ...
"Fast-learning, earnest and hard-working graduate student" (professor Joan Roberts) ...
"Smart, friendly, outgoing — real stick-to-it-iveness" (professor Tim Horrell)...

Education   San Diego State University, San Diego, CA
Degree: Masters of Science in Engineering   Major: Electrical Engineering
GPA: 3.0/4.0   Graduation: December 2005

Degree: Bachelor of Science   Major: Electrical Engineering
GPA: 3.86/4.0   Minor: Mathematics
Honors: Magna Cum Laude   Graduation: May 2004

Honors   National Dean's List, Dean's List at San Diego State University, Member of College's National Engineering Honor Society, Member of Alpha Chi National Honor Society

Software Skills   MathCAD, MathLab, Pspice, Microcap, Fortran, Altera Logic Design System, programming M68HC11 microcontroller using Assembly language, C Language and other software utilities (word processing, spreadsheets)

Includes keywords in skills and courses sections.

Relevant Courses
- Systems, Signals and Noise
- Data Communications
- Fiber Optics Communication
- Digital Image Processing
- Random Signal Theory 1 and 2
- Transform Theory and Application
- Digital Spectral Analysis
- Communication Network Design

Work   **Tutoring Lab Supervisor**   **Experience**   San Diego
State University   Fall 2000-present
- Tutor students in Engineering, Mathematics, and Science courses

Assistant Engineer
Rilerad Projects Engineering, Hong Kong   Summers 2000-2004
- Collected data from engineers, produced progress reports
- Assisted bidding team, preparing documents and breakdown quotations

Administrator
National Service Hong Kong Armed Forces   March 1995-June 2000
- Scheduled military training and vocational upgrading courses
- Improved mobilization system to increase Reserve Corps processing rate during mobilization exercise

Activities   Vice President, Institute of Electrical and Electronic Engineers (IEEE), student chapter
Secretary of student chapter of National Society of Professional Engineers (NSPE)
Society of Physics Students
Intercultural Club
Intramural sports at San Diego State University
Fluent in Chinese

This is not a StandOut resume. What's wrong? Hint: Other than GPA, not high at master's level, where are measurements? Where are achievements? How could this resume be kicked up a couple of notches?

Career Changer
PROFESSIONAL & KEY WORD

REANNA DUMON

123 Dane Street, Portland, OR 97504

(503) 456-7891

E-mail: rdumo@aol.com

Qualifications Highlights:

Seek physical therapist position using eight years' physical therapy and nursing experience in Canada, Switzerland, and the United States. Fluent in French, English, and Spanish. Trauma life-support, ECG, pediatrics, obstetrics, emergency and general nursing, internal medicine.

Includes keywords in summary.

Education:

- Laval University, Quebec, Canada, Physical Therapy Certificate, 2003-2005
- Ste-Foy College, Ste-Foy, Quebec, Canada, D.E.C. in Technical Nursing (equivalent to RN diploma in U.S.), 1992-1995
- Garneau College, Ste-Foy, Quebec, Canada, D.E.C. in Physical Therapy, 1988-1990

Experience:

Ungava Hospital, Nunavik, Canada, 2000-20XX
- Designed 25-page physical therapy clinic manual distributed to injured patients regarding methods of therapy and preventative procedures to eliminate further injury.
- Nurse: Clinical work: physical therapy, pediatric, obstetrical, and long-term follow-ups, child vaccination, laboratory procedures, home visiting, physical exams, medical evacuations, mutidisciplinary case discussions.
     Community Health: school vaccination programs.
     Administration: patient transfers, medical visits, arranging meetings.

Includes keywords in job descriptions.

Ungava Hospital, Nunavik, Canada, 1998-2000
- Coordinated physical therapy schedule and program for 16 patients.
- Pediatrics, obstetrics, general medicine nurse. Monitored staff of 30 pediatric nurses; managed 57 patients.
- Coordinated schedule for 37 nurses in general medicine unit, maximizing hospital efficiency in patient care and personal organizational skills.

Canntonnal Hospital of Fribourg, Fribourg, Switzerland, 1997-1998

Gives results.

- Nurse, Department of Internal Medicine. Managed 26 patients, 8 with PT needs.
- Trained 11 interns on internal medicine procedures, enhancing leadership, management, and interpersonal skills to implement teamwork ideal of hospital.

Bassee-Nord Health Center, Quebec, Canada, 1995-1997
- Performed daily physical therapy sessions with 13 pediatric patients.
- Head Nurse – emergency care, general medicine and pediatrics nurse.
- Promoted to Head nurse in emergency-care unit within first eight months.
- Supervised 23 nursing interns and coordinated medicine schedules for 35 patients.

Because physical therapy, not nursing, is goal, Dumon leads with physical therapy experience, although nursing experience is dominant. Dumon moves in and out of the two professions – PT and nursing.

Seasoned Ace
ACCOMPLISHMENT

Romero Cortez

42 Plains Road
Mystic, CT 06493
(203) 555-6932
E-mail: romeroc@drd.sfi.com

Senior Creative/Marketing Executive

Experienced in major account management, new product and strategic concept development, advertising and promotion; spearheaded revenue growth from $13 million to $180 million in 5 years.

Omits section headings for more direct impact.

- Increased one company's value from $50 million to sales price of $225 million
- Revitalized company by effecting $10 million sales increase

Effective leader skilled in building, training, and motivating highly profitable creative teams and directing major projects to completion on time with strong cost control. Track record of developing and maintaining corporate relationships.

Creative/Marketing Success Highlights

"Advertises" marketing achievements.

Marketing Theme	Client
Tannik's Capitalist Tool	Tannik's Magazine
Call them with clarity	RTO Telephones
Fly us	Abroad Airlines
Oil No More	Oil Gleaners Inc.
Let Our Machines Work, You Think	Mattison Products
Feel sensitive	Crimson Skin Products
Every Bit Crystal Quality	Crystal Diskettes
Moist and Flavorful Food	New-Taste Dog Food

Awards

Clio, American Institute of Graphic Arts, Rissoli Award, Best Read Ad-Rosser Reeves, Communications Arts Award, Outdoor Billboard Design Award, and Andy Award, International Film Festival Silver Medal, Connecticut Art Directors Club Gold Medal

(1 of 2)

Can change to computer friendly by switching "Creative Marketing Success Highlights" with "Professional Experience." That's the order in which computers expect to find data. But for human viewing, current presentation is different and effective.

Romero Cortez

Developed all RTO-TV Network advertising for 2 years. Directed turnaround of Morning brand cereal division. Other creative assignments in advertising, direct marketing and new product development launches for:

Generative Appliances	American Bottling Co.
International Athletics Association	New Foods
Sweet Candy Company	Crystal

Sells industry reputation before employment history.

Professional Experience

Vice President, **Creative Director**	Wilton Marketing & Communications, Wilton, CT 1996-Present	
Vice President, **Associate Creative Director**	McConnell and McCarthy, Inc., Manhattan, NY 1993-1996	
Vice President, **Associate Creative Director**	Mark Jenkins Company Advertising, Inc., Manhattan, NY 1986-1993	

Romero Cortez shows he's a pro by using advertising skills on his resume — in this model, Cortez makes a virtue of open white space, citing only a few standout achievements.

(2 of 2)

Seasoned Ace
ACCOMPLISHMENT

Dana M. Brigham

123 Teal Way, Tujunga, California, 91042   (714) 222-4985
e-mail: dbrigham@infonet.com

Urban Planner: 15 years' experience in urban planning with substantial management experience in public and private sectors. Experienced in preparing and managing: general plan revisions; zoning code administration; redevelopment plans; environmental projects.

> *Different typeface than body text for more attention.*

Qualifications and Accomplishments:

- Planner for city of Laguna Niguel, managing review of large-scale urban projects.

- Managed general plan preparation for Irvine, Palmdale, and San Jose including environmental analysis of plans' impacts, surviving court challenge.

> *Gives results.*

- Supervised zoning section of Irvine Planning Department for over four years, developing commission agenda and preparing staff reports to commission and City Council.

- Supervised 37 planners in public sector for Irvine, Palmdale, and San Jose.

- Assisted in establishing plan in Palmdale immediately following its incorporation.

> *Brigham departs from template by combining qualifications and accomplishments.*

- Directed task force in designing and implementing new hillside grading/development standards for Palmdale, developing builder sensitivity to community goals.

- Organized Hillside Development Panel for 2002 American Planning Association.

- Managed preparation of E. Santa Monica Boulevard Strategic Plan and East Irvine Specific Plan for Pasadena; coordinated with 56 planners, presented to large groups.

Employment:
CITY OF IRVINE, Irvine, California, 2003-Present
Special Projects Planner, Planning and Community Development Department.

> *Maximizes white space.*

LOCKEN AND CO., Santa Monica, California, 2000-2003
Director of Planning Department.

CITY OF PALMDALE, Palmdale, California, 1996-2000
Senior Project Manager, Planning and Research Section.

KLO ASSOCIATES, Palmdale, California, 1994-1996
Senior Project Manager of preparing environmental impact reports.

WOLHBAHN & SONS, Santa Monica, California, 1992-1994
Senior Planning Consultant providing advisory services to local municipalities.

CITY OF SAN JOSE, San Jose, California, 1988-1992
Supervising Associate Planner, Zoning Division, Planning Department.

Education:
Bachelor of Arts, Political Science, University of Sacramento, Sacramento, California, 1987
Master of Science, Public Administration, California State University, Sacramento, California 1990

Professional Affiliations:
American Planning Association, American Institute of Certified Planners

Seasoned Ace
ACCOMPLISHMENT

Older human resource pro wishes to re-enter private sector after government stint; limits work history to 10 years.

ANDREW WALLACE
P.O. BOX 123, NEWPORT, LONG ISLAND, 11413
(212) 456-1997
awall@aol.com

**Human Resource position using recruitment, appraisal
and benefit skills, accumulated over 10 years**

QUALIFICATIONS:

➤ Directed human resource systems for two mid-sized corporations
➤ Worked inside EEOC structure; bulletproof employee management
➤ Expert in recruiting, benefits, evaluations, training, and outplacement
➤ Use computer — or manual — applicant/employee tracking systems
➤ Can manage contingent workforce

ACCOMPLISHMENTS:

➤ Investigated and negotiated resolutions of 400 allegations of employment discrimination. Led investigation teams and instructed on negotiation procedures to maximize resolution success.

➤ Performed EEO consultation, trained more than 60 employer and university organizations in human resource skills to establish increasingly effective management-staff working relationship.

➤ Received 12 annual merit-based promotions; managed staff of 15 recruiters.

RECENT PROFESSIONAL EXPERIENCE:

➤ 11/01 to 12/04 — **Employment Equality Commission, New York, NY** — Federal Investigator
➤ 9/00 to 6/04 — **University Of New York City, Queens, NY** — Adjunct Faculty
➤ 11/00 to 11/01 — **Swanky Interiors, New York, NY** — Human Resources Director
➤ 6/94 to 9/00 — **Lucrative Corporation, Buffalo, NY** — Human Resources Manager

EDUCATION:

➤ **Central New York University** — Master of Sciences, Human Resource Administration
➤ **Mariner College** — Bachelor of Arts, Management of Human Resources
➤ **New York College of Law** — Continuing coursework toward Juris Doctor degree

PROFESSIONAL ASSOCIATIONS:

➤ Human Resource Association of New York
➤ Society for Human Resource Management
➤ American Society of Training & Development

➤ American Bar Association Student Division
➤ State Bar of New York Student Division
➤ Kiwanis International

New Graduate
REVERSE CHRONOLOGICAL & TARGETED

> Lutwig's research on the target showed they wanted an energetic, young person with his degrees. Objective and education centered for formal look and to highlight degrees that employer favors.

DALE K. LUTWIG
12 West 34th Street , Los Angeles, CA 91121
(213) 567-8910   E-mail: twig@nnn.gov

Objective : CONGRESSIONAL AIDE

JURIS DOCTOR INTERNATIONAL LEGAL STUDIES
Occidental University, College of Law 20XX

MASTER OF ARTS, POLITICAL SCIENCE
Adele School of Citizenship and Public Affairs, 20XX
Concentration in Government Planning & International Negotiation
Teaching Assistant in International Negotiation

BACHELOR OF ARTS, POLITICS AND SOCIOLOGY
University of California, Los Angeles, 20XX, Dean's List

Bar Admission: CA and NJ Passed entrance examinations. Admissions pending.

WORK EXPERIENCE

> Summary omitted: saved for cover letter.

2002-2005   **Office of the United States Trade Representative**
Assisted Deputy Assistant US Trade Representative in analyzing House and Senate bills. Reconstructed 25 legislative provisions which complicated international trade obligations. Corresponded with corporations, trade associations, congressional staff members and other Federal agencies. Developed working dexterity with international negotiations. Trade representative John Katan compliments my work: "Best intern we have."

> Complimentary quotes accentuate skills and promise.

2001   **Los Angeles Department of Consumer Affairs**
Assisted investigators in enforcing Attorney General's Guidelines for Fair Advertising. Accumulated strong background in advertising ethics proceedings.

2000   **Charles Swabb**
Assisted 19 account executives in management activities, including investor research, telemarketing, mass mailings, computerized clerical operations and communications. Tremendous experience with intercompany and public communications. Praised for follow- through and organization (office manager Tom Cannon).

1997-2000   **Reese, Riley & Thorne**
Assisted library staff, paralegals and attorneys with all library functions, including organization and research. Modernized 14 computers. Compiled legal information for 32 lawsuits from cases and articles, acquiring early experience with legal negotiations.

> Technical skills detailed to target employer's needs.

MISCELLANEOUS

- Proficient with all applications, including LEXIS/NEXIS/WESTLAW databases.
- Hobbies include sailboat racing and golf.

> Personal interest included; Lutwig's research shows target company's recruiters value interest in sports.

New Graduate
LINEAR

Grades speak for themselves. Testimonial backs up claim of favorable faculty comments.

Herman Ling

123 Northrop Avenue #4, Ft. Lauderdale, Florida 33308
(305) 566-6789   E-mail: hling@jkuafu.edu

Objective Marketing position in Agribusiness or Chemicals

Qualifications Focus: plant pathology. MBA/Master's in Plant Pathology/ agriculture undergraduate degree. Two years' international marketing experience. Bilingual — Chinese and English. Computer literate. Rated tops by grades and favorable faculty comments in graduate studies: ("Herman Ling is the most industrious student to come through here in several years" — U. of Colorado marketing professor Karl Weber.)

Communications Skills
- Computer: MS Word, Excel, Powerpoint, WordPerfect, Lotus 123, Freelance, Harvard Graphics, PSI-Plot, SAS JUMP, QBasic programming, and main frame
- Language: Chinese (Mandarin and several dialects)

Gives details on bilingual and computer claims in summary.

Experience

8/01-7/04   **Graduate Research Assistant**
University of Colorado, Department of Plant Pathology, Boulder, CO
- Designed and implemented experiments in greenhouse, growth chamber, and field
- Developed weather-based advisory for improving control of plant disease with reduced fungicide

7/99-8/01   **Account Manager, Department of Marketing and Sales**
Detect Bio-Pharmacy Group, Beijing, PR China
- Developed channel strategies for entering Chinese marketplace
- Managed and developed sales accounts
- Developed promotion plan for marketing new medicine
- Participated in joint venture for manufacturing ingredients

Prior experience in China. This experience is for U.S. job, thus quote from U.S. professor; for a job in China, would emphasize China connections.

9/96-6/99   **Social Coordinator, Department Student Association;**
Co-editor, Department Student Journal
Beijing Agricultural University, Beijing, PR China

Education   **Master of Business Administration,** 2001, GPA 4.0/4.0
University of Miami, Miami, FL

Master of Science, Plant Pathology, 1999, GPA 3.8/4.0
University of Colorado, Boulder, CO

Bachelor of Science, Plant Protection, 1999, GPA (comparable) 4.0/4.0
Beijing Agricultural University, Beijing, People's Republic of China

Publications   **Ling, Herman,** Grant, P., and Milton, F. 2000 "Effects of precipitation and temperature on garden crop infection." *Plant Disease.*

Ling, Herman, and Kilkenny, E. 2000 "Comparison of weather-dependent crops based on soil concentration." *Plant Disease.*

Activities   American Phytopathological Society

Despite advanced degrees, placed experience first to show market orientation.

Re-Entry Homemaker
REVERSE CHRONOLOGICAL

Faith Marks

167 Vanderbilt Road   (916) 779-1434
Harrisburg, PA 12101   E-mail: fmarks@cts.com

> Space between text and line.

Objective
Social Studies Teacher, grades 5-12
Teaching is my life. Comfortable with computers, daily communication and research via
e-mail and the Internet. Computer focus promises that children taught will not be left
behind in a competitive era.

> Objective mixed with summary: concentration on e-mail & Internet shows stay-at-home is up-to-date.

Education
Bachelor of Science in Secondary Education
Pennsylvania State University, 2002

Pennsylvania Teaching Credential:
Economics, Geography, United States and
World History, Grades 5-12

Honors
• National Dean's List, 2000
• Alpha Lambda, 1999, Freshman Honor Society
• Phi ETA Sigma, 1999, Freshman Honor Society

> Fast-learning, willingness to put self-interest aside for team good.

Teaching Experience

Substitute Teacher, Townville Elementary School   Fall 2002
• Became expert at instant lesson plan preparation. Never refuse last-minute assignments.
• Work with diverse student groups, expanding range of teaching capabilities. Not
  intimidated by challenge of middle-school behavioral problems.
• Use considerable experience with children, ages five - twelve. Create exciting and
  motivational lesson plans. Principal Morgan Rathbone says "Faith Marks gives
  110% to her substitute teaching assignments. Her students get energized by her
  classroom technique. I only wish we had a staff opening. I'd hire her in a second!"

> Complimentary quote used to explain why she was not hired here if she's so great.

Student Teacher, Townville Middle School, 10 weeks   Spring 2002
                          Grant Middle School, 6 weeks
• Taught US History, Geography, and Government; developed multi-faceted
  daily lesson plans for each course.
• Perfected computer fluency. Strengthened supervisory roles, delegation ability,
  organizational skills and motivational techniques. Worked full-time while parenting.
• Instructed extracurricular activities, including softball and computer club.

Additional Experience
Advised graduate students, worked as student financial aid liaison. Analyzed student
financial information and matched to available funding.

Seasoned Ace
LINEAR

Alternative heading for Objective.

Lee Ralston

7702 Ridge Road   Tacoma, Washington 90543
(206) 555-9876   E-mail: lralst@aol.com

Ampersand okay — familiar phrase.

Profile: Property Management professional seeks to use high-quality history in supervisory position. More than 15 years' solid experience A to Z in property management.

Qualifications:
- Skilled in profit & loss, reductions, distribution, and financial administration
- Restructure marketing plans strategically, advancing returns in excess of 20%
- Record of enthusiastic achievement of corporate objectives
- LIHTC (tax credit), Bond, Section 8, HODAG, New Construction and Renovations
- Managed multi-family properties in Washington, California, Oregon, Arizona, Colorado, and Utah

Quantifies achievements.

keywords throughout.

Education and Training:
- **Bachelor of Arts in Education,** University of Puget Sound, Tacoma, Washington
- **College of Certified Property Managers,** Apartment Management, Real Estate Finances and Management

Designations:
- Certified Apartment Property Supervisor
- Washington Real Estate License

White space and bullets improve readability.

Professional Experience:

2000-Present   **Senior Asset Manager**   Greengrove Point Properties, Inc.

Quantifies and gives results of achievements.

- Manage marketing and operations programs for over 2,000 units.
- Recruit, train, and hire over 100 employees, maximizing $2M in capital improvements.
- Consult on all EEOC and fair housing issues, minimizing legal consultation costs by $2,000.

1999-2000   **Regional Manager**   Builder Companies of Washington

- Facilitated marketing programs for 10-12 properties throughout Washington.
- Superintended successful lease-up and operation of 23-story luxury hi-rise property in Seattle.
- Directed $2 million renovation of 25-year-old property on coast of Washington.

1997-1999   **District Manager**   Washington Property Management

- Created marketing and operations programs for two properties in Tacoma, WA.
- Facilitated $2 million renovation with lease-up three months ahead of schedule.
- Maintained 98% occupancy in New Construction lease.

Ampersand okay — company name.

1992-1997   **Area Manager**   Benedict, Young, Dalton, & McMillan

Assistant Manager on 1,672-unit property in Seattle, Washington.
- Led company nationally for two years in leasing, averaging over 120 new leases per month.
- Portfolio consisted of 2,000 units and over 100 employees.
- Directed monthly regional sales meetings, initiated energy savings program that accomplished $150,000 work done to 14 properties with profit exceeding $12,000.

Grouping Temporary Jobs
ACCOMPLISHMENT

BETH SHELTON

1849 Warner Road, Newark, Delaware 19905   **Phone: (302) 555-6778**
                                              E-mail: shelton@khl.com

Objective

Position as **Administrative Assistant/Executive Secretary** — using detail-oriented skills and experience accumulated over 9 years

Qualifications

- More than 10 years' secretarial/administrative experience; keyboard speed of 90 wpm
- Proficient in Microsoft Word, WordPerfect, Windows, Lotus, Excel, FileMaker Pro

Accomplishments

- Responded promptly to technical requests from Parker clients (account average: $25,000), advising on hardware and software issues, ensuring client satisfaction

- Supported office operations of 35-bed hospital ward; developed substantial ability to prioritize duties and service large numbers of people in high-pressure environment

- Researched, compiled and prepared crucial data, independently and with little supervision — developing strong self-management skills

- Organized meetings and workshops, arranged travel for conferences averaging 20 executives; as noted by Tom Rogers, corporate vice president: "Beth fits together all the cogs and wheels here; without her, it's chaos."

- Tracked 250 medical admissions, discharges, and transfers on computer

- Resolved issues after hours and on weekends, meeting challenges with commitment

Job History

Combined temporary jobs under one heading to avoid looking like job hopper.

Administrative Assistant and Secretary, Hammond Temporaries, Dover, Del.   2001-Present
Assistant Database Manager, Parker Regional Medical Systems, Newark, Del.   1998-2001
Assistant Office Manager, Hyde Transport Company, Dover, Del.   1996-1998
Secretary to Computing Manager, Range Systems, Newark, Del.   1989-1996

Education

Bachelor of Arts in Business Management, 3.8/4.0 GPA   Awarded 2000
Newark College, Newark, Del.

Seasoned Ace
KEYWORD & LINEAR

Objective woven into keyword summary.

Griffin T. Stenner

2345 Fremont Blvd.   Santa Fe, NM 87501
(505) 555-0006   Messages taken at (505) 333-8000
E-Mail: griffsten@aol.com

Senior-level sales and distribution management position

12 years' experience in supervisory positions. Sales and distribution experience. Budgeting. Profit & loss responsibility. Customer service. Materials and product management. Employee selection and training. Strategic and tactical planning. Marketing. Facility location. Product training. Labor relations. Manufacturing plant management. Computerized environment and pricing.

Business Experience

Divides jobs by titles, highlighting upward mobility over long period with single employer.

1991-Present DUNCAN TRANSIT COMPANY, Santa Fe, New Mexico
2001-Present **Director of Aftermarket Business**

Amper-sand OK here — familiar phrase.

Profit & loss responsibility for $40 million aftermarket parts division. Supervise 16 sales and 35 distribution staff for sales, marketing, materials management, customer service, distribution and product management. Serve on Executive Committee for policy making and strategizing.
- Facilitated strategic plan increasing sales 30%, exceeding 25% assets return
- Chaired integrated software system committee
- Edited sales literature and media campaign for $3 million retail expansion
- Sharpened inventory accuracy to 97.5% with new bar code system, significantly reducing manufacturing downtime

1997-2001   **Corporate Distribution Manager**
Managed warehouse, distribution and traffic functions for two locations of more than 10,000 stockkeeping units. Assumed plant responsibility for distribution of product to 860 retail stores weekly.
- Designed and relocated new distribution center on schedule and $200,000 under budget
- Received **Star of the Year** award from employer for product quality and distribution service levels
- Lowered total distribution cost 24%, saving $1.8M over five years

1991-1997   **Account Manager**
Developed first- and second-level distribution and manufacturing accounts in 30 key market areas, while maintaining in excess of 40 existing accounts in eight states. Conducted sales, product, and technical meetings for distributorship managers and sales staff.
- Top company salesperson in 1992, 1993, and 1995
- Increased sales by 220% to $4.4M in two years

Achievement numbers combined for over one year to show high-impact results.

Education

No years given.

Bachelor of Science, Business Administration, University of New Mexico, Santa Fe
Senior Executive Management Course, Santa Fe Community College, New Mexico

Part VI
The Part of Tens

The 5th Wave   By Rich Tennant

"I've sent my resume to nine accounting firms, and not <u>one</u> of them has responded! I put my e-mail address right there under my name, too — 'Dminus@math.com'."

In this part . . .

You see why the famous *For Dummies* Part of Tens is treasured for putting information quickly and simply on your table. Find out what really ticks off recruiters, simple ways to upgrade your resumes, how to back up your claims, and how to choose a professional resume writer (not that you'll need one). Plus, you get a detailed checklist you can use to score your own StandOut resumes.

Chapter 19

Ten (x3) Ways to Prove Your Claims

So you have excellent communications skills, or you meet people well, or you can make a computer slam dance with ease. At least, that's what you assert. How can I (an employer) believe you?

I am more likely to believe your claims of skills and accomplishments when you back them up with specifics. A good start on backing up your statements is *quantifying* them with numbers, percentages, and dollar amounts.

Decide for yourself. Compare the following statements labeled A with the statements labeled B. Which is the strongest, most attention-grabbing, most convincing?

A. Easy Ways to Be More Popular

B. 50 Easy Ways to Be More Popular

A. Towels on Sale

B. Towels 40% Off

A. Designed internal company insurance plan to replace outside plan at great savings.

B. Designed $30 million self-insured health plan, saving estimated $5 million per year over previous external plan.

I think you'll agree with me that the B statements win hands down! The take-home message is *quantify, quantify, quantify.* Look at the following statements in the three categories of numbers, percentages, and dollar amounts. Fill in the blanks as an exercise to remind yourself to quantify your accomplishments and results.

Say It with Numbers

1. __ (#) years of extensive experience in _____ and
   _____.

2. Won ____ (#) awards for _____.

3. Trained/Supervised ____ (#) full-time and ____ (#) part-time employees.

4. Recommended by _____ (a number of notable people)
   as a _____ (something good that they said about you) for
   excellent _____ (an accomplishment or skill).

5. Supervised a staff of ____ (#).

6. Recruited ____ (#) staff members in _____ (period of time),
   increasing overall production.

7. Sold ____ (# of products) in _____ (period of time), ranking ____
   (1st, 2nd, 3rd) in sales in a company of ____ (#) employees.

8. Exceeded goals in __ (#) years/months/days, establishing my employer
   as ____ (1st, 2nd, 3rd, or whatever number) in industry.

9. Missed only ____ (#) days of work out of ____ (#) total.

10. Assisted ____ (#) (executives, supervisors, technical directors, others).

Say It with Percentages

1. Excellent_____(your top proficiency) skills, which resulted in ____ (%) increase/decrease in _____ (sales, revenues, profits, clients, expenses, costs, charges).

2. Recognized as a leader in company, using strong skills to effect a/an ____ (%) increase in team/coworker production.

3. Streamlined _____ (industry procedure), decreasing hours spent on task by ____ (%).

4. Used extensive _____ (several skills) to increase customer/ member base by ____ (%).

5. Financed __ (%) of tuition/education/own business.

6. Graduated within the top ____ (%) of class.

7. Responsible for an estimated __ (%) of employer's success in _____ (functional area/market).

8. Resolved customer relations issues, increasing customer satisfaction by ____ (%).

9. Eliminated _____ (an industry problem), increasing productivity by ____ (%).

10. Upgraded _____ (an industry tool), resulting in ____ (%) increase in effectiveness.

Say It with Dollar Amounts

1. Supervised entire _____ (a department) staff, decreasing middle-management costs by ____ ($).

2. Purchased computer upgrade for office, saving the company ____ ($) in paid hours.

3. Eliminated the need for _____ (one or several positions in company), decreasing payroll by __ ($).

4. Averaged ____ ($) in sales per month.

5. Collected ____ ($) in memberships and donations.

6. Supervised the opening/construction of new location, completing task at ____ ($) under projected budget.

7. Designed entire _____ program, which earned ____ ($) in company revenues.

8. Implemented new _____ system, saving ____ ($) daily/weekly /monthly/annually.

9. Reduced cost of _____ (substantial service) by developing and implementing a new _____ system at the bargain price of ____ ($).

10. Restructured _____ (organization/system/product) to result in a savings of ____ ($).

Chapter 20

Ten Pet Peeves of Recruiters

Check out what recruiters say when they think no "civilians" (job seekers) are reading. Both third-party (independent) recruiters and inside corporate recruiters share their thoughts freely on various Internet forums.

Here are ten categories of transgressions that various e-recruiters cite as making them grumpy. Some categories contain comments from different recruiters. I report them anonymously to protect their privacy. My comments conclude each category.

Resume-Free Pitches

I bristle at applicants who e-mail me a general question, "Do you have any technical positions open in Kansas City?" instead of a resume.

Comment: Spare yourself a non-answer for a non-resume. Attach a resume to your question.

Major Mismatches

I find it extremely annoying when people send resumes without reading our job posting. If we advertise for a pizza chef, a bike mechanic is just as likely to self-nominate himself for the job, leaving us to figure it out. We don't have time for goose chasing.

Our management positions require a background in a certain industry plus experience. We get responses from people with one year of experience and no management background. We get resumes that claim their experience is ideal or that they read the position and found it to fit their skills exactly, when in reality they have none of the experience detailed in the job posting.

We advertised for a telecommunications consultant with call center experience and received a resume of someone with experience in movie production and no experience in anything we look for. I am sure applicants would have a more positive outcome if they applied for positions that are relevant to their experience, although I doubt this will ever change.

Comment: Some job seekers, particularly in technical fields, operate on the lottery theory and scatter resumes everywhere. A number of job seekers adhere to the 80 percent strategy (if you fit 80 percent of the job's requirements, give it a go) or believe that if you can manage one thing, you can manage anything.

Others seek ways to apply viable transferable skills to new environments and, failing to make a strong enough case, are rejected because some recruiters are too inexperienced, overworked, or insular to recognize the legitimacy of transitioning skills.

Still other job seekers just don't get it and waste everyone's time in applying for jobs for which they're dramatically unqualified.

E-Stalking

One applicant e-mailed his resume and a few days later sent another, saying he was waiting for a response. I replied that we would contact him if we are interested. A few days later, and once a week for a few months, he sent e-mails that only said, "Still waiting." Creepy.

I would like to tell job seekers to send only one resume. If someone is "open" to all appropriate positions, just say so!

Comment: Checking back periodically works best if you send new information of interest to the recruiter. You may scan and send a relevant news article with a brief "In case you missed this" note, adding that you continue to look forward to the right timing for an interview.

Censor before sending your complaint

This is the true story of what can happen when you give into feelings of stress, frustration, irritation, and anger and call it like you see it. The following is an actual e-mail letter to a major defense contractor that employs tens of thousands of people:

To Whom It May Concern:

In response to the job openings posted at your Web site, I have applied for numerous jobs (probably over 100 different positions) by sending my resume to you along with e-mails during the last 4 to 5 weeks. I am extremely disappointed by the way my online job applications have been handled by [company name withheld].

If this is common practice in your company, sooner or later, people will find out how *irresponsible and unprofessional you are and as a result, you will lose a lot of talented people.*

Please take this matter very seriously. I think that your CEO or COO should know what's going on within the company. Sincerely, [job seeker's name withheld].

The recruiter who handled the complaint replies:

"This person was interviewed at a job fair and told that if he qualified for any positions, we would notify him. He then submitted 111 actual resumes for more than 40 different career positions. I have never met anyone who could qualify for that many positions. This individual doesn't get it. We now have removed him from all job searches in our company."

Saying that you're available for any appropriate position carries the risk that you'll be seen as too much of a generalist and expert at nothing, or desperate. If you do it, define the field — "appropriate in the accounting field" or "appropriate in the retail financial field," for example.

Staffing and technical systems consultant Jim Lemke says that stuffing the recruitment box with your resumes may become moot:

"Many of the major applicant tracking system vendors have released software that companies can use to require answers to online screening questions before permitting job seekers to attach a resume.

"If the questions are answered correctly (according to the company's standards), the recruiter or hiring manager is notified by e-mail that a new qualified resume is available for review. If the applicant doesn't pass the litmus test for qualification, the applicant's resume stays in the company's database and is searched on for future openings.

"This online screening technology (more fully described in Chapter 1) does not stop the persistent applicant from sending additional resumes or e-mail or making phone calls. The trick is not to become a pest," Lemke explains.

Caps and Taps and Typos

My sore spot is receiving e-mails with no use of capitalization whatsoever, or with some words mysteriously capitalized and those that should be (proper names, beginning of a sentence) are not capitalized.

For heaven's sake, use spell check. A neat resume will always be my preference over one that is not.

Comment: Every single book or article on resume writing I've ever seen recommends impeccable work. It would be a crying shame to put together a StandOut, well-researched resume only to have it discarded because of misspellings and typos throughout the text.

Too Much Information

I give bad marks to people who think that sending their resume multiple times will increase their chance of getting a call for an interview. It won't.

I dislike it when the applicant puts several addresses in the "To" e-mail box and mass mails the resume. This unprofessional shortcut looks like no care is taken in applying to each individual position.

Comment: Another practice to avoid is postal mailing a hard copy of your e-mailed resume. Carry hard copies to an interview, but don't mail or fax an additional copy because doing so is unnecessary. Not only is it disrespectful to mass mail your resume addressed to multiple names, but it's no one's business but your own where you're applying for work.

Date Grate

What annoys me is when job seekers send resumes and don't specify start and end dates for jobs. As if this won't be at the top of my list to ask in an interview and a reference check — if they get to the interview process at all.

Two old dodges don't fly with me: (1) Trying to hide a resume gap by listing employment dates at the end of the summaries rather than in the left-hand margin and (2) substituting the number of years at a company for the real dates.

Comment: Reporters are taught to put the most important facts at the lead of a story. Using the same theory of first things first, you would list your experience in this order: title of position, name and locale of employer, and dates of employment.

Dates of employment don't have to be placed in the left margin. The right margin is perfectly acceptable and even preferred by some resume experts.

Guess Who

It's a pain when I get incomplete resumes and cover letters without contact information. We have offices in several countries and a hotmail.com address doesn't suffice.

A pet peeve of mine is receiving resumes without the current employer listed — "confidential" resumes. I can understand this treatment for Web job site postings but when sending a resume to a specific employer, the current employer should be identified.

Comment: As for the first comment, you can add to the "hotmail.com" (or other free mailbox established for a job search) a post office box and a dedicated telephone answering machine. That combination will protect your privacy but make it easy for a recruiter to contact you.

As for the second comment, you can use a generic description of your current position and skills, noting that you'll reveal the current employer's name in a job interview. I urge caution in fully revealing your identity and personal workplace information on the Internet (see Chapter 2).

File Style

I can't imagine why, but some people have to be told to submit a resume as a normal attachment in a common program (Word, WordPerfect, Notepad, and so forth). I have received two-page Word documents as zip files! I have the software to handle zips, but many people do not.

Comment: Zip files are for documents the size of Connecticut, not resumes or CVs. No one wants to bother unzipping.

Useless and Uninformative

I grow peevish when forced to read through fluff that does not relate to a workforce position. It doesn't matter to anyone in my office that you were the local beauty queen. It doesn't matter to anyone in my office that when you are 35, out of college, and have held several jobs and that you attended a prestigious prep school as a teenager. It doesn't matter to anyone in my office that your wife is the vice president of a well-known company.

Another thing that bugs me is the use of fancy graphics and poems on resumes.

Comment: Stick to information related to your ability to do the job for which you are applying.

Probable Prevarication

I hate wasting my time on resumes from people who claim to have attended a school they never saw the inside of and to have worked for a company that they didn't.

Comment: Lying about a point of fact easily proved or disproved is riskier than ever in today's era of fact-checking background investigations (see Chapter 1).

Chapter 21

Ten Simple Ways to Improve Your Resume

In This Chapter

▶ Walking in a recruiter's shoes

▶ Discovering that, in little words, less is more

▶ Finding success in the 5 percent rule

So you've finished your resume, and disappointment could etch lines across your brow. No way does your resume show what you've got. When you desperately need the equivalent of a java jolt, your resume seems to have as much punch as a decaf soy latte.

Possibly your resume needs a factory recall, and you should start over. Or, with luck, you may be able to power it up with just a kiss of makeover secrets like those I describe in this chapter.

Use Bulleted Style for Easy Reading

As the accomplishment and linear formats in Chapter 9 show, the use of one- or two-liners opens up your resume with white space, making it more appealing to read. Professional advertising copywriters know that big blocks of text suffocate readers. Let your words breath!

Discover Art of Lost Articles

Although using articles — "a," "an," and "the" — in your resume isn't *wrong*, try deleting them for a crisper and snappier end result. Recruiters and employers expect to read resumes in compact phrases, not fully developed sentences.

The first person "I" is another word that your resume doesn't need. Look at the following examples:

With Articles	*Without Articles*
I report to the plant manager of the largest manufacturer of silicone-based waxes and polishes.	Report to plant manager of largest manufacturer of silicone-based waxes and polishes.
I worked as the only administrative person on a large construction site.	Worked as only administrative person on large construction site.

Sell, Don't Tell

Forget sticking to the old naming-your-previous-responsibilities routine. Merely listing, "Responsible for XYZ" doesn't assure the recruiter that you met your responsibility or that the result of your efforts was worth the money someone paid you.

By contrast, read over your resume and make sure you have answered that pesky "So what?" question, which is lying in ambush for each bit of information you mention. Try to imagine what's running through a recruiter's mind when you relate that you were responsible for XYZ: *So what? Who cares? What's in it for me?* Anticipate those questions and answer them before a recruiter actually has a chance to ask them.

Frame your resume in results, not responsibilities.

As famous salesman Elmer Wheeler said, "Sell the sizzle, not the steak." Here are some examples of how to do just that:

- ✔ Perform preventive maintenance on 14 machines on daily basis; reduced repair costs 8% over previous year.

- ✔ Monitor quality control, identify problems, find solutions; lab insurance rates, related to mistakes, lowered this year by 3%.

- ✔ Organize daily work distribution for effective teamwork of 12 lab workers; absorb and solve workload issues from previous shift.

The Five Percenters

Recruiters are wild about snaring the cream of the crop. If you're in the top 5 percent of any significant group (graduation, sales, attendance record, performance ratings) make sure that fact appears prominently on your resume.

Verbs, Nouns, and Writing

Old wisdom: Use lots of action verbs to perk up reading interest in resumes (see StandOut Words in Chapter 11). Later wisdom: Cash in the action verbs for nouns, the keywords that ward off anonymity in sleeping resume databases. New wisdom: With the return of the handsome resume, fully formatted for online attachments, use both verbs and nouns.

Use the nouns to construct a keyword profile at the top of your resume (see Chapter 9). Use the action verbs in the body of your resume to liven up your achievements.

Just don't mix noun and verb phrases in the same resume section. The following example explains.

> ### *Highlights:*
>
> • Founded start-up, achieving positive cash flow and real profits in the first year. [verb]
>
> • President of point-of-sale products. [noun]
>
> • Proven ability for representation of high technology products. [noun]
>
> • Consistently achieved highest profit in 45-year-old company history. [verb]

Change the noun statements to be consistent with the verb statements:

> • Founded point-of-sale vending company, generating positive cash flow and real profits in the first year.
>
> • Proved ability to represent high technology products.

Writing instructors call this agreeable notion *parallel construction*.

Strip Out Sad Stories

If your career history looks like the fall of the Roman Empire, don't try to explain a long stretch of disasters on a resume. Save your explanations for an interview. Make the resume as adversity-free as you legitimately can.

An exception is when you have suffered multiple layoffs or a company closing within a short period of time. You don't want recruiters to think you are a job hopper. Instead, add brief notes at the end of comments for each employer that cut short your tenure — (Company ceased operation.) (Company downsized 70%.) (Company moved out of state.).

And never apologize on your resume for any weakness that you may observe in your professional self. Shortcomings don't belong on your resume. Eliminate any negative information on your resume that can dull a recruiter's interest in meeting with you.

Reach Out with Strength

Select the qualifications and past job activities that speak to the kind of job you want and the skills you want to use. Highlight these. If, for instance, you want to transition from military training to civilian training, remain riveted on your training skills without diluting your message by mentioning your ability to use several simple computer programs. If you've muddled your resume's message with minor skills or skills you no longer wish to use, get rid of them. Stay on message.

Object to a Wimpy Objective

Imagine an actor striding onto a stage, stopping, then standing there like a log addressing the audience: "I came to find out what you can do for me."

Not exactly a curtain raiser — any more than beginning your resume with simply awful objective statements like: "Seeking a chance for advancement," or "where my skills will be utilized."

Trash the trites: "To obtain a responsible (does someone want an irresponsible?) job with "challenging and rewarding (does anyone want dull and unrewarding?) duties."

Be an editor! Draw a line through wussy wording that leaves everyone wondering if you're a washout. Your statement can be simple, yet effective: "Management position in finance where more than 10 years' experience will strengthen the bottom line."

My Fair Resume

Pick up the phone and call the HR department where you want to work and are about to submit your resume. Ask: "Before I send you my resume online, I want to get the facts. Do you accept MS Word attachments, store them as formatted documents, and route them to line managers as images?" If the answer is *yes*, wrap fish in that ugly ASCII plain text resume and throw it away, reveling in the fact that you'll get to send the attractive version of your resume. If the answer is *no,* well, good try in this era of transition. After all, ugly is still better than unreadable.

Ditch the Cat

If you've included references to your spouse, significant other, domestic partner, or even a family pet on your resume, free your resume from certain shunning by deleting them. These non-workplace references won't help a recruiter see how you're perfect for the job and, in many cases, they work against you.

From the annals of recruiters' funniest resumes: a song-and-dance recital about how a man's wife and he are Mets fans and want to get out of California and back to New York; a medical history of how a man's spouse is wracked with headaches, backaches, and sinus congestion — although it doesn't affect his ability to give all of himself to the job; and a chatty background account by a woman who got a cat for her husband and considered it a good trade.

Chapter 22

Solutions to the Top Ten Resume Problems

In This Chapter

▶ Fixing the outward appearance of your resume

▶ Resurrecting a resume deadened with job duties

▶ Checking your resume for errors

▶ Tapping into professional skills

*D*oes your job search seem to be marching and marching and marching but never getting anywhere? Find a few quiet moments to look back over your resume to see if it's the problem. Maybe it is and maybe it isn't. In either case, you're too close to the issue to see where your self-marketing tool needs improvement. Use these lightly written but heavy-hitting possibilities to stay focused.

Smoothing Out Tattered Pages

Does your paper resume look as though it's been in someone's backpack on a rock band's road tour? Does it seem less than professional in appearance, with handwritten updates — or, heavens to Betsy, does it sport a coffee stain or ink smudge? Does your resume subliminally suggest that your work may be as careless as your paper introduction?

The solution: When your document looks like an Ozzy Osbourne moment, go the whole nine yards and freshen it up completely: Experiment with a different typeface. Print it on bright-white paper. Use a little bold type or a bulleted format to call attention to your accomplishments. Break up paragraphs. Try a linear format (see Chapter 9). Wrap your resume in white space.

Letting Go of the Big Squeeze

Does your resume look like an overloaded furniture consignment shop with your information squeezed onto one chock-full page? Does it seem as difficult to read as a parachute company's guarantee that you'll get a full refund if the parachute doesn't open? Does your resume cause anyone older than 10 to head for a low-vision clinic?

The solution: Forget what you learned in fifth grade, that "all resumes should be limited to one page." By cramming everything onto one page, you probably leave out impressive achievements. The litmus test about what to include is to ask yourself, "Does this fact support my qualifications for the job I'm chasing? Will it help me get an interview?" If so, don't leave it on the cutting room floor.

Cleaning Up Musty, Dusty Buzzwords

Does your resume hark back to language of yesteryear — like "affirmative action plan," when today's buzzword is "diversity?" Does it mention that you are a "go-getter" rather than "action-oriented?" Does your resume speak of "paradigm" and "proactive" instead of "new principle" and "action motivated?"

The solution: Thumb through appropriate trade publications, newspapers, and general business magazines. Notice the words that describe experiences you want to put on your resume. If you're not sure what a business word means, try looking it up on Word Spy (www.logophilia.com/wordspy). Word Spy notes that some resumes are "buzzword-compliant," which means littered with jargon and buzzwords.

Making your resume buzzword-compliant is effective only when the phrasing is up-to-date. Contemporary jargon identifies you as being an insider, not an outsider. (Chapter 11 identifies some StandOut Words.)

Looking Too Old in a Youth Culture

Does your resume look as though the person it describes fought in the American Revolution? Does it seem weary because 20 years later you're still showing your first job after graduation? Does your resume exhibit middle-aged creep because it's padded with irrelevant experiences that bear little relationship to the job you want?

The solution: Condense your background that's older than 10 to 15 years. Consolidate other nonrelevant experience under an "Other Experience" heading.

Should you omit graduation years? Opinions vary. One school says revealing graduation years is akin to prehistoric carbon dating, and therefore you should leave them off. Another school says that's "fool's-paradise thinking," meaning that leaving off dates red flags your age, making recruiters assume you're an old coot — even older and "cootier" than you really are. See Chapter 4 for more ideas on how to put a spring into your resume's step.

Seeming Excessively Vague

Does your resume obscure your qualifications? Does it cloud the clues to the kind of work you want to do? Does your resume go too far in trying to keep your options open and, as a result, suggest you're willing to take any kind of job?

The solution: Offer an objective or profile of qualifications that defines your area of expertise. Expecting a recruiter to sift through your resume hoping to discover whether your qualifications match a job's requirements is expecting too much. Chapter 10 says more on objectives and summaries.

Reorganizing Slovenly Structure

Does your resume look way too complicated? Does it consume too much time to figure out? Does your resume ramble all over the map, forcing the reader to take a wild guess as to where your interests and abilities lie?

The solution: Improve the organization of your resume. Even if you've had four jobs in four different career fields, search for a common theme — a focus. Once you find the theme, make sure that every item in your resume supports that theme. A lack of focus is one of the biggest blunders a job seeker can commit. Check out Chapter 12 for tips on focusing.

Including Missing Achievements

Does your resume read like your inner mountain climber never learned to yodel? Does it present a fleshless skeleton that puts a reader to sleep faster than chamomile tea? Is your resume as dull as a page from a tax manual?

The solution: Stop talking responsibilities and start talking results. Measure your results — numbers, percentages, dollar amounts — that show how you successfully reached high points in your work efforts, how you made a difference at each company. (Use the worksheets in Chapter 19.) If you don't list your results with your job duties, the employer may miss the fact that you are the perfect candidate for the job. Use a measurement, make an impact.

Adding Essential Keywords

Does your resume seem just fine with lots of action verbs, but it consistently disappoints you by producing too few, if any, invitations to drop by for an interview? Perhaps the problem is a dearth of keywords.

The solution: Fill your resume with all the keywords that count toward the job you seek. Otherwise, your resume will remain sleeping in a database until Mars is colonized. For lots of help on keywords, turn to Chapter 11.

Checking For the Unrepentant Typo

Does your resume consistently come through with typos and grammatical mistakes? Does it look as though you forgot to proofread it? Does your resume reflect the imperfect you?

The solution: Even the sharpest eyes miss mistakes (as I well know), so ask a friend to double-check your resume after you proofread for errors in four steps:

1. **Spell and grammar check on the computer.** That's a good start, but don't stop there. Spell- and grammar checkers won't find words that aren't there, ones inadvertently left out.

   Check the punctuation and grammar. A period often looks like a comma, a he like a she, and an extra space is often overlooked; a computer doesn't catch these types of errors. Furthermore, checkers approve spellings that represent the wrong word, as this comical but true example:

   As indicted, I have over five years of analyzing investments.

2. **Slow down.** Use a ruler to read the entire document aloud, line by line. Speed kills StandOut resumes.

3. **Read backward, from the bottom up.** Start at the lower right-hand corner, reading backward from the bottom to the top, word by word. You may be a little goofy when you're finished, but because you're not reading for content, you're likely to spot word warts and other blemishes.

4. **Read for content.** Do one more read-through, this time for clarity. To illustrate how words can trip over themselves, smile at these signs discovered by travelers in England:

- **In a laundromat:** "Automatic washing machines. Please remove all your clothes when the light goes out."

- **In a dry cleaner's store:** "Anyone leaving their garments here for more than 30 days will be disposed of."

- **In a conference room:** "For anyone who has children and doesn't know it, there is a day care center on the first floor."

- **In a rural pasture:** "Quicksand. Any person passing this point will be drowned. By order of the District Council."

- **In a safari park:** "Elephants Please Stay In Your Car."

Understanding that the Problem May Not Be the Resume

Does your resume continue to fail in your job search? Does it seem that no matter how often you revise it — or have experts revise it — that it fails to excite interest? Does your resume seem to be an insurmountable problem

The solution: The factors keeping you from employment may have nothing to do with your resume. A variety of obstacles — from an excess of better-qualified applicants and hiring freezes to poisoned references and interview errors — may be holding you back.

Do you feel like you are wasting your time, fixing your resume and not getting the results you want? If you sense you're chasing your own tail, then it's time to seek a professional opinion. Free advice is available at the public job service's One-Stop Career Centers. For the locations of the One-Stop Career Centers, visit the Department of Labor Web site, www.usworkforce.org/onestop. For the names of fee-based career coaches and consultants, inquire at the Career Planning and Adult Development Network (www.careernetwork.org).

A resume's job is to lasso job interviews, or to support your performance in interviews. Beyond that, your resume may not bear responsibility for your employment problems.

Chapter 23

Tips for Choosing Professional Resume Help

*T*o use a professional resume writer or not? That is the question.

"No!" answers one recruiter, "I don't recommend professional services. Write your own. Interviewers have certain expectations from the resume. When a professional writer creates an overblown image that you can't live up to, the interview will crash because the interviewer feels she's been fooled. That wastes everyone's time, including yours."

Yes! Another career counselor disagrees: "Seldom would I recommend that job seekers write their own resumes, regardless of their intelligence or writing ability. They lack objectivity. They often spin their wheels focusing on the wrong things, either over- or under-reacting to their experiences."

These two opinions differ because effectively packaging yourself on paper is not a naturally acquired ability, but a skill you purposely set out to learn.

I come down on the side of the second counselor's opinion — use a pro to write your resume, if you wish. You should, however, organize your own material to present to the professional writer just as you organize your taxes to hand over to an accountant. The reason is simple: Organizing your information primes your mind for job interviews.

In today's volatile job market where job-change is a growth industry, you, you need a StandOut resume. When you need help producing such a document, talented resume writers are your friends.

Using a Resume Pro

In an age of personalization — personal financial advisers, personal trainers, personal tax preparers, personal career coaches — why not a personal resume pro? Prime candidates for resume services are first-time resume writers, people with a checkerboard history, and people who haven't thought about resumes in years. Follow these tips to choose a personal resume pro wisely.

Resume firm or clerical service

Many *clerical services* do a nice job of word processing your resume for a fair price of $80 or more. A clerical service is a good option if that's all you need.

Most people need more, and clerical services are in a different business than *professional resume firms*. Clerical services sell clerical processes. Resume firms sell specialized knowledge in fluently articulating what you want to do and the evidence that proves you can do it.

A resume pro knows a great deal about the business of marketing you to employers, has the latest trends and buzzwords on tap, and coaches you through old potholes in your history. A resume pro knows how to do online as well as paper resumes.

Signs of reliability

After you've decided to use a resume professional, how can you find a good one?

1. **One of the two best ways to choose a resume pro is a referral from a satisfied customer.**

2. **The other best way is asking for a referral from a local career center consultant, recruiter, employment agency consultant or outplacement consultant.**

If you're being laid off, inquire within your corporate human resource department. These people often know who is doing the best work.

The fact that a resume firm has been in business for a long time and has done thousands of resumes is no guarantee of competence — but it's a sign that some customers must like what they do and have spread the word. The acceptance of major credit cards is another indicator of stability. Check with the local Better Business Bureau for the number of unresolved complaints; if the number is more than a couple, move on. Merely asking the firm for its interview success rate wastes time — how can the rate be proven?

Free initial consultation

Request a free, brief, get-acquainted meeting. A telephone encounter serves the purpose, but you may prefer a face-to-face session. Speak not to the boss or a sales representative, but to the writer. The same firm can have good and poor writers. Ask the writer what general strategy will be used to deal with your specific problems. If you don't hear a responsible answer, keep looking.

A responsible answer does not imply discussion of the specifics of how your resume will be handled. Much like people shop retail stores to look at the merchandise and then order from a discount catalog, people shop professional resume services to pick writers' brains and then write their own resumes. Resume pros caught on to this move and developed laryngitis. Moreover, it is irresponsible for a resume pro to go into detail about how your resume will be handled until more is known about you. You want to know the general approach — the kinds of strategies discussed in this book.

Another tip-off is the technology issue. Ask prospective resume writers: *Do you know how to prepare and send resumes by e-mail? Do you know how to add lots of keywords to make resumes searchable?* Positive responses suggest the professional is on the leading edge of technology and, by inference, on the leading edge of the employment industry.

Dependence on forms

Most resume pros ask you to fill out a lengthy, detailed form — much like the one new patients fill out in a doctor's office. (You can substitute the worksheets in Chapter 13.) The form is a good start, but it's far from enough. Eliminate the firms that don't offer dialogue with the writer. The resume pro should interview you to discover your unique experience and strengths. You and the resume pro are colleagues, sharing a task.

The problem with form dependency is you may merely get back your own language prettied up in a glitzy format. That's not what you want a resume pro to do for you.

The cost issue

Prices vary by locale, but expect to pay between $100 and $500 for a core resume. Never pay by the page — longer isn't better. Find out the rate for branching out from a core resume to create a targeted resume specifically for an individual employer or occupation. Perhaps you'll want to target in several directions, requiring several resumes — can you get a fleet price? What is the charge for minor alterations? What is the charge for an update two years later? What is the cost for extra copies?

Speaking of copies, don't be persuaded by an offer of, say, 100 copies for a discount price. Even if it seems like a bargain, you may want to make changes long before your inventory is gone.

Beware of a resume professional who gives lifetime free updating — it's unrealistic to expect quality work when the professional isn't being paid.

Serving alumni is a trend sweeping across the country in college and university career services. Most of these services offer some form of resume writing assistance free or at a low cost.

Samples

Ask the resume pro to show you samples of his resumes. Look not only at content, but at production values. Choose a resume pro who has invested in state-of-the-art technology: a good computer and a laser printer. The resume pro doesn't need showy graphics programs or 30 typefaces with 300 fonts. Nor does the resume pro need a high-end copier — copy shops are plentiful. You judge the quality of the content, layout, word processing, paper, and printing.

Taking aim

For maximum impact, target each resume you send out to a specific employer or career field. Do it either by customizing your resume or by using a core resume in tandem with a targeted cover letter.

Make sure your resume pro understands this concept. You need a resume that has "you" written all over it — *your* theme, *your* focus, and *your* measurable achievements — all matched to a career field you want. Skip over those who sell the same cookie-cutter resume over and over.

Avoid resume pros who offer assembly-line presentations, virtually indistinguishable from thousands of others created by the service. Ignore resume pros who plug your information into a fill-in-the-blanks standard form, garnished with prefab statements. Double ignore those who try to cover the sameness of their work by printing out resumes on 11 x 17-inch parchment paper and folding them into a pretentious brief. Employers use these resumes for kindling.

Also, be careful of the pro who caters to you instead of to your target audience. A heavyweight resume pro warned me that some resume services cater to their customers, not their customers' customers — with fancy brochures, excessive color, and whimsical paper.

About certification

The *Professional Association of Resume Writers & Career Counselors* (parw.com) is a for-profit organization. The organization was the first in the resume-writing industry to certify professionals who meet the required criteria of experience and examination. Those who become certified are allowed to use the title Certified Professional Resume Writer (CPRW) after their names. The association maintains a membership directory on its Web site from which you can choose a member to construct your resume. Now that distance communication opportunities are available, you can easily work with any resume writer, regardless of location.

The *National Resume Writers' Association* (nrwa.com) is a not-for-profit organization. It started as a spin-off of PARW but is now totally independent. Many professional resume writers maintain memberships in both organizations. Those who become certified through this group are allowed to use the title Nationally Certified Resume Writer (NCRW) after their names. Visit the organization's Web site to locate members who are well qualified to write your resume.

A number of noncertified resume writers are excellent professionals as well. Look at work samples, not at certification.

Using Online Resume Builders

On the theory that you get what you pay for, you may be wondering how good are the resume builders offered online at virtually all substantial Web sites? Not great, but not bad.

The online resume builders can be very useful with one Big If:

> *If you remember to think for yourself and not assume the technology will bring to light your most marketable qualities.*

The automated resume builders are designed to benefit the recruiting side of the employment industry, not the job seeking side. So if you use a free resume builder as your chief template offline as well as online, be alert to making amendments as needed. For example, if the template calls for a section on references, delete it. If you prefer to use a skills summary, lose the job objective section if it calls for much more than a position title.

A Poor Resume Is No Bargain

Appreciate the hidden costs of a poor resume: A hack job can cost you good job interviews. When the finished product is in your hands, you should be able to say:

- ✔ This is a StandOut resume — it makes me look great! It looks great!

- ✔ This resume doesn't leave out any skills that are targeted to the jobs I'm after.

- ✔ I like reading my resume; it won't put the recruiter to sleep.

Chapter 24

Your Ten-Point Resume Checklist

In This Chapter

▶ Developing a StandOut resume

▶ Making sure your StandOut resume stands out

▶ Eliminating errors in your StandOut resume

*B*efore going public with your resume, make sure it's a StandOut. Check the box in front of each item only when your resume meets StandOut standards. Give yourself 10 points for each checkmark. If you don't get a score of 100, it's back to the keyboard for you.

Format and Style

☐ You select the best format for your situation. For example, *reverse chronological* when staying in the same field, or *functional* when changing fields. If you select a resume alternative, such as a targeted letter, portfolio, or special report, you go all out to make it a hard-hitting, effective document. (Chapter 9 explains resume formats.)

Focus and Fit

☐ You consider the overall impression of your resume. You present yourself as focused — not desperate to accept just any job. Your resume has a theme. It says what you want to do and proves you have the qualifications to do the work. Your resume is aimed at the employer you want, or at minimum, at the specific occupation or career field in which you seek employment.

Achievements and Skills

☐ Your skills relate to the skills needed for the job. You cite at least one achievement for each skill. When you answer a want ad, you make an effort to match skill offered for skill required. You quantify by using numbers, percentages, or dollar amounts for each achievement. You quantify any statement you can. You highlight results, not just responsibilities.

Language and Expressions

☐ You use adequate keywords (nouns) to make your resume searchable. You use StandOut words (action verbs) to put vitality in your resume. You eliminate words that don't directly support your bid for the job you want, as well as such meaningless words and phrases as "Resume" or "References available." You use industry jargon where appropriate, but you translate acronyms, technical jargon, or military lingo into easy-to-understand English.

Contents and Omissions

☐ You begin with either a skills profile or a job objective. Next, you state your experience. You only begin with your education if you're a new graduate with virtually no experience, or if your target job is related to education and training. Don't list personal information that isn't related to the job you seek, such as marital status, number of children, or height. Your content supports your objective.

Length and Common Sense

☐ You limit your resume to one or two pages if you're lightly experienced, or two or three pages if you're substantially experienced. These page counts are only guidelines; your resume can be longer if necessary to put your qualifications in the best light. Additionally, your resume can exceed three pages if it's a professional resume or a CV (curriculum vitae). *Remember:* Don't jam pack a jumble of text on one page because it discourages reading.

Appearance: Attached and Paper Resumes

❑ Your e-resume in a fully formatted Word document (or equivalent) looks much like a fully formatted paper resume. You use an open layout with white space, minimum one-inch margins, headings in bold typeface or capital letters, bullets and other low-key graphic elements that make your resume look professional. Your paper resume is printed on white or eggshell paper, both for a business impression and because it may be scanned into a database.

Appearance: Plain Text Resumes

❑ The e-resume that you send to online job sites (Monster, HotJobs, and so on), and to recruiters whose older technology doesn't accept attachments is dispatched in plain text (ASCII) with no graphic frills. You do not send a *cover note* (very brief cover letters) with your resume to job sites — unless your resume does not match a specific job for which you're applying. In contacting recruiters with older technology, compose a unified e-mail message that contains a cover note, which is immediately followed by your ASCII resume.

Note an important exception in this era of transition: In responding to a job posting or initiating contact through a company Web site, notice whether the site's applicant portal has a button by the text box labeled "browse." If you see a browse button, you can assume that your MS Word resume can be attached and that everyone can look at the document on the site. If the site doesn't have a browse button, the company applicant portal probably can't accept attachments. In that case, follow the instructions on the applicant portal, which is likely to cut and paste your resume, or e-mail it as ASCII text.

You take the correct submission action based on your alertness to the technology.

Sticky Points and Spin

❑ You thoughtfully handle all problem areas, such as grouping irrelevant jobs, long-ago, part-time, and temporary jobs. You account for all the gaps in the timeframe of your resume. You scour your resume for possible hidden negatives and eliminate them as described in Chapter 12.

Proofreading and More Proofreading

☐ Your resume contains no typos, no grammar disasters — no errors of any kind. You not only use your computer's spell-checker, but you also double-check (and triple-check) it. You also ask others to carefully read it. Typos are hot buttons to many employers — two goofs and you're gone!

Launch Your StandOut Resume

Let me put it this way: Technology and I will never be in hot sync. I am frankly relieved that good-looking resumes are roaring back in style. Write, attach, and send. Effectively, that's about all you have to do as the new recruiting software replaces trailing technology of the past decade.

Drawing from these pages, start now — if you haven't already begun — to craft your own core resume. Your core resume is the basis from which you can devise targeted StandOut versions as you need them.

Let me be the first to wish you good hunting in a new era.

Joyce Lain Kennedy, *Resumes For Dummies, 4th Edition,*
Carlsbad, California

Index

NOW AVAILABLE!

FOR DUMMIES™ Videos & DVDs

"The best video I have ever seen to introduce brand new students to yoga." - YogaBasics.com

Basic Yoga Workout FOR DUMMIES

with Sara Ivanhoe

An Easy-to-Follow Yoga Practice

Instructor Sara Ivanhoe offers step-by-step instruction of the 12 essential yoga postures. This workout shows you proper technique, as well as tips on modifying postures for your fitness level. Today, many people use yoga to help alleviate back pain, reduce stress, and increase flexibility.

VHS - 45 Mins. $9.99
DVD - 70 Mins. $14.98

"Sara Ivanhoe makes yoga enjoyable and accessible for people at all levels... you'll love every minute." - Fitness Magazine

Beyond Basic Yoga FOR DUMMIES

with Sara Ivanhoe

An Easy-to-Follow Workout

The *Beyond Basic Yoga Workout For Dummies* is the next step for anyone who has enjoyed *Basic Yoga Workout For Dummies* and is ready to enhance their practice with 12 more postures. This workout is a little more advanced than the basic yoga program but still features the *For Dummies* format.

VHS - 45 Mins. $9.99
DVD - 55 Mins. $14.98

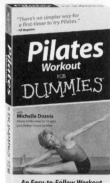

"There's no simpler way for a first-timer to try Pilates." - Fit Magazine

Pilates Workout FOR DUMMIES

with Michelle Dozois

An Easy-to-Follow Workout

Instructor Michelle Dozois offers step-by-step instruction of 18 popular Pilates mat exercises to help you strengthen and lengthen your muscles, improve your posture, and tone and tighten your midsection.

VHS - 40 Mins. $9.99
DVD - 60 Mins. $14.98

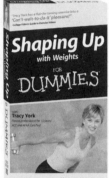

"Tracy York has a flair for turning exercise into a 'Can't-wait-to-do-it' pleasure!" - College Videos Guide to Exercise Videos

Shaping Up with Weights FOR DUMMIES

with Tracy York

An Easy-to-Follow Workout

Instructor Tracy York offers step-by-step instruction of 12 key strength-training exercises and makes it easy to work out at any level. This workout incorporates both upper- and lower-body exercises to help tone muscles and burn more calories per day, which leads to fat loss.

VHS - 51 Mins. $9.99

"Gay Gasper helps you get the most out of each move." You'll see a major difference in your abs." - Fitness Magazine

Basic Ab Workout FOR DUMMIES

with Gay Gasper

An Easy-to-Follow Workout

Instructor Gay Gasper demonstrates her top 10 exercises to tone and flatten your tummy. Throughout this workout, she gives you more advanced options for the exercises so you can start at any level and then advance as you become more fit.

VHS - 45 Mins. $9.99
DVD - 55 Mins. $14.98

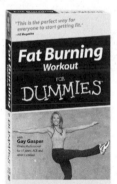

"This is the perfect way for everyone to start getting fit." - Fit Magazine

Fat Burning Workout FOR DUMMIES

with Gay Gasper

An Easy-to-Follow Workout

In this workout, instructor Gay Gasper offers step-by-step instructions of the 10 basic exercises that make up any aerobic routine. She incorporates both high- and low-impact choices in an effective workout to help you burn more fat, use more calories every day, and meet your fitness goals.

VHS - 45 Mins. $9.99

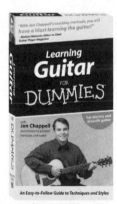

"With Jon Chappell's teaching methods, you will have a blast learning the guitar!" - Michael Molenda, Editor in Chief, Guitar Player Magazine

Learning Guitar FOR DUMMIES

with Jon Chappell

An Easy-to-Follow Guide to Techniques and Styles

Instructor Jon Chappell provides step-by-step instruction of all of the skills you need to become an accomplished guitar player! By simply watching the instructor onscreen and following along, you can learn to play songs — without reading music.

VHS - 75 Mins. $12.98
DVD - 75 Mins. $16.98

To Order Call: 1-800-546-1949

FOR DUMMIES®

The easy way to get more done and have more fun

PERSONAL FINANCE

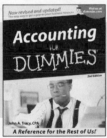

0-7645-5231-7

0-7645-2431-3

0-7645-5331-3

Also available:

Estate Planning For Dummies
(0-7645-5501-4)

401(k)s For Dummies
(0-7645-5468-9)

Frugal Living For Dummies
(0-7645-5403-4)

Microsoft Money "X" For Dummies
(0-7645-1689-2)

Mutual Funds For Dummies
(0-7645-5329-1)

Personal Bankruptcy For Dummies
(0-7645-5498-0)

Quicken "X" For Dummies
(0-7645-1666-3)

Stock Investing For Dummies
(0-7645-5411-5)

Taxes For Dummies 2003
(0-7645-5475-1)

BUSINESS & CAREERS

0-7645-5314-3

0-7645-5307-0

0-7645-5471-9

Also available:

Business Plans Kit For Dummies
(0-7645-5365-0)

Consulting For Dummies
(0-7645-5034-9)

Cool Careers For Dummies
(0-7645-5345-3)

Human Resources Kit For Dummies
(0-7645-5131-0)

Managing For Dummies
(1-5688-4858-7)

QuickBooks All-in-One Desk Reference For Dummies
(0-7645-1963-8)

Selling For Dummies
(0-7645-5363-1)

Small Business Kit For Dummies
(0-7645-5093-4)

Starting an eBay Business For Dummies
(0-7645-1547-0)

HEALTH, SPORTS & FITNESS

0-7645-5167-1

0-7645-5146-9

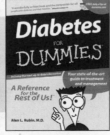

0-7645-5154-X

Also available:

Controlling Cholesterol For Dummies
(0-7645-5440-9)

Dieting For Dummies
(0-7645-5126-4)

High Blood Pressure For Dummies
(0-7645-5424-7)

Martial Arts For Dummies
(0-7645-5358-5)

Menopause For Dummies
(0-7645-5458-1)

Nutrition For Dummies
(0-7645-5180-9)

Power Yoga For Dummies
(0-7645-5342-9)

Thyroid For Dummies
(0-7645-5385-2)

Weight Training For Dummies
(0-7645-5168-X)

Yoga For Dummies
(0-7645-5117-5)

Available wherever books are sold.
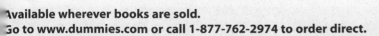
Go to www.dummies.com or call 1-877-762-2974 to order direct.

FOR DUMMIES®

A world of resources to help you grow

HOME, GARDEN & HOBBIES

Feng Shui
0-7645-5295-3

Gardening
0-7645-5130-2

Guitar
0-7645-5106-X

Also available:

Auto Repair For Dummies
(0-7645-5089-6)

Chess For Dummies
(0-7645-5003-9)

Home Maintenance For
Dummies
(0-7645-5215-5)

Organizing For Dummies
(0-7645-5300-3)

Piano For Dummies
(0-7645-5105-1)

Poker For Dummies
(0-7645-5232-5)

Quilting For Dummies
(0-7645-5118-3)

Rock Guitar For Dummies
(0-7645-5356-9)

Roses For Dummies
(0-7645-5202-3)

Sewing For Dummies
(0-7645-5137-X)

FOOD & WINE

Cooking
0-7645-5250-3

Cookies
0-7645-5390-9

Wine
0-7645-5114-0

Also available:

Bartending For Dummies
(0-7645-5051-9)

Chinese Cooking For
Dummies
(0-7645-5247-3)

Christmas Cooking For
Dummies
(0-7645-5407-7)

Diabetes Cookbook For
Dummies
(0-7645-5230-9)

Grilling For Dummies
(0-7645-5076-4)

Low-Fat Cooking For
Dummies
(0-7645-5035-7)

Slow Cookers For Dummies
(0-7645-5240-6)

TRAVEL

Italy
0-7645-5453-0

Hawaii
0-7645-5438-7

Las Vegas
0-7645-5448-4

Also available:

America's National Parks For
Dummies
(0-7645-6204-5)

Caribbean For Dummies
(0-7645-5445-X)

Cruise Vacations For
Dummies 2003
(0-7645-5459-X)

Europe For Dummies
(0-7645-5456-5)

Ireland For Dummies
(0-7645-6199-5)

France For Dummies
(0-7645-6292-4)

London For Dummies
(0-7645-5416-6)

Mexico's Beach Resorts For
Dummies
(0-7645-6262-2)

Paris For Dummies
(0-7645-5494-8)

RV Vacations For Dummies
(0-7645-5443-3)

Walt Disney World & Orlando
For Dummies
(0-7645-5444-1)

Available wherever books are sold. Go to www.dummies.com or call 1-877-762-2974 to order direct.

FOR DUMMIES®

Plain-English solutions for everyday challenges

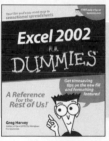

FOR DUMMIES®

Helping you expand your horizons and realize your potential

INTERNET

0-7645-0894-6

0-7645-1659-0

0-7645-1642-6

Also available:

America Online 7.0 For Dummies
(0-7645-1624-8)

Genealogy Online For Dummies
(0-7645-0807-5)

The Internet All-in-One Desk Reference For Dummies
(0-7645-1659-0)

Internet Explorer 6 For Dummies
(0-7645-1344-3)

The Internet For Dummies Quick Reference
(0-7645-1645-0)

Internet Privacy For Dummies
(0-7645-0846-6)

Researching Online For Dummies
(0-7645-0546-7)

Starting an Online Business For Dummies
(0-7645-1655-8)

DIGITAL MEDIA

0-7645-1664-7

0-7645-1675-2

0-7645-0806-7

Also available:

CD and DVD Recording For Dummies
(0-7645-1627-2)

Digital Photography All-in-One Desk Reference For Dummies
(0-7645-1800-3)

Digital Photography For Dummies Quick Reference
(0-7645-0750-8)

Home Recording for Musicians For Dummies
(0-7645-1634-5)

MP3 For Dummies
(0-7645-0858-X)

Paint Shop Pro "X" For Dummies
(0-7645-2440-2)

Photo Retouching & Restoration For Dummies
(0-7645-1662-0)

Scanners For Dummies
(0-7645-0783-4)

GRAPHICS

0-7645-0817-2

0-7645-1651-5

0-7645-0895-4

Also available:

Adobe Acrobat 5 PDF For Dummies
(0-7645-1652-3)

Fireworks 4 For Dummies
(0-7645-0804-0)

Illustrator 10 For Dummies
(0-7645-3636-2)

QuarkXPress 5 For Dummies
(0-7645-0643-9)

Visio 2000 For Dummies
(0-7645-0635-8)

Available wherever books are sold. Go to www.dummies.com or call 1-877-762-2974 to order direct.

FOR DUMMIES®

The advice and explanations you need to succeed

SELF-HELP, SPIRITUALITY & RELIGION

 0-7645-5302-X

 0-7645-5418-2

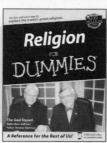 0-7645-5264-3

Also available:

The Bible For Dummies
(0-7645-5296-1)

Buddhism For Dummies
(0-7645-5359-3)

Christian Prayer For Dummies
(0-7645-5500-6)

Dating For Dummies
(0-7645-5072-1)

Judaism For Dummies
(0-7645-5299-6)

Potty Training For Dummies
(0-7645-5417-4)

Pregnancy For Dummies
(0-7645-5074-8)

Rekindling Romance For
Dummies
(0-7645-5303-8)

Spirituality For Dummies
(0-7645-5298-8)

Weddings For Dummies
(0-7645-5055-1)

PETS

 0-7645-5255-4

 0-7645-5286-4

 0-7645-5275-9

Also available:

Labrador Retrievers For
Dummies
(0-7645-5281-3)

Aquariums For Dummies
(0-7645-5156-6)

Birds For Dummies
(0-7645-5139-6)

Dogs For Dummies
(0-7645-5274-0)

Ferrets For Dummies
(0-7645-5259-7)

German Shepherds For
Dummies
(0-7645-5280-5)

Golden Retrievers For
Dummies
(0-7645-5267-8)

Horses For Dummies
(0-7645-5138-8)

Jack Russell Terriers For
Dummies
(0-7645-5268-6)

Puppies Raising & Training
Diary For Dummies
(0-7645-0876-8)

EDUCATION & TEST PREPARATION

 0-7645-5194-9

 0-7645-5325-9

 0-7645-5210-4

Also available:

Chemistry For Dummies
(0-7645-5430-1)

English Grammar For
Dummies
(0-7645-5322-4)

French For Dummies
(0-7645-5193-0)

The GMAT For Dummies
(0-7645-5251-1)

Inglés Para Dummies
(0-7645-5427-1)

Italian For Dummies
(0-7645-5196-5)

Research Papers For
Dummies
(0-7645-5426-3)

The SAT I For Dummies
(0-7645-5472-7)

U.S. History For Dummies
(0-7645-5249-X)

World History For Dummies
(0-7645-5242-2)

Available wherever books are sold. Go to www.dummies.com or call 1-877-762-2974 to order direct.

FOR DUMMIES®

We take the mystery out of complicated subjects